Beginning
Backdrop CMS

■ ■ ■

Todd Tomlinson

Apress®

Beginning Backdrop CMS

Todd Tomlinson
Tigard
Oregon, USA

ISBN-13 (pbk): 978-1-4842-1969-0   ISBN-13 (electronic): 978-1-4842-1970-6
DOI 10.1007/978-1-4842-1970-6

Library of Congress Control Number: 2016943317

Managing Director: Welmoed Spahr
Acquisitions Editor: Ben Renow-Clarke
Development Editor: Matthew Moodie
Technical Reviewer: Eric Goldman
Editorial Board: Steve Anglin, Pramila Balen, Louise Corrigan, James DeWolf, Jonathan Gennick, Robert Hutchinson, Celestin Suresh John, Nikhil Karkal, James Markham, Susan McDermott, Matthew Moodie, Ben Renow-Clarke, Gwenan Spearing
Coordinating Editor: Nancy Chen
Copy Editor: Tiffany Taylor
Compositor: SPi Global
Indexer: SPi Global

Distributed to the book trade worldwide by Springer Science+Business Media New York, 233 Spring Street, 6th Floor, New York, NY 10013. Phone 1-800-SPRINGER, fax (201) 348-4505, e-mail orders-ny@springer-sbm.com, or visit www.springer.com. Apress Media, LLC is a California LLC and the sole member (owner) is Springer Science + Business Media Finance Inc (SSBM Finance Inc). SSBM Finance Inc is a Delaware corporation.

For information on translations, please e-mail rights@apress.com, or visit www.apress.com.

Apress and friends of ED books may be purchased in bulk for academic, corporate, or promotional use. eBook versions and licenses are also available for most titles. For more information, reference our Special Bulk Sales–eBook Licensing web page at www.apress.com/bulk-sales.

Any source code or other supplementary materials referenced by the author in this text is available to readers at www.apress.com. For detailed information about how to locate your book's source code, go to www.apress.com/source-code/.

Printed on acid-free paper

To my beautiful and amazing wife Misty,
who cheerfully sacrifices time together as I pursue my passion for writing.

Contents at a Glance

About the Author xvii

About the Technical Reviewer xix

Foreword xxi

Acknowledgments xxiii

Introduction xxv

■Chapter 1: Introduction to Backdrop CMS 1

■Chapter 2: Creating and Managing Content 7

■Chapter 3: Creating and Managing Users 23

■Chapter 4: Taxonomy 35

■Chapter 5: Content Types 51

■Chapter 6: Creating Layouts 77

■Chapter 7: Using Backdrop Themes 89

■Chapter 8: Creating Menus 99

■Chapter 9: Backdrop Blocks 107

■Chapter 10: Views 115

■Chapter 11: Creating Pages 133

■Chapter 12: Backdrop Modules 143

■Chapter 13: Anatomy of a Module 149

■Chapter 14: Creating Themes 155

■Chapter 15: Multilingual Capabilities 165

■Chapter 16: Using Git.. 177

■Chapter 17: Putting It All Together 185

■Chapter 18: Administering Your Backdrop Site... 191

■Chapter 19: Creating a Blog Site 205

■Chapter 20: Building a Company Site.. 219

■Appendix A: Installing Backdrop 243

■Appendix B: Contributing to Backdrop 251

■Appendix C: Additional Resources.. 253

Index... 255

Contents

About the Author xvii

About the Technical Reviewer xix

Foreword xxi

Acknowledgments xxiii

Introduction xxv

■Chapter 1: Introduction to Backdrop CMS 1

Content Management Systems 1

    Backdrop CMS 2

    Backdrop Core 2

    Contributed Modules 3

    Backdrop Layouts and Themes.. 3

Creating Content 4

Summary... 6

■Chapter 2: Creating and Managing Content.. 7

Understanding the Basics 7

Creating Content in Backdrop 7

    Teasers and Full Nodes.. 11

Editing Content... 11

Other Content Options 13

    Publishing Options... 13

    Authoring Information... 14

    Revision Information... 15

URL Settings 17

Comment Settings 18

Deleting Content 20

Finding Content 21

Summary 22

■Chapter 3: Creating and Managing Users 23

Users, Roles, and Permissions 23

User Accounts 24

Configuring User Account Settings 24

Creating Roles 25

Assigning Permissions 27

Creating User Accounts 29

User-Generated Accounts 31

Resetting Users' Passwords 32

Summary 33

■Chapter 4: Taxonomy 35

Taxonomy Overview 35

Using Tagging to Categorize Content 35

Using Structured Taxonomy 38

Implementing Structured Taxonomy 38

Creating Vocabularies 39

Assigning a Taxonomy Vocabulary to a Content Type 42

Selecting a Taxonomy Term When Creating Content 44

Creating Human- and Search Engine–Friendly Lists 47

Hierarchical Terms 47

Assigning More Than One Vocabulary 49

Summary 50

■Chapter 5: Content Types 51

The Page and Post Content Types 51

Defining a Custom Content Type 52

Creating a Custom Content Type 52

Customizing Your Content Type 59

Other Field Types 64

List Fields 65

File Uploads 68

Text Area 71

Numeric Fields and Other Field Types 72

Formatting the Input Form for a Custom Content Type 72

Formatting the Output of a Custom Content Type 73

Summary 75

■Chapter 6: Creating Layouts 77

Default Layouts 77

Creating Custom Layouts 79

Installing Other Layouts 85

Creating a Custom Layout Template 85

Creating the Layout's .Info FIle 86

Creating the Layout's .tpl.php File 86

Creating the Layout's .css File 88

Changing Layouts 88

Summary 88

■**Chapter 7: Using Backdrop Themes** **89**

How a Backdrop Theme Works 91

Finding a New Theme 92

Installing a Theme 94

The Administration Theme 96

Configuration Options 97

Summary 97

■**Chapter 8: Creating Menus** **99**

Ordering from the Menu 99

Adding an Item to a Menu 100

    Adding a Content Item to a Menu 100

    Adding a Menu Item Through the Administrative Interface 102

Creating a New Menu 103

Summary 105

■**Chapter 9: Backdrop Blocks** **107**

Blocks, Blocks, and More Blocks 107

Making Blocks Appear on Layouts 107

Finding the List of Available Blocks 108

Rearranging Blocks 109

Removing Blocks from a Region 109

Configuring Blocks 109

Using Blocks from Contributed Modules 110

Creating Custom Blocks 111

Summary 113

■Chapter 10: Views 115

The Views Module 115

Creating Your First View 116

    Page Display 121

    Block Display 125

    Filtering 127

Advanced View Output 130

    Creating RSS Feeds 130

    Creating Tables 131

Views Add-on Modules 132

Summary 132

■Chapter 11: Creating Pages 133

Foundation for Creating Pages 133

    Creating Landing Pages 136

    Creating Views 137

Summary 141

■Chapter 12: Backdrop Modules 143

Locating Backdrop Contributed Modules 143

Downloading Backdrop Modules and Themes 143

Customizing Contributed Modules 146

Summary 147

■Chapter 13: Anatomy of a Module 149

Your First Backdrop Module 149

    Step 1: Create the Module's Directory 149

    Step 2: Create the Module's info File 150

    Step 3: Create the Module File 150

    Step 4: Enable the Module 152

Other Module Files 152

Summary 153

■**Chapter 14: Creating Themes** **155**

Contents of a Theme 155

The Theme .info File (Required) 156

Template Files (.tpl.php) 156

The template.php File 156

Sub-themes 156

The screenshot.png File 156

The theme-settings.php 156

The color Directory 156

Use a Sub-theme Instead of Copying 157

Writing Theme .info files 157

Theme Name Requirements 157

Encoding 157

Contents 158

Example: Creating a Theme 159

Create the Theme Directory 159

Create the Theme's .info File 160

Add Your Own Style 160

Add Custom JavaScript If Needed 160

Add Custom Code in template.php 160

Add Template Files 160

Add Your Own Screenshot 161

Creating a Sub-theme 161

Create a Theme Directory 161

Create an .info File, or Copy and Modify the Parent Theme's .info File 161

Copy Color Module Settings If Needed 162

Add Your Own Style 162

Override JavaScript If Needed 162

Add Your Custom Code in template.php 162

Override Template Files 163

Add Your Own Screenshot 163

Copy the Parent Theme's Color Module Settings 163

Copy the Parent Theme's Settings 163

Summary 163

■Chapter 15: Multilingual Capabilities 165

Getting Started with Multilingual 165

Configuring Multilingual Capabilities 166

Specifying Languages 166

Configuring Language Activation 167

Content Translation Example 169

Configuring Entities 171

Detecting the Language and Filtering Content 173

Setting Block Visibility by Language 174

Summary 175

■Chapter 16: Using Git 177

Installing Git 177

Installing Git on Linux 177

Installing Git on OS X 178

Installing Git on Windows 178

Using Git 178

Using GitHub 180

Summary 183

■Chapter 17: Putting It All Together 185

Now What? 185

Look at Other Backdrop-Based Sites for Ideas 185

Keep Tabs on Backdrop and Contributed Modules 185

A Methodology for Building Your Site on Backdrop 186

Summary 190

■Chapter 18: Administering Your Backdrop Site 191

Backing Up and Restoring Your Site 191

Backing Up with the Backup and Restore Module 192

Backing Up with the Command Line...196

Checking the Log Files 196

Recent Log Messages...197

Top 'Page Not Found' Errors 198

Status Report 199

Checking for Updates and Security Patches 200

Approving Requests for User Accounts 201

Summary.. 204

■Chapter 19: Creating a Blog Site 205

Requirements for a Blog Site 205

Installing Backdrop 206

Installing and Creating a Theme... 206

Creating Taxonomy 208

Updating the Post Content Type 209

Creating Views... 211

Assigning Blocks 212

Adding Other Pages.. 217

Summary.. 218

■Chapter 20: Building a Company Site 219

Requirements for a Company Site... 219

Installing Backdrop 220

Installing and Creating a Theme... 220

Creating Taxonomy 222

Updating the Post Content Type 223

Creating the Client Portfolio Content Type.. 225

Expanding Backdrop's User Profile 229

Contact Form 231

Assembling the Site 232

The About US Page 232

The Client Portfolios Page 232

The Service Offerings Page 234

The Key Staff Members Page 236

News Posts 237

The Staff Blog Page 238

Adding the Contact Form to the Main Menu 239

Creating the Footer 239

Creating the Home Page 240

Summary 241

■Appendix A: Installing Backdrop 243

System Requirements 243

Downloading Backdrop 243

Installing Backdrop 244

Creating the Database 244

Setting File Permissions 244

Running the Backdrop Installer 245

File and Directory Structure Differences 248

■Appendix B: Contributing to Backdrop 251

Contributing to core 251

Contribute a Module, Layout, or Theme 251

Contributed Development Branches 252

Contributed Releases 252

■Appendix C: Additional Resources 253

Issue Queue: GitHub 253

API Documentation and Change Records 253

Contributing to Backdrop 253

Weekly Meetings: Google Hangouts 253

Video Archives: YouTube 253

Reddit 254

Live Chat: IRC 254

Twitter 254

Facebook 254

LinkedIn 254

Index **255**

About the Author

Todd Tomlinson is recognized globally for his expertise in Drupal and Backdrop. He is the author of *Pro Drupal 7 Development, Beginning Drupal 7, Beginning Drupal 8, Migrating from Drupal to Backdrop,* and this book, *Beginning Backdrop CMS*. Todd is a frequent contributing author to *Drupal Watchdog,* the Drupal magazine, and has been the featured guest on several podcasts, including Acquia and Drupal Easy.

Todd has worked with Drupal for the past 12 years and has built hundreds of Drupal sites for large media companies, global publishers, higher education organizations, manufacturers, retailers, and state and local governments. His involvement in the Internet began in the late 1980s, when he led the technology team at one of the National Science Foundation's supercomputing centers, and became the primary focus of his consulting career in the early 1990s. He developed Netscape Communications' training programs and trained the early pioneers in the Internet and continued with Netscape as he marched around the world implementing Netscape's server products. Todd was also the senior director of Oracle Corporation's eBusiness Strategic Services practice and has travelled the world speaking on the future of business on the Internet and helping organizations adopt new business strategies, models, and technologies. Today you will find him filling the role of Senior Enterprise Drupal Architect, helping multi-billion-dollar corporations fully embrace the capabilities of Drupal as an enterprise application platform.

About the Technical Reviewer

Eric Goldman is a solution architect and technical project manager residing in Gilbert, AZ. He holds a BS in managerial economics from the University of Massachusetts and has been involved in the IT industry for more than 25 years. He has worked for various companies such as BBN, American Express, and Charles Schwab. He has held project manager, web developer/admin, consultant, and director of IT roles. Eric has been part of the Web since its early days, starting with his DEC Rainbow 100; he discovered Drupal three years ago and has been immersing himself in all its glory ever since. He is currently working on several Backdrop sites and has become very active in the community. He is glad to be back working again with Todd and the vast knowledge Todd brings to the Backdrop/Drupal universe.

When not at work, Eric likes to spend time with his family, goes camping, is an avid reader, and is pursuing his newest hobby, photographing the dark skies of Arizona. His family calls him "the computer whisperer," because he always seems to make things "just work" when others cannot!

Foreword

All around us, from our phones to cars, software shapes our everyday lives. Software is incredibly powerful. It allows people who have never met to collaborate on common interests. It allows the near-instantaneous spread of information. And with so much accessible information, we depend on software to filter the information we receive.

The free-software movement is one of the most important social movements of our time. Software has become a force. And it is a force so powerful that it is too dangerous to leave in the hands of only a few, whether they be individuals, corporations, or governments. Software and the capabilities it brings should belong to all of us. The beliefs of the free-software movement have popularized free software to the extent that it is found in nearly every computing project in existence.

Born from the Drupal project, Backdrop is a tool that helps spread information. The freedoms permitted by the GNU Public License (GPL) made it possible for us to take the code that powers hundreds of thousands of sites (Drupal 7) and tailor it with different goals in mind, thus creating Backdrop CMS.

Backdrop continues to value flexibility and extensibility as does its parent project, but it puts a focus on learnability, longevity, and lower costs. This lower cost emphasis is particularly important for Backdrop. Free software can be surprisingly expensive. In the case of free software for building web sites, there is the cost of the initial site building as well as the expense of hosting, ongoing maintenance, security updates, and site-specific customizations. Most people expect an up-front cost, but it's the long-term costs that can catch them off guard.

Backdrop has expanded the feature-rich capabilities of Drupal but done so in a way that minimizes the costs for existing Drupal web sites. Backdrop treats Drupal 7 as its previous version, providing an upgrade path for your content and configuration. Porting a module from Drupal 7 to Backdrop can be done in a few hours. And existing Drupal developers can pick up all the critical differences in Backdrop in as little as a few days.

Making Backdrop accessible to existing Drupal developers is just one goal. The Backdrop community is working constantly to decrease the learning curve of our software. Although Backdrop will be familiar to Drupal developers, it strives to attract all people who share our mission: enabling people to build highly customized web sites, affordably, through collaboration and open source software.

With the release of this book, Todd has created the first comprehensive guide to Backdrop CMS. This book is a major part of fulfilling our goal to reduce the cost of creating and maintaining a highly customized web site. By providing a comprehensive guide, *Beginning Backdrop CMS* will help new and existing developers jump in to the exciting new world of Backdrop. We're excited to have you with us on this journey and hope that you enjoy using Backdrop!

—Nate Haug
Backdrop CMS Co-Founder, Oakland, California, US

Acknowledgments

I would like to acknowledge my grandmother, who at age 97 authored her first book and sparked my desire to write.

My parents, who always stood behind me as I wandered my way through life.

My mother- and father-in-law, for being so supportive and for raising an amazing daughter: my wife.

My daughters Anna and Emma, for sacrificing time together as I pursued my career.

Eric Goldman, for suffering through yet another book as my technical reviewer.

Nate Haug, founder and creator of Backdrop CMS, for having the vision for something bigger and better.

Introduction

In its relatively short life, Backdrop CMS (Backdrop) is beginning to have an impact on the landscape of the Internet. As a web content management system (CMS), Backdrop enables the creation of feature- and content-rich web sites for organizations large and small. As a web application framework, Backdrop changes the way people think about web application development. When I experienced the power of the Backdrop platform for the first time, I knew that it was something more than just another content management solution. When I saw how easily and quickly I could build feature-rich web sites, I shifted gears and began to focus on Backdrop as one of my preferred platforms for developing web sites and web-enabled applications.

If you are new to content management systems or are investigating Backdrop as an alternative to your current platform, then this book is for you. As you journey through this book, you'll see how easy it is to quickly build functionally rich and robust web sites. The Backdrop team used the millions of hours of work performed on the Drupal platform as the foundation for Backdrop and took the platform to a new level. Ease of use, simplifying the complex and confusing steps required to build a site, and making it affordable to host Backdrop were key tenets when Nate Haug and others began the planning and creation of Backdrop, and they succeeded. If you are new to the CMS landscape, you'll find the process and interface intuitive and easy to use. If you're moving from another CMS, you'll find yourself grinning from ear to ear as you see how the Backdrop team simplified the overall process.

As someone who has focused his career over the past 12 years on content management systems, I applaud the Backdrop team and look forward to the amazement of my clients as I build and transition those sites into their support organizations. Buckle up and get ready for an amazing experience. The journey starts now.

## CHAPTER 1

Introduction to Backdrop CMS

This chapter provides a basic overview of what a content management system (CMS) is, how Backdrop CMS fills the role of a CMS, the major building blocks of Backdrop, and how to create content on your new Backdrop-based web site.

Content Management Systems

In its simplest form, a CMS is a software package that provides tools for authoring, publishing, and managing the content on a web site. *Content* includes anything from a news story, a blog post, a video, or a photograph, to a podcast, an article, or a description of a product you are selling. In more general terms, *content* is any combination of text, graphics, photographs, audio, and video that represents something visitors to your site will read, watch, or hear.

A CMS typically provides a number of features that simplify the process of building, deploying, and managing web sites, including the following:

- An administrative interface
- A database repository for content
- A mechanism for associating information that is stored in the database with a physical page on the web site
- A toolset for authoring, publishing, and managing content
- A component for creating and managing menus and navigational elements
- The tools required to define and apply themes
- User management
- A security framework
- Social networking capabilities such as forums, blogs, wikis, and surveys
- Taxonomy and tagging
- Online forms
- E-commerce capabilities

Hundreds of CMSs are available (check out www.cmsmatrix.org). They range from simple blogging-centric platforms, such as WordPress, to complex enterprise-class content management solutions, such as Backdrop.

© Todd Tomlinson 2016
T. Tomlinson, *Beginning Backdrop CMS*, DOI 10.1007/978-1-4842-1970-6_1

Backdrop CMS

Backdrop is a free and open source CMS written in PHP and distributed under the GNU General Public License. Backdrop stems from a project by a Belgian university student, Dries Buytaert, called Drupal. The goal of the project was to provide a mechanism for Buytaert and his friends to share news and events. Buytaert turned Drupal into an open source project in 2001; the community readily embraced the concept and has expanded on its humble beginnings, creating what is now one of the most powerful and feature-rich CMS platforms on the Web. Individuals, teams, and communities use Drupal's features to easily publish, manage, and organize content on a variety of web sites, ranging from personal blogs to large corporate and government sites. But Drupal continued to grow and, with the latest release, Drupal 8, turned its focus from small and medium-sized organizations to large, enterprise-scale web sites. Drupal 8's level of complexity and infrastructure may overwhelm many small to medium-sized organizations, driving hosting and support costs beyond what they can afford. Nate Haug, founder of Backdrop, was a highly visible member of the Drupal community; he saw the direction Drupal was heading and believed there was a significant need to still support those small to medium-sized organizations. So, he created Backdrop, using Drupal 7 as the foundation. Organizations familiar with Drupal will find that the transition to Backdrop is a relatively simple process, and those just beginning the CMS experience will find Backdrop CMS an easier solution to host and manage.

The standard release of Backdrop, known as *Backdrop core*, contains basic features that can be used to create a classic brochure web site, a single- or multiuser blog, an Internet forum, or a community web site with user-generated content. Features found in Backdrop core include the ability to author and publish content; to create and manage users, menus, and forums; and to manage your site through a web browser–based administrative interface.

Backdrop was designed to be enhanced with new features and custom behavior by downloading and enabling add-on modules. A growing inventory of additional modules (known as *contributed* or *contrib* modules) extend Backdrop core's functionality and cover a broad spectrum of capabilities, including e-commerce, social networking, integration with third-party applications, and multimedia.

Backdrop can run on any computing platform that supports both a web server capable of running PHP version 5.3.2 or higher (including Apache, IIS, lighttpd, and nginx) and a database (such as MySQL, SQLite, or PostgreSQL) to store content and settings.

Backdrop Core

When you download and install Backdrop, you are installing what is commonly called *Backdrop core*. Core represents the "engine" that powers a Backdrop-based web site, along with a number of out-of-the-box features that enable the creation of a relatively full-featured web site. The primary components of Backdrop core include capabilities to create and manage the following:

- Content
- Fle uploads/downloads
- Menus
- User accounts
- Roles and permissions
- Taxonomy
- Views to extract and display content in various forms such as lists and tables
- WYSIWYG-based content editor

Backdrop core also includes a feature-rich search engine, multilingual capabilities, and logging and error reporting.

Contributed Modules

Although Backdrop core can be used to build feature-rich web sites, there are situations where it lacks the functionality needed to address specific requirements. In such cases, the first step is to search the inventory of custom modules contributed by developers from around the world to the Backdrop CMS project, for a solution that meets your needs. It's very likely that someone else has had the same functional requirement and has developed a solution to extend Backdrop core to provide the functionality that you need.

To find a contributed module, visit `www.backdropcms.org/modules`. You will find a list of contributed modules (for all versions of Backdrop.

A few of the most popular contributed modules, and the ones you will probably want to install, include the following:

- *Google analytics*: Adds a Google Analytics JavaScript tracking code to every page

- *Webform*: Adds a webform content type to your Backdrop site

- *References*: Enables you to add node reference and user reference fields to your content types

Backdrop Layouts and Themes

A *layout* is the Backdrop component that defines how the pages on your web site are structured, and the *theme* defines the visual aspects of those pages. A Backdrop layout defines attributes of your web site such as these:

- How many columns of information are presented on a page (a three-column layout with left, center, and right columns; a two-column layout with a narrow left column and a wide right column for content; a one-column layout; and the like)

- Whether a page has a banner at the top

- Whether a page has a footer

- Where navigational menus appear (at the top of the page, under the banner, in the right column, and so on)

The Backdrop theme defines attributes such as

- The colors used on the page

- The font and font size used for various elements on a page (such as headings, titles, and body text)

- Graphical elements, such as logos

Backdrop core includes a number of off-the-shelf layouts and themes that you can use for your new web site. You can also download free layouts and themes from `www.backdropcms.org/layouts` and `www.backdropcms.org/themes`, or create your own layouts and theme by following the directions found at backdropcms.org/guide/layouts and backdropcms.org/guide/themes.

Creating Content

A web site without content would be like a book without words, a newspaper without news, or a magazine without articles: hardly worth the effort of looking at. Backdrop makes it easy to create, publish, and manage content on your web site. Let's look at how simple it is by creating your first piece of content. If you haven't installed Backdrop yet, please visit the book's appendix and follow the step-by-step process for installing and configuring Backdrop core.

There are multiple paths for getting to the content-authoring screens in Backdrop. This chapter focuses on the simplest, and Chapter 2 discusses other methods.

On the front page of your new web site is an Add New Content link beneath the Welcome post (see Figure 1-1). Clicking it takes you to the content-editing form where you can create your first piece of content.

Figure 1-1. *Click the Add New Content link to get started*

Next you see a list of the content types you can use (see Figure 1-2). Backdrop comes with two basic content types: posts and pages. Both provide a text field for entering the title of the content item and a body text area where you can write. Different content types provide additional elements. In the case of a post, you can enter tags for categorizing the content, along with an image. The book covers tagging and several other content types later, as well as how to create custom content types.

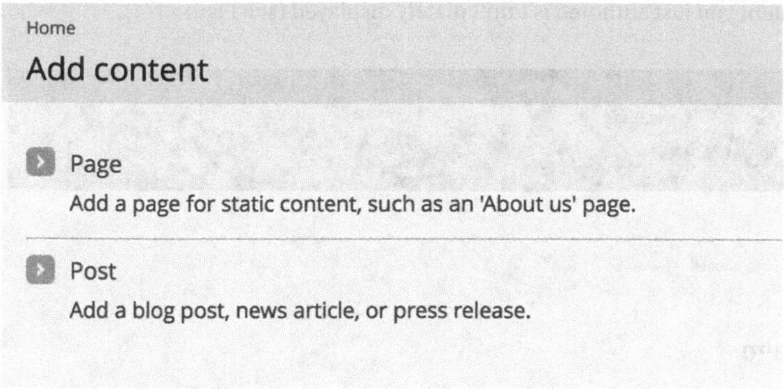

Home

Add content

▶ **Page**
Add a page for static content, such as an 'About us' page.

▶ **Post**
Add a blog post, news article, or press release.

Figure 1-2. *Selecting your content type*

Start with the simplest content type, a page, as the basis for your content item. Click the Page link, which opens the form for creating that content type (see Figure 1-3). On this form, enter the title of your first article, and type some text in the Body area. After you have entered the title and body, scroll down to the bottom of the page and click the Save button.

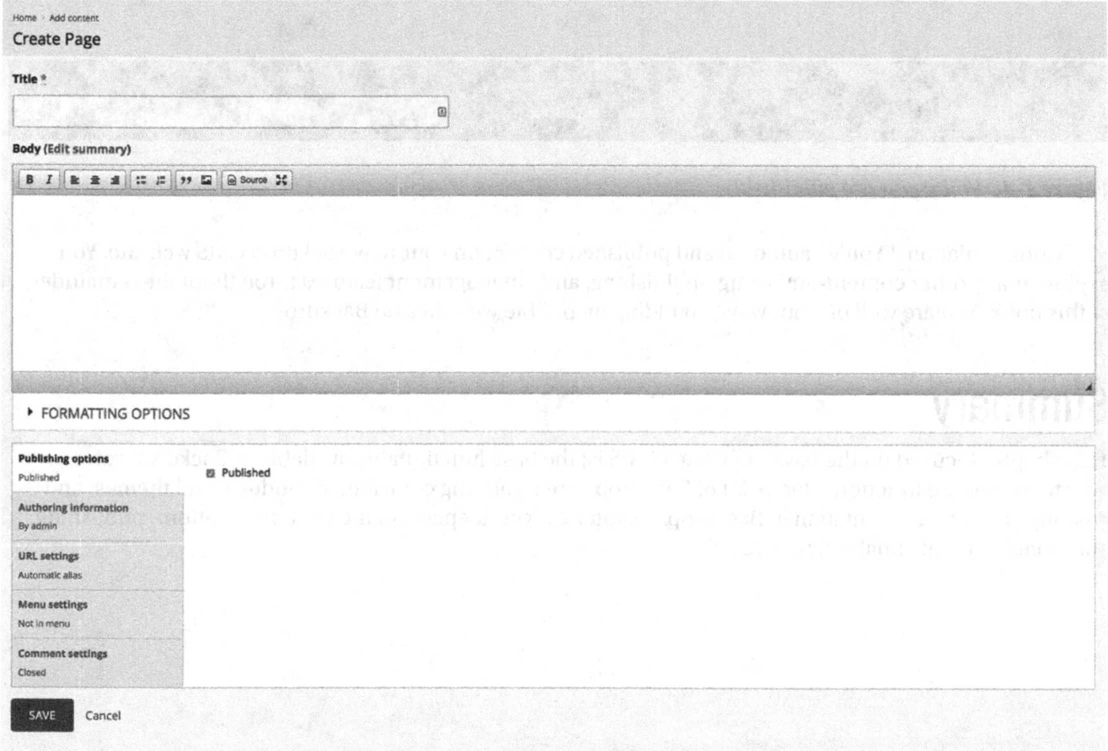

Home › Add content

Create Page

Title *

Body (Edit summary)

B I | 🔲 🔲 🔲 | ≔ ≔ | 99 🖼 | 🔲 Source 🔀

▶ FORMATTING OPTIONS

Publishing options
Published
☑ Published

Authoring information
By admin

URL settings
Automatic alias

Menu settings
Not in menu

Comment settings
Closed

SAVE   Cancel

Figure 1-3. *Creating a page*

When you click Save, the content you just authored is immediately displayed (see Figure 1-4).

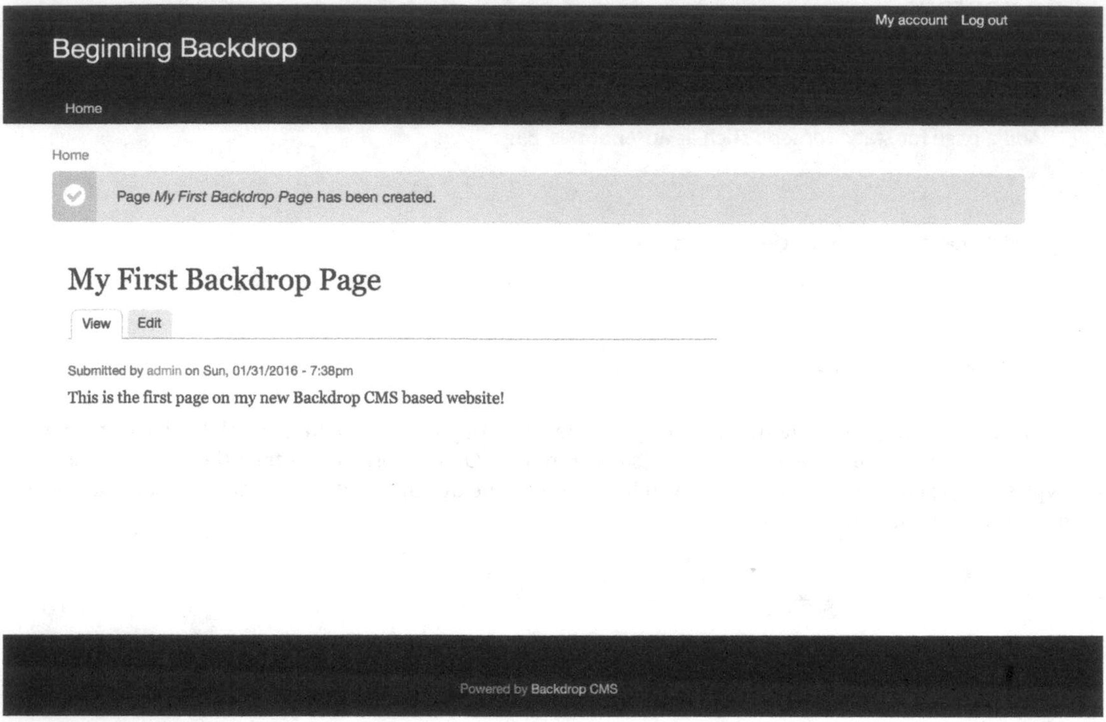

Figure 1-4. *Voila: you are published!*

Congratulations! You've authored and published content on your new Backdrop CMS web site. You explore many other content-authoring, -publishing, and –management features throughout the remainder of this book. You are well on your way to building incredible web sites on Backdrop.

Summary

This chapter focused on the basics of what a CMS is; the base functionality available in Backdrop core; how to extend the functional footprint of Backdrop core by adding contributed modules and themes; and creating your first content item in Backdrop. Chapter 2 dives deeper into the content-creation, -publishing, and -management capabilities of Backdrop.

CHAPTER 2

■ ■ ■

Creating and Managing Content

Remember, a web site without content is as interesting and informative as a book without words. This chapter focuses on Backdrop's features for creating, publishing, editing, and managing content, providing you with the knowledge necessary to venture out and create, publish, and manage a wide variety of content on your new Backdrop web site. You started that process in the previous chapter; now let's see what you can add.

Understanding the Basics

Content is the primary building block of any web site, whether it is constructed using Backdrop or any other tool in the marketplace. Content is what visitors come to a web site to find, and a lack of content is often the reason visitors fail to return to a web site. In its most basic form, *content* is any combination of text, pictures, video, audio, and graphics. An individual piece of content may take a variety of forms:

- News story

- Blog post

- Product description

- Company overview

- Photograph

- Wiki entry

Content on a Backdrop-based web site often starts with a title followed by body text. In Chapter 1, you created a page that consisted of content with just a title and body. Backdrop provides the ability to expand on this with a custom content type. A custom content type enables you to create additional fields that can be used to capture other relevant and related information. A common example is a calendar event. An event includes a title and body text (the description of the event), as well as other pertinent information, such as the date and time, the location, and possibly a map or photo. Chapter 5 covers creating custom content types.

Creating Content in Backdrop

Chapter 1 introduced Backdrop's content-creation capabilities by showing you how to create your first content item and publish it to your web site. The content type you used in Chapter 1 was the *page*. Backdrop includes a second content type: the *post*.

A post is identical to a page, with the single exception that a post has an image-upload feature and an additional field where you can enter *tags*. Tags are simply words that help classify, organize, and search for related content on your site. They are a powerful Backdrop feature and are covered in detail in Chapter 4.

© Todd Tomlinson 2016
T. Tomlinson, *Beginning Backdrop CMS*, DOI 10.1007/978-1-4842-1970-6_2

To create and publish your new post, click the Add Content link on the home page of your web site, and select Post from the list of content types. The form that is used to create a post looks identical to the form used to author a page, plus the image-upload and tags fields. Proceed with the content-creation process by entering a title. Next, upload a picture by clicking the Browse button and finding a picture on your computer to upload and include in the post (see Figure 2-1).

Image

| Browse... No file selected. | UPLOAD |

Upload an image to go with this post.
Files must be less than **32 MB**.
Allowed file types: **png gif jpg jpeg**.

Figure 2-1. *Browse your computer for the image you wish to add to your post*

After you locate and upload an image, the content-creation form should display a miniature version of the image (see Figure 2-2) along with an Alternate Text field. It is a good idea to enter text into this field, especially if you expect to have visitors with visual disabilities.

Image

📄 Parthenon.jpg **(57.56 KB)**   REMOVE

Alternate text

| The Parthenon in Greece |

This text will be used by screen readers, search engines, or when the image cannot be loaded.

Upload an image to go with this post.

Figure 2-2. *The image you wish to upload appears, and you are given the chance to add descriptive text*

The next step is to create the body text and tags associated with your post (see Figure 2-3). Tags can be any list of words or phrases, separated by commas, that describe the general concepts covered in your post. Chapter 4 discusses tags in more detail.

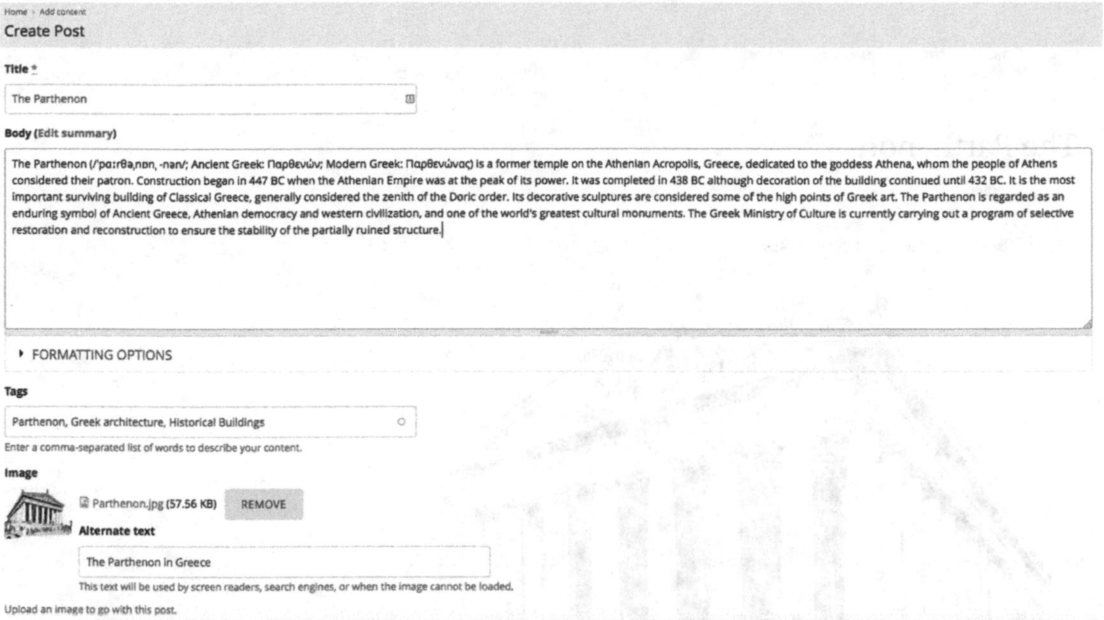

Home › Add content
Create Post

Title *

The Parthenon

Body (Edit summary)

The Parthenon (/ˈpɑːrθəˌnɒn, -nən/; Ancient Greek: Παρθενών; Modern Greek: Παρθενώνας) is a former temple on the Athenian Acropolis, Greece, dedicated to the goddess Athena, whom the people of Athens considered their patron. Construction began in 447 BC when the Athenian Empire was at the peak of its power. It was completed in 438 BC although decoration of the building continued until 432 BC. It is the most important surviving building of Classical Greece, generally considered the zenith of the Doric order. Its decorative sculptures are considered some of the high points of Greek art. The Parthenon is regarded as an enduring symbol of Ancient Greece, Athenian democracy and western civilization, and one of the world's greatest cultural monuments. The Greek Ministry of Culture is currently carrying out a program of selective restoration and reconstruction to ensure the stability of the partially ruined structure.

▸ FORMATTING OPTIONS

Tags

Parthenon, Greek architecture, Historical Buildings

Enter a comma-separated list of words to describe your content.

Image

🖾 Parthenon.jpg (57.56 KB)   REMOVE

Alternate text

The Parthenon in Greece

This text will be used by screen readers, search engines, or when the image cannot be loaded.

Upload an image to go with this post.

Figure 2-3. *Creating the post's body text, and adding tags*

Next, click the Save button at the bottom of the page. Backdrop displays the post you created (see Figure 2-4).

Home

 Post *The Parthenon* has been created.

The Parthenon

View | Edit

Submitted by admin on Sun, 02/07/2016 - 5:44pm

The Parthenon (/ˈpɑːrθəˌnɒn, -nən/; Ancient Greek: Παρθενών; Modern Greek: Παρθενώνας) is a former temple on the Athenian Acropolis, Greece, dedicated to the goddess Athena, whom the people of Athens considered their patron. Construction began in 447 BC when the Athenian Empire was at the peak of its power. It was completed in 438 BC although decoration of the building continued until 432 BC. It is the most important surviving building of Classical Greece, generally considered the zenith of the Doric order. Its decorative sculptures are considered some of the high points of Greek art. The Parthenon is regarded as an enduring symbol of Ancient Greece, Athenian democracy and western civilization, and one of the world's greatest cultural monuments. The Greek Ministry of Culture is currently carrying out a program of selective restoration and reconstruction to ensure the stability of the partially ruined structure.

Tags:
Parthenon   Greek architecture   Historical Buildings

Figure 2-4. *Your completed post*

As you can see in Figure 2-4, a post displays the image that was uploaded as well as the list of tags entered. Chapter 4 covers tagging and taxonomy in detail, but as a preview, clicking one of the tags automatically generates a list of all posts tagged with that same term.

Teasers and Full Nodes

One of Backdrop's key content-related features is the ability to automatically display a content item in either teaser mode or full-node view mode. A *teaser* is a shortened version of a post, typically the first 600 characters, whereas *full node* refers to the entire length of the content. Teaser mode is great when you're displaying a list of posts and you want visitors to be able to read the introductory paragraph(s), thus enticing them to click the Read More link to see the entire post. You can modify the length of the teaser as well as several other aspects of a view mode. Chapter 10 covers the details.

Return to your site's home page by clicking the Home link in the main navigational menu. On the home page, you see the post you just created rendered in teaser mode, with a Read More link at the bottom that takes you to the full version of the post (see Figure 2-5). If you compare the body of the post in Figure 2-4 with the body of the post in Figure 2-5, you see that the content was shortened to 600 characters and the Read More link was added.

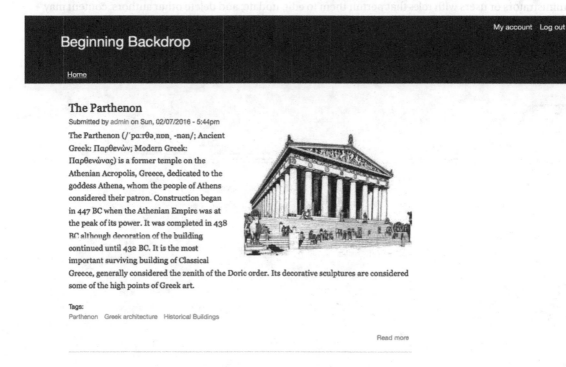

Figure 2-5. *The teaser mode of a post*

Editing Content

At some point, you will need to change something about a piece of content you've posted on your site. The process for editing content is nearly identical to the process of creating it, the only difference being the need to find the content you want to change. To find content, click the Content link in the menu at the top of the page. The Content page lists all the content that appears on the site and is filterable by published status and type of content (such as post or page); there is also a title search feature.

To edit a content item from the list presented on the Content page, simply click the Edit button for that item, and Backdrop displays the content-editing form. If you are on the page where the content you need to change resides, and you are logged in as a user who has the correct permissions (see Chapter 6), you see View and Edit tabs (see Figure 2-6) at the top of the edit form and a Delete button at the bottom to remove that content item from your site.

Figure 2-6. *You can edit the content of your site by clicking Edit*

By default, Backdrop allows the author of a content item to edit, update, and delete that item. Only site administrators or users with roles that permit them to edit, update, and delete other authors' content may make changes to your content. If you do not see Edit next to the title of a content item, you are not logged in with an account with the proper permissions to make changes to that item.

To change a content item, click the Edit tab. Backdrop displays that content item in editing mode, where you can change or delete the item (see Figure 2-7).

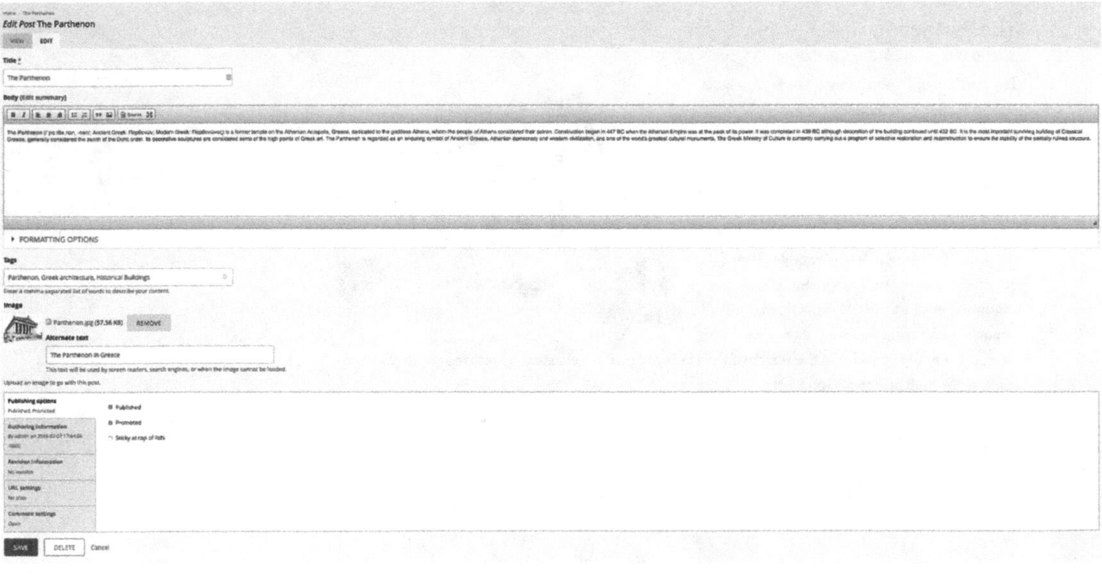

Figure 2-7. *Content is displayed in editing mode*

There's also another way to edit your posts. Try updating the post you created in the previous step by navigating back to your home page. To navigate back to the home page, click the Home icon button at upper left on the page. On the home page, hover over the post you wish to change. A gear icon appears to the right of the title as you hover (see Figure 2-8). Click the gear icon, and select the Edit option.

The Parthenon

Submitted by admin on Sun, 02/07/2016 - 5:44pm

The Parthenon (/ˈpɑːrθəˌnɒn, -nən/; Ancient
Greek: Παρθενών; Modern Greek:
Παρθενώνας) is a former temple on the

Figure 2-8. *Gear icon and Edit option*

Clicking Edit takes you to the node edit page for that content item. Make changes to the text in the editor, and click Save. The new version automatically appears on the home page after you've saved it. This is a great way to perform quick text touch-ups or fix errors you've spotted.

Other Content Options

At the bottom of the content-editing form in Figure 2-7 are several options associated with the content item that allow you, as the content author, to control aspects of that item. Return to the edit form for your post by using one of the techniques described earlier, and scroll to the bottom of the content-editing form. Examine the vertical tabs at the bottom of the form, and you find the following:

- Publishing options
- Authoring information
- Revision information
- URL settings
- Comment settings

The options associated with each of these items are described in the sections that follow.

Publishing Options

As the author of the content item, you can specify whether the content should be published, promoted, or sticky at the top of lists. If you check the box next to Published, your article is immediately viewable by site visitors the moment you click the Save button. Unchecking the Published box saves the content in a state that is viewable by site administrators/editors, but not by visitors to your site—a great option if your content is a work in progress and isn't ready to be viewed by site visitors.

The Promoted option specifies that the content you authored should be displayed on your site's home page. By default, Backdrop displays a list of published content in descending order by date published, a style that is common on blog sites. You look at how to change what appears on the home page in Chapter 11. Unchecking the box directs Backdrop to not display the content on your home page.

On most sites, the list of content is sorted either by the date it was published (for example, most recent content at the top of the list) or by an attribute of the content, such as the title. There may be cases when you have a content item that is important and that you want to ensure always appears at the top of any list it appears in on the site. The Sticky At Top Of Lists check box provides that mechanism to ensure that the content you authored always appears at the top of a list. If the Sticky At Top Of Lists check box is unchecked, the content item appears based on the sort order you have defined for your list.

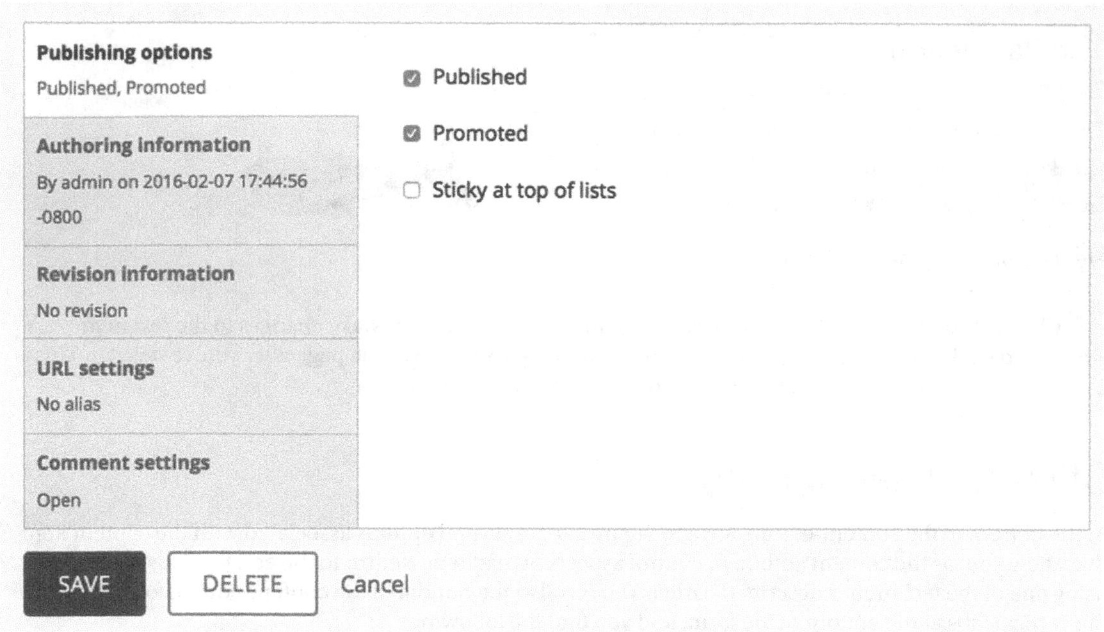

Figure 2-9. *Publishing options*

Authoring Information

The Authoring Information tab (see Figure 2-10) provides two options to override the default information that is set by Backdrop when you create a new content item. By default, the Authored By field is populated with the username of the person who was logged in and created the content. The Authored On field represents the original date and time the content was authored. Sometimes you may wish to attribute the content to a different user, or you may want to change the date and time the content was published.

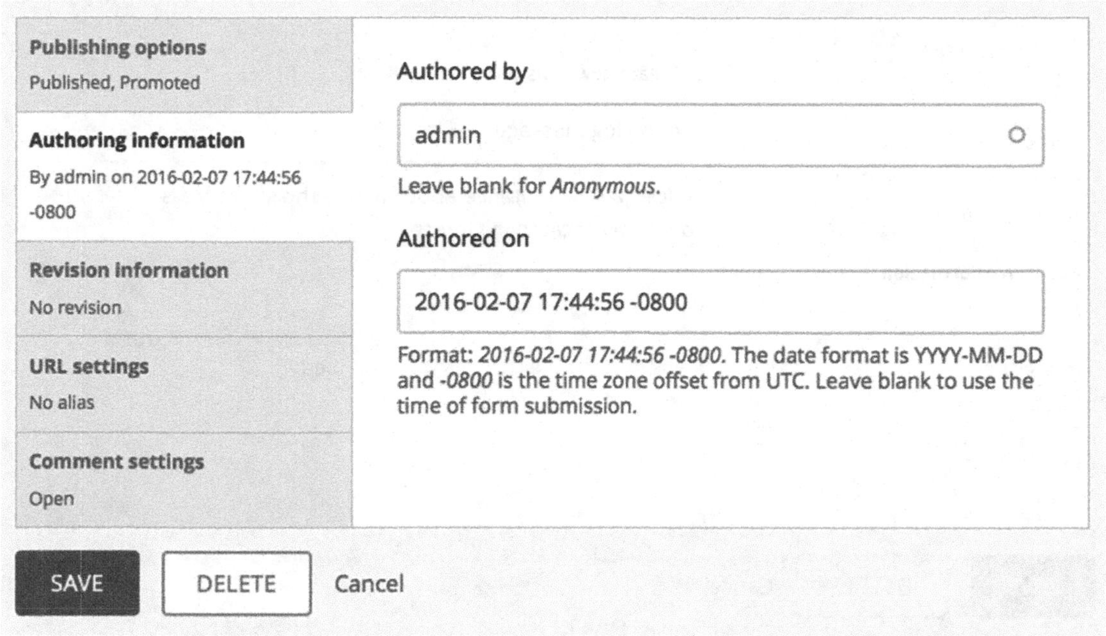

Publishing options
Published, Promoted

Authoring information
By admin on 2016-02-07 17:44:56 -0800

Revision information
No revision

URL settings
No alias

Comment settings
Open

Authored by

admin

Leave blank for *Anonymous*.

Authored on

2016-02-07 17:44:56 -0800

Format: *2016-02-07 17:44:56 -0800*. The date format is YYYY-MM-DD and *-0800* is the time zone offset from UTC. Leave blank to use the time of form submission.

SAVE   DELETE   Cancel

Figure 2-10. *Authoring Information tab*

To change the author of the content item, begin typing the username of the person to whom you wish to attribute the article. If the username exists in the database, it appears in a drop-down list. If the username does not exist, you can attribute the article to a person's name—but that person can't log on to the site and maintain that content item, because they do not have a valid user account on the Backdrop site. More about user accounts in Chapter 3.

To change the date and time the content item was authored, follow the format shown below the text box: for example, *2016-02-07 17:44:56 -0800* represents February 2, 2016 at 17:44:56 in a time zone that is 8 hours behind GMT.

Revision Information

Backdrop provides a feature that allows a content author to create a new revision of an existing content item, retaining the old version of that item in the database. This is a good option for sites where a content author can revise content but an editor must approve those changes before the new content is published and made available to site visitors. Clicking the Revision Information tab displays a Create New Revision check box and a text area (Revision Log Message) for describing the changes that were made (see Figure 2-11).

Publishing options Published, Promoted	☑ Create new revision
Authoring information By Anonymous on 2016-02-07 17:44:56 -0800	Revision log message Added a new sentence about where the structure is physically located in Greece.
Revision information New revision	
URL settings No alias	Briefly describe the changes you have made.
Comment settings Open	

SAVE   DELETE   Cancel

Figure 2-11. *Revision Information tab*

After selecting the Create New Revision check box and entering a description of the changes, click Save. A new Revisions tab appears at the top of the content item in addition to the View and Edit tabs (see Figure 2-12). Clicking the Revisions tab displays a list of all the revisions made to the content, including the date, time, and author of the previous revisions. You can revert a revision to the current version of the content item if someone made a change that shouldn't have been made and you need to revert the content back to the previous state.

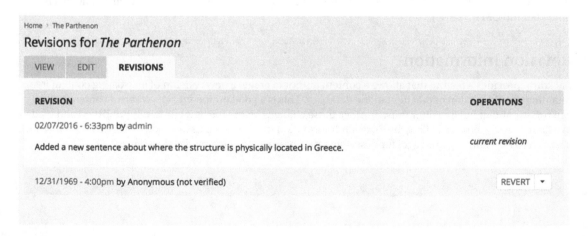

Home > The Parthenon
Revisions for *The Parthenon*

VIEW	EDIT	**REVISIONS**

REVISION	OPERATIONS
02/07/2016 - 6:33pm **by** admin Added a new sentence about where the structure is physically located in Greece.	*current revision*
12/31/1969 - 4:00pm **by** Anonymous (not verified)	REVERT ▾

Figure 2-12. *Viewing revisions*

You can view a previously published version of the post by clicking the date and time for the version.

Clicking the Back button in your browser returns you to the previous page, where you can click the Revert link to change the currently published version to a previously published version. When you click Revert, Backdrop displays a page that asks you if you are sure you want to revert to a previously published version. Clicking the Revert button results in Backdrop unpublishing the current version and publishing the selected version.

URL Settings

The default URL structure for a content item is `http://yoursitename.com/node/nodeid`, where `nodeid` is a number that is automatically assigned by Backdrop to your content item. In the previous example, the post's URL is `node/2`. There may be cases where you may want to override the default URL generated by Backdrop with a more meaningful URL structure that is search engine and human friendly. For the article about the Parthenon, that might be `/parthenon`. Click the URL Settings tab, and enter the URL you wish to use (without the leading slash) for your content item (see Figure 2-13).

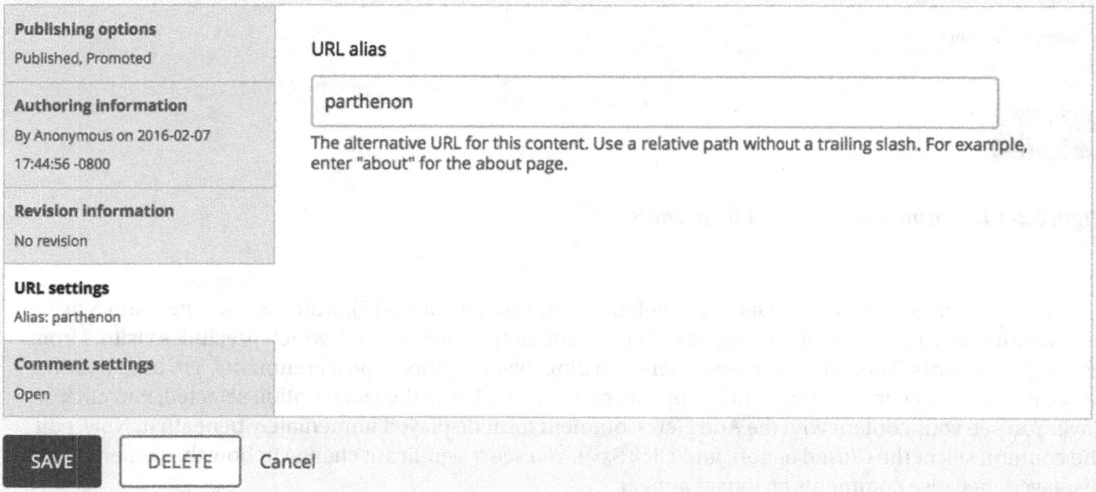

Publishing options	URL alias
Published, Promoted	
Authoring information	parthenon
By Anonymous on 2016-02-07 17:44:56 -0800	The alternative URL for this content. Use a relative path without a trailing slash. For example, enter "about" for the about page.
Revision information	
No revision	
URL settings	
Alias: parthenon	
Comment settings	
Open	

SAVE   DELETE   Cancel

Figure 2-13. *Setting a URL alias*

■ **Caution**   You must use hyphens, underscores, periods, or other characters to separate the words in your URL. Spaces between words do not work.

After entering the URL alias, click the Save button. The new URL that is displayed in the browser for your content item.

Creating alias URLs is an important aspect of creating content on your web site. However, manually creating an alias for every content item is tedious. Fortunately, there is a Backdrop module called Pathauto that automatically creates a URL alias for every content item saved on your site. Chapter 12 covers the installation of modules like Pathauto.

Comment Settings

Backdrop provides the capability for visitors to your web site to post comments about the site's content. By default, every content item is open for commenting by site visitors. You can change how comments are handled by clicking the Comment Settings tab as shown in Figure 2-14.

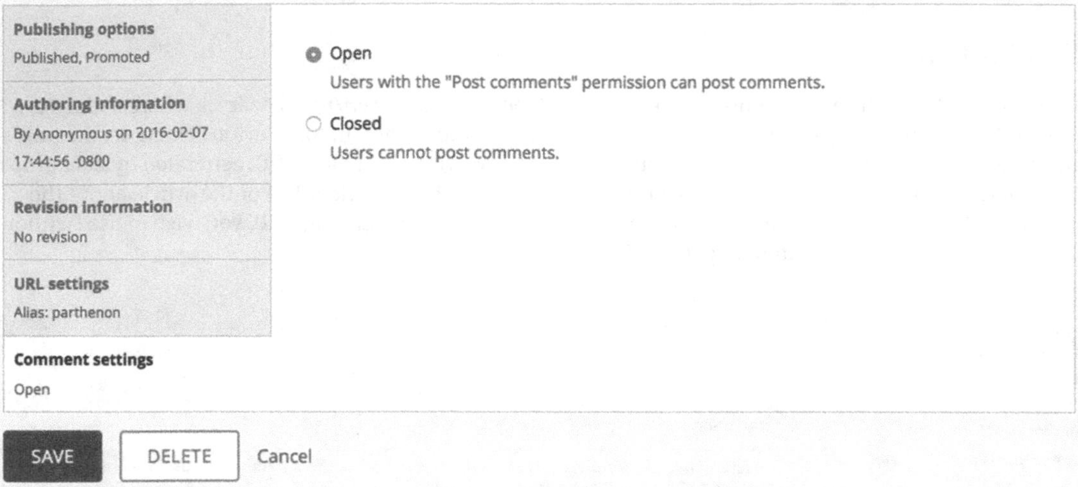

Publishing options
Published, Promoted

Authoring information
By Anonymous on 2016-02-07
17:44:56 -0800

Revision information
No revision

URL settings
Alias: parthenon

Comment settings
Open

● Open
    Users with the "Post comments" permission can post comments.

○ Closed
    Users cannot post comments.

SAVE   DELETE   Cancel

Figure 2-14. *Setting your comment preferences*

Two options are presented: Open, the default option (see Figure 2-15), which allows site visitors to post comments to a content item created with this content type; and Closed, which precludes visitors from posting comments. There may be cases where you don't want visitors to post comments. Try both options to see the difference in how the content appears on your site. Leave the Open option selected, and click Save. You see your content with the Add New Comment form displayed immediately beneath it. Now, edit the content, select the Closed option, and click Save. You see a significant change in how the content item is displayed, because comments no longer appear.

greatest cultural monuments. The Greek Ministry of Culture is currently carrying out a program of selective restoration and reconstruction to ensure the stability of the partially ruined structure.

Tags:
Parthenon   Greek architecture   Historical Buildings

Add new comment

Your name   admin

Comment *

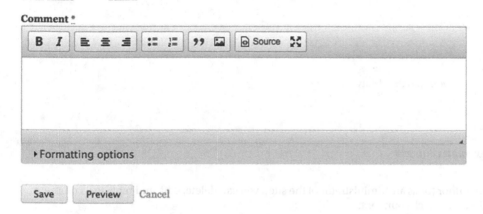

Figure 2-15. *With the default setting of Open, users can post comments on your site*

With the default Open setting, visitors to your site can write and publish comments in response to content items (assuming you have set the permissions to allow anonymous users to post comments, as covered in Chapter 5). Try entering a comment, and then click Save. Your comment should appear in the Comments section (see Figure 2-16).

Ancient Greece, Athenian democracy and western civilization, and one of the world's greatest cultural monuments. The Greek Ministry of Culture is currently carrying out a program of selective restoration and reconstruction to ensure the stability of the partially ruined structure.

Tags:
Parthenon   Greek architecture   Historical Buildings

Comments

Figure 2-16. *An example comment*

As the content author (or as an administrator of the site), you can delete, edit, and reply to a comment by clicking the links under each comment.

Comments typically appear in chronological order. As the site administrator, you can specify how comments are displayed: either the newest comment at the top of the list or the first comment posted at the top of the list. Chapter 10 covers how to set the default order.

Turning comments on and off at the individual content item provides absolute control over which items accept comments. You can also set whether to accept comments at the content-type level, meaning every content item created using that content type inherits that setting. Chapter 10 discusses setting global parameters, such as accepting comments.

Deleting Content

You now know how to create and edit content, but not how to delete it. Sometimes you have a piece of content that is no longer relevant to your site, and you want to delete it. The process is fairly simple. First create a new post, following the steps covered earlier in the chapter. The title and content aren't important, because you're going to delete the post immediately after you create it. When you're finished, click the Save button. If you are viewing that piece of content, you may do the following:

- Click the Edit tab, and, on the node edit form, click the Delete button at the bottom of the form.

- If the content item is being displayed as part of a list, hover over the title, and click the gear icon. Select the Delete option from the drop-down list that appears.

- On the content listing page (click Content on the menu), click the Delete button in the Actions column.

All of these methods permanently remove the content item from the Backdrop database. If you created a menu link for that content item, that menu item is also removed.

Sometimes you may not want a content item to appear on the site, but you wish to retain the post for future reference; or perhaps you're working on a long post and need to finish it later. In those situations, to effectively hide that content item from site visitors, simply edit the content item and click the Publishing Options tab. Uncheck the Published check box, and then click Save. The content remains in the database but is not viewable by visitors.

Finding Content

It is likely that your site will have dozens or hundreds of content items, and at some point you'll need to look for an item that you want to view, change, or delete. To do so, you can do any of the following:

- Navigate to the page where that item resides, and click the Edit tab above the content item. Or, if the content is displayed in a list, click the gear icon.

- If you know the URL of the content item, enter the URL in the address bar of your web browser.

- Search for that item using your site's search feature.

- Use the content listing page.

Any of these methods will work, but using the content listing page is probably the most common. To view this page, click the Content link in the administrator's toolbar (assuming you are logged in to the site as a site administrator). You see the screen shown in Figure 2-17.

Figure 2-17. *Viewing the content listing page*

On this page, you can sort the list by clicking the Title, Content Type, Name (author), Status, or Updated column heading and then clicking the up and down triangles to sort in ascending or descending order. You can also *filter* the results (limit what is shown) by selecting the status from the Published drop-down menu (for example, Published or Unpublished) and/or the content type drop-down menu (such as Post or Page). Clicking the Filter button refreshes the list to show only those items that meet the criteria you selected.

From any item in the list, you can click the title of the content item to view it, or you can click the arrow to the right of Operations to reveal Edit and Delete options. You may also update the node alias values, remove content from the front page, delete content, promote content, unpublish content, publish content, make content unsticky, or make content sticky, for multiple content items at the same time. Just click the check box to the left of each content item, select from the Operations drop-down menu the option that you want to apply to all items you checked, and then click Execute.

Summary

This chapter focused on creating content, setting the various options that are available when creating a content item, and updating and deleting content. You learned how to view content, how to create search-engine- and user-friendly URLs, change authoring information, publish and unpublish content, change comment settings, and make a content item stay at the top of a list.

At this point, you have the basic skills and understanding necessary to create a basic Backdrop web site, but stopping now means you would miss out on all the other rich and powerful features that Backdrop has to offer. The chapters that follow describe the processes for creating complex page layouts, rendering lists of content, and controlling who has access to various features and functions on your web site. You also learn tips and tricks for managing your new site.

CHAPTER 3

■■■

Creating and Managing Users

Now that your site is up and running, you have a couple of decisions to make. First, will your site have any administrators other than yourself? Second, will your site be open to everyone, or will users need to log in to view content and other features? This chapter discusses how Backdrop treats visitors to your site, and how you as a site administrator can configure Backdrop's user account features to restrict the capabilities of those who have user accounts on your system.

Users, Roles, and Permissions

You can control who has the ability to do what on your web site by using Backdrop's security features. These features let you define who can view, create, update, delete, and participate through a combination of individual user accounts, user roles, and permissions.

Users (or site visitors) in Backdrop are divided into two general categories: anonymous users and authenticated users. Anonymous users are individuals who visit your web site and do not log in using a user ID and password. For example, if you visit www.cnn.com and don't log in, you're classified as an anonymous user. With Backdrop, you can support anonymous users, and you also can restrict what an anonymous user can do on your site. Authenticated users are visitors to your site who log in using a unique user ID and password. You see how user IDs and passwords are created shortly, but understanding the difference between the two categories of users is important.

Roles are a Backdrop mechanism that allow you, the site administrator, to define categories of authenticated users of your web site. You may define roles on your web site that are department specific (for example, a role each for human resources, purchasing, sales, marketing, and customer service), roles that are functionally oriented (for example, content authors, content reviewers, content publishers), roles that are associated with a specific section of your web site (for example, products, support, sales, home page), or any other definition you can dream up. Roles are simply a way of putting authenticated users into categories associated with specific permissions. Any authenticated user of your web site may be assigned to none, one, or more than one role (for example, you may have a user who is assigned the roles *sales department*, *content author*, and *products*).

Permissions in Backdrop are a mechanism for controlling what a user assigned to a specific role can do. There are dozens of permissions that you can enable or revoke for each user role you have defined. Examples of permissions that you might set for a specific role include the ability to create a new page, the ability to create a new article, the ability to edit any article regardless of who authored it, the ability to search content on the web site, and the ability to add a new user account. The combination of permissions that you set for each role defines what a user assigned to that role can do on your web site once they have successfully logged in.

When you combine user roles with permissions and individual user accounts, you end up with a highly configurable solution for securing access to key features and content on your web site.

© Todd Tomlinson 2016

T. Tomlinson, *Beginning Backdrop CMS*, DOI 10.1007/978-1-4842-1970-6_3

User Accounts

All Backdrop web sites have at least one user account: the system administrator. This account is created automatically during the installation process and is the account you use to administer the site. If the site owner is the only one who creates content and administers the site, then the site administrator account is all that is required. If you anticipate that other people will administer or create content, you need to decide which Backdrop mechanism to use to create user accounts. Backdrop provides three alternatives for you to pick from:

- Only administrators can create user accounts.

- Visitors can create their own accounts without an administrator's approval.

- Visitors can request a new account, but an administrator has to approve the account before it is activated.

Which approach you should take depends on how you anticipate visitors using your web site. If your site is informational in nature and visitors don't need to log in to see content or participate in site features (for example, posting comments), then the first option is the best approach, because it doesn't confuse visitors by making them think they have to log in to see content. If your site has content or features that are considered "not for public consumption" and require a user account, then you want to pick an approach that works for you, depending on whether you want visitors to be able to create their own accounts without verifying their credentials (second option), or you want an administrator to perform some form of verification before a user's account is activated (third option).

Specifying the approach you wish to use is part of the process of determining the various settings for user accounts on your system.

Configuring User Account Settings

Before creating your first user account, it is advisable that you visit the Account Settings page and review or modify the general user account configuration settings, of which there are many (see Figure 3-1).

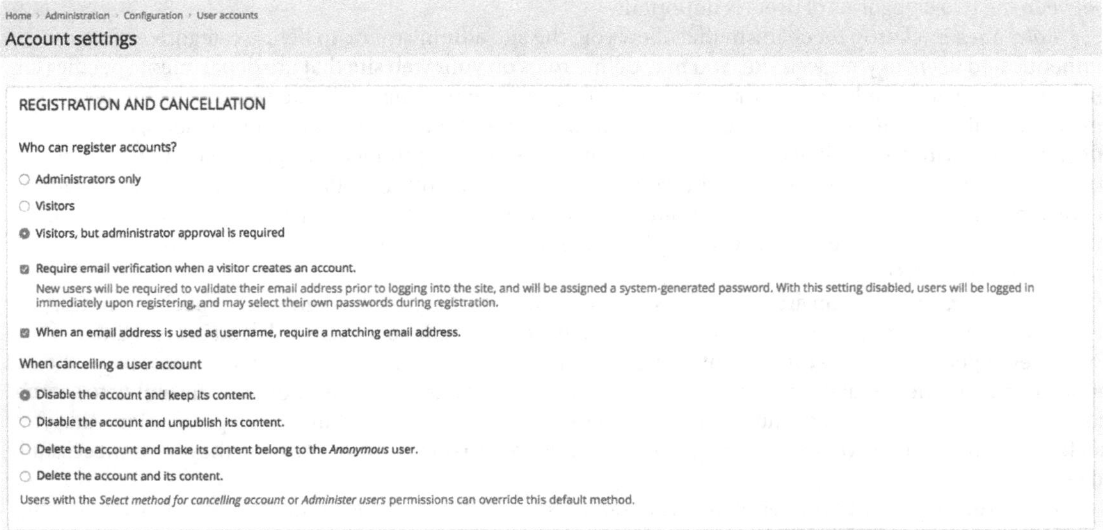

Home › Administration › Configuration › User accounts
Account settings

REGISTRATION AND CANCELLATION

Who can register accounts?

○ Administrators only

○ Visitors

◉ Visitors, but administrator approval is required

☑ Require email verification when a visitor creates an account.
New users will be required to validate their email address prior to logging into the site, and will be assigned a system-generated password. With this setting disabled, users will be logged in immediately upon registering, and may select their own passwords during registration.

☑ When an email address is used as username, require a matching email address.

When cancelling a user account

◉ Disable the account and keep its content.

○ Disable the account and unpublish its content.

○ Delete the account and make its content belong to the *Anonymous* user.

○ Delete the account and its content.

Users with the *Select method for cancelling account* or *Administer users* permissions can override this default method.

Figure 3-1. *Account Settings page*

To access the Account Settings page, choose Configuration ➤ User Accounts ➤ Account Settings (assuming you are logged in as the administrator). On this page are a number of configuration options:

- *Registration And Cancellation*: Defines who can register new accounts on the site. The options are Administrators Only; Visitors; and Visitors, But Administrator Approval Is Required. The most common options are Administrators Only and Visitors, But Administrator Approval Is Required. These two are the most common due to spam accounts being created on sites that let the general public create accounts. Other options in this section include whether to require e-mail verification when a user creates an account; ensuring that when an e-mail address is used as an account's username, the e-mail address entered matches the account's e-mail address; and what to do when cancelling a user account. The default options are appropriate for most sites.

- *User Login*: Mechanisms users may use to log in to the site. Options are to allow a user to log in with their username or e-mail address, or only their username, or only their e-mail address. The most common option is a username or e-mail address.

- *URL Pattern*: URL structure for user account pages.

- *Administrator Role*: Defines which role is assigned to the capabilities associated with a site administrator. By default, Backdrop creates a role named Administrator. You may use that for all accounts that should have administrative access to the site, or you may create a new role (described later in this chapter).

- *Anonymous Users*: Name associated with an anonymous user, typically Anonymous.

- *Personalization*: Defines which options are available to authenticated users on the site, such as signatures, and a user picture that is used as an avatar on the site.

Now that you have completed the definition of user accounts, you are ready to define roles and set permissions.

Creating Roles

User roles are a mechanism for categorizing groups of users with similar responsibilities and capabilities on your web site. If your site is for an elementary school, you may have roles for teachers, students, and staff. If it is a community web site, you may have roles for content authors, content reviewers, publishers, and forum administrators.

The hardest part about creating user roles is deciding what roles you need for your site. In general, it is easier to administer a site that has fewer roles than one that has lots of roles, because you must set the permissions for each individual role. However, fewer roles means less flexibility, so it is a balancing act, and often one that you have to adjust over time as you become more familiar with the types of users on your site. Unfortunately, there isn't a formula you can use to determine how many roles you need, but there also isn't a right or wrong answer. For this chapter's example, you'll create two general-purpose roles:

A role for users who are part of the organization and who will have responsibility for authoring, publishing, and managing content and menus on the site.

A role for site visitors who are provided access to non-public content that is intended only for authenticated users (visitors who have been assigned a user ID and password). These users can view content and add comments to content, but they cannot author, edit, or delete content.

To create a new user role, assuming you are logged in with the Administrator account, visit Configuration ➤ User Accounts ➤ Roles. On this page, you see a list of roles that already exist. By default, Backdrop creates three roles during the installation process:

- *Anonymous:* Assigned to site visitors who have not logged on to the site

- *Authenticated:* A role associated with every site visitor who is logged on to the site

- *Administrator:* Typically assigned to user accounts that you wish to have administrative privileges. Assign this role judiciously, because it provides the ability to manage users, modules, comments, content, and pages on your site.

To create a new role, enter a descriptive name in the text box at the bottom of the list of existing roles. For example, enter **Company user** as the name of the new role (see Figure 3-2).

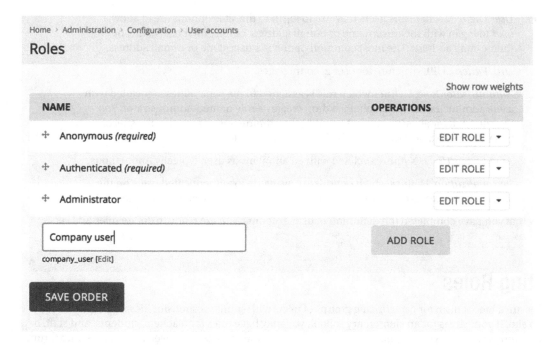

Figure 3-2. *Working with roles*

Click the Add Role button. This results in the creation of the Company User role, as shown in the list of defined user roles in Figure 3-3.

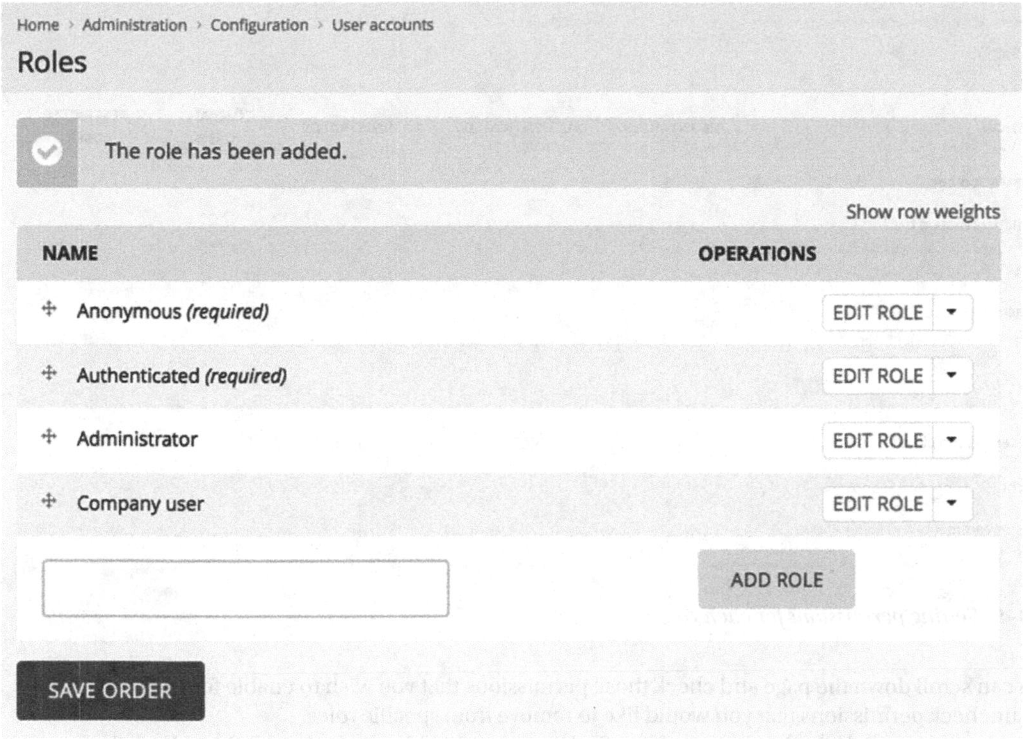

Home › Administration › Configuration › User accounts

Roles

✓ The role has been added.

Show row weights

NAME	OPERATIONS
✛ Anonymous *(required)*	EDIT ROLE ▾
✛ Authenticated *(required)*	EDIT ROLE ▾
✛ Administrator	EDIT ROLE ▾
✛ Company user	EDIT ROLE ▾
	ADD ROLE

SAVE ORDER

Figure 3-3. *The list of defined roles*

As a second example user role, let's create a *restricted user*: a user who has an account on the web site and who can view restricted content and post comments to that content, but cannot create, edit, or delete content or perform any administration functions. Enter the value **Restricted user** in the text box, and click the Add Role button to continue.

With both of these new roles defined, you're ready to assign permissions to them.

Assigning Permissions

Permissions provide a mechanism for controlling what users assigned to specific roles on the web site can and cannot do. Backdrop core and each contributed module provides a set of predefined permissions that you must either enable or disable on a role-by-role basis.

To assign permissions to a role, visit Configuration ➤ User Accounts ➤ Permissions. The Permissions page reveals the assigned permissions for each of the roles you have defined (see Figure 3-4).

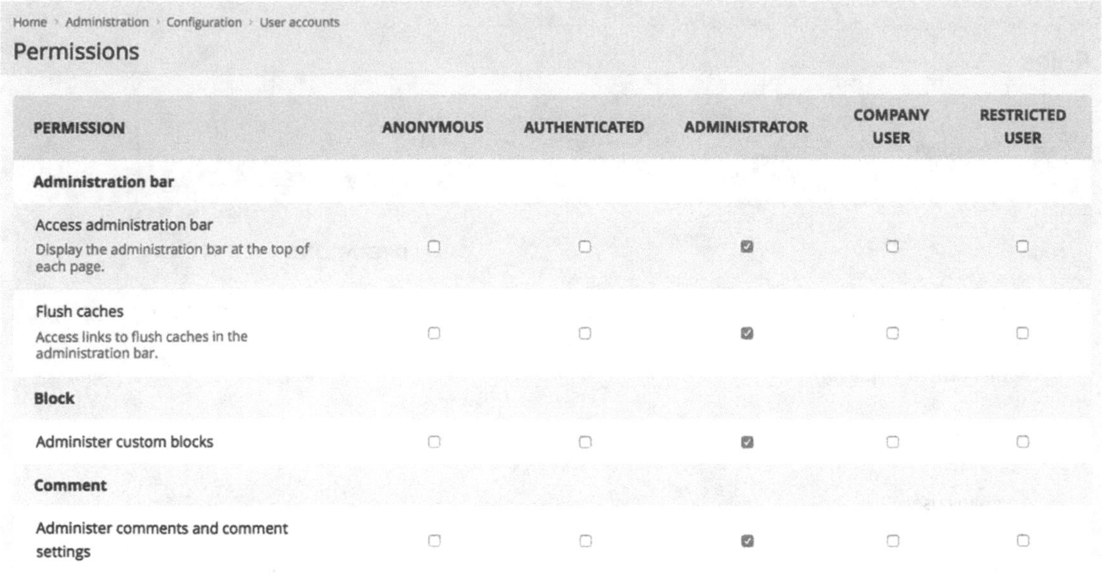

PERMISSION	ANONYMOUS	AUTHENTICATED	ADMINISTRATOR	COMPANY USER	RESTRICTED USER
Administration bar					
Access administration bar Display the administration bar at the top of each page.	☐	☐	☑	☐	☐
Flush caches Access links to flush caches in the administration bar.	☐	☐	☑	☐	☐
Block					
Administer custom blocks	☐	☐	☑	☐	☐
Comment					
Administer comments and comment settings	☐	☐	☑	☐	☐

Figure 3-4. *Setting permissions for each role*

You can scroll down the page and check those permissions that you wish to enable for each role. You can also uncheck permissions that you would like to remove from specific roles.

For example, scroll down the page until you find a section titled Node. In that section, check the following boxes for the Company User role:

- Administer Content
- Access The Content Overview Page
- View Published Content
- View Own Unpublished Content
- View Content Revisions
- Revert Content Revisions
- Delete Content Revisions
- Page: Create New Content
- Page: Edit Own Content
- Page: Delete Own Content
- Post: Create New Content
- Post: Edit Own Content
- Post: Delete OCn content

For the Restricted User role, scroll up to the Comment section and ensure that the following permissions are checked:

- View Comments

- Post Comments

- Skip Comment Approval

- Edit Own Comments

Once you have checked the boxes for the required permissions, scroll to the bottom of the page and click the Save Permissions button. At this point, you have created roles and assigned permissions to them. You are now ready to create user accounts.

Creating User Accounts

You have defined user roles and set appropriate permissions. Next, you can create user accounts. To do so, choose User accounts ➤ Add User Account to see the page shown in Figure 3-5.

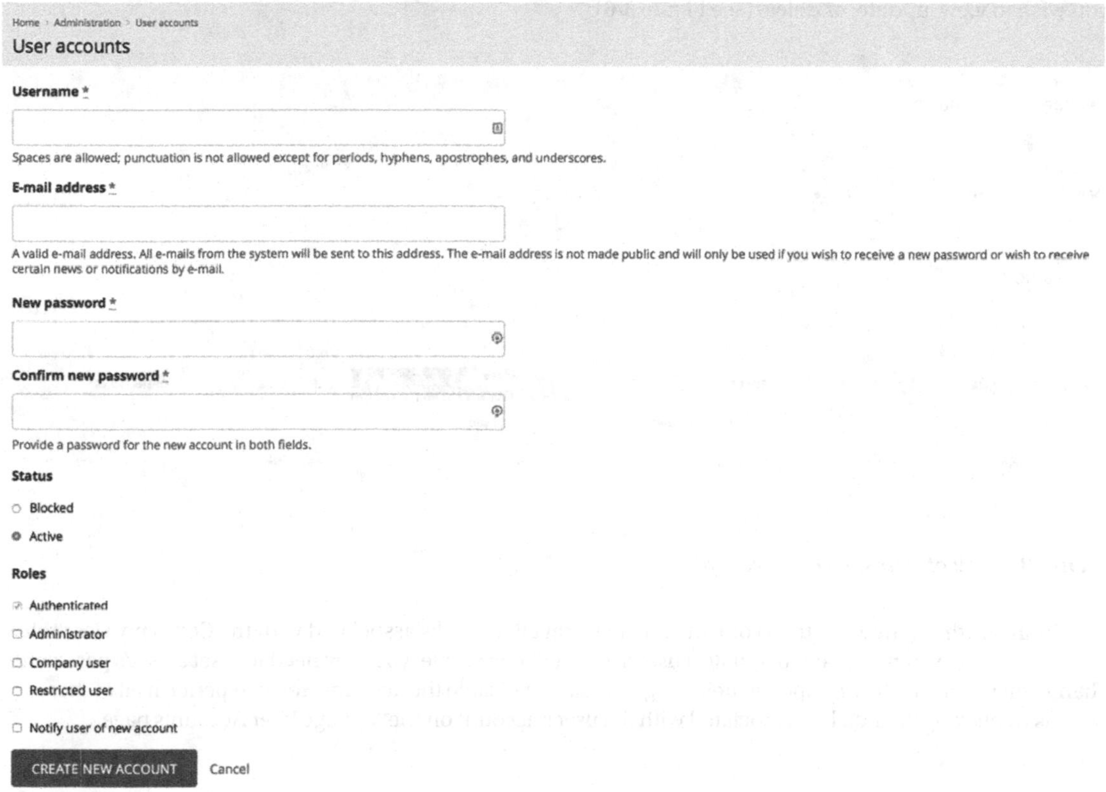

Figure 3-5. *Creating user accounts*

For example, create a new user account by entering the following values:

- In the Username field, enter **johnsmith**.

- In the E-mail Address field, enter: **johnsmith@example.com**.

- In the Password field, enter **12johnsmith34**.

- In the Confirm Password field, re-enter the password: **12johnsmith34**.

- For Status, make sure Active is selected.

- For Roles, check the Company User box.

- Check the Notify User Of New Account box (doing so causes Backdrop to send an e-mail to the user, notifying them of their new account).

- Click the Create New Account button to save the account.

As soon as you click Create New Account, an e-mail is sent to the new user, notifying them that their account has been created. The e-mail includes a link that takes them to the site's login page.

To see a list of all the user accounts on your site, click the User Accounts link in the administrator's menu. This page displays all the user accounts and is filterable and sortable to help you locate the account you wish to view, update, or delete (see Figure 3-6).

Figure 3-6. *All of your site's user accounts*

John Smith can now log in to your site and perform all the tasks associated with the Company User role.

Sometimes you may need to update a user account. For example, you may need to reset a user's password, change their e-mail address, update their assigned roles, or disable the account. You can perform all of these actions by clicking the Edit link associated with the user's account on the Manage User Accounts page.

User-Generated Accounts

If you configured your site so that visitors can create their own accounts, the process is slightly different than when an administrator creates accounts. The login form on the home page has an additional option under the Log In button: Create New Account. See Figure 3-7.

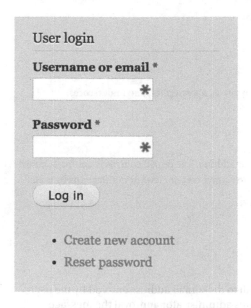

Figure 3-7. *The Create New Account option*

Clicking this link (while not logged in to the site) brings you to a screen where a visitor can enter their requested username and their e-mail address (see Figure 3-8). For this example, enter a username and an e-mail address for the new account, and click Create New Account. (Note: Backdrop only allows you to use an e-mail address once across the entire site. Attempting to reuse an e-mail address that is already assigned to an account on your system will result in an error message.)

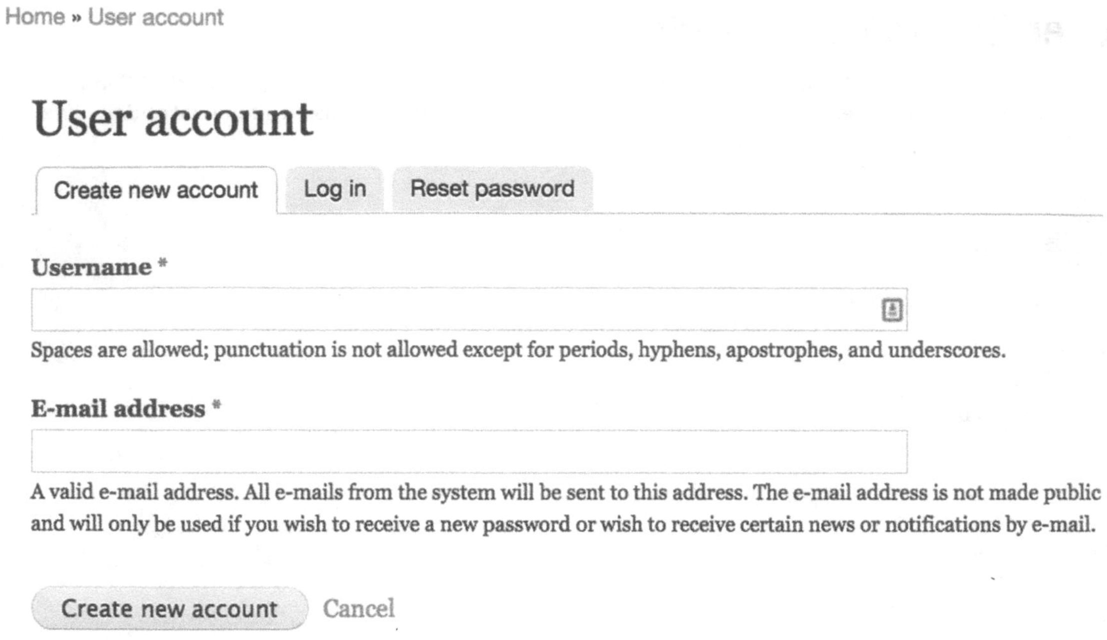

Home » User account

User account

| Create new account | Log in | Reset password |

Username *

[   ]

Spaces are allowed; punctuation is not allowed except for periods, hyphens, apostrophes, and underscores.

E-mail address *

[   ]

A valid e-mail address. All e-mails from the system will be sent to this address. The e-mail address is not made public and will only be used if you wish to receive a new password or wish to receive certain news or notifications by e-mail.

(Create new account) Cancel

Figure 3-8. *Entering new account information*

As soon as the account is created, Backdrop sends an e-mail to the e-mail address entered by the user and displays a success message on the screen. If your site requires administrator approval the message thanks the user for applying for an account is pending approval by the site administrator and to check their email for a message with further instructions. If you site does not require administrator approval the message instructs the visitor to check their email for further instructions.

If you configured your system so that users can create an account but an administrator must manually approve that account, you need to visit the Manage User Accounts page and edit the account, changing the user's status from Blocked to Active. Until the user's status has been changed, they will be unable to log in to the site with their user ID and password. If you selected the option that lets users create an account without administrator approval, the user can log in immediately.

Resetting Users' Passwords

One of Backdrop's features that saves site administrators hours of work is the ability for users to reset their passwords without having to e-mail a site administrator and ask for help. If you log out of your site (click the Logout link at upper right on the page), note that in the right column, under the Log In button, there is a link for resetting your password (refer to Figure 3-7). Clicking this link reveals a page where the user can enter either their user ID or e-mail address.

Entering either a valid username or a valid e-mail address (where *valid* means it exists as either a valid user ID on your site or a valid e-mail address associated with a user account on your site) results in Backdrop generating an e-mail that is sent to the user with a one-time login link that allows them to reset their password.

Summary

This chapter covered the process for configuring how Backdrop handles user accounts, creating user roles, and assigning permissions to those roles. You learned about the decisions that you as the site owner must make when setting up your site, including whether you are the only person who can administer the site and create content, or whether you others will be responsible for those areas.

If others are assigned to create content or manage the site, then you want to configure the base settings for user accounts, create roles for those who perform activities on the site, and set the appropriate permissions. You also want to define whether only administrators can create accounts, visitors can create their own accounts without an administrator's approval, or visitors can create an account but an administrator must approve it. Once you've made those decisions and set the parameters discussed in this chapter, you're ready to begin adding users to your site.

You can have all the visitors you can handle, but they probably won't stick around long if they can't find the content they're interested in. That's where taxonomy comes in, which is what the next chapter talks about.

CHAPTER 4

Taxonomy

One of the Backdrop features new Backdrop users often underuse and misunderstand is taxonomy. New Backdrop users are overwhelmed with all the other features and functions provided by the platform, and they bypass what may be one of the most powerful and useful features that Backdrop has to offer. In this chapter, you learn and use taxonomy terms to categorize content so that visitors can easily find information related to a specific topic.

Taxonomy Overview

Although many of you may not be able to define the word *taxonomy*, the reality is that you use taxonomy on a daily basis as a means for categorizing things in your life. If you open the doors to your kitchen pantry, you might find an orderly assemblage of food items: all of your spices on the top shelf, canned food on the second shelf, pastas and other boxed foods on the third shelf, and cereal boxes on the fourth. Categorizing food items and putting things away in an orderly fashion so that you can easily find them when you need them to prepare a meal is, in its simplest form, the use of taxonomy. Without this kitchen taxonomy system, you may have everything you need to prepare dinner jammed randomly in the pantry; but finding it may be a challenge, leading to frustration and a phone call to the local pizza delivery restaurant when you're not able to find the ingredients you need to make a meal.

In Backdrop, taxonomy is divided into two general capabilities: tagging and structured taxonomy. Both are powerful solutions and can be used simultaneously on your site.

Using Tagging to Categorize Content

Tagging is a simplified yet powerful use of the taxonomy system, enabling content authors to enter keywords that describe the content in a text field on the content-editing form. As an example of tagging content, an author who writes a post about alternative energy could use keywords, or *tags*, such as *solar*, *wind*, and *geothermal* to categorize the article. The keywords created by the author are typically displayed as hyperlinks at the end of the article and can be used by site visitors to locate other content tagged with the same keywords. In chapter 1, I created a new post about the Parthenon and used several tags to categorize the content (see Figure 4-1).

© Todd Tomlinson 2016
T. Tomlinson, *Beginning Backdrop CMS*, DOI 10.1007/978-1-4842-1970-6_4

The Parthenon

Submitted by Anonymous (not verified) on Sun, 02/07/2016 - 5:44pm

The Parthenon (/ˈpɑːrθəˌnɒn, -nən/; Ancient Greek: Παρθενών; Modern Greek: Παρθενώνας) is a former temple on the Athenian Acropolis, Greece, dedicated to the goddess Athena, whom the people of Athens considered their patron. The template is located in central Athens. Construction began in 447 BC when the Athenian Empire was at the peak of its power. It was completed in 438 BC although decoration of the building continued until 432 BC. It is the most important surviving building of Classical Greece, generally considered the zenith of the Doric order.

Tags:
Parthenon   Greek architecture   Historical Buildings

Figure 4-1. *A tagged post*

A site visitor can find all references to historical buildings on the site by clicking Historical Buildings in the list of tags. When a visitor clicks a tag, Backdrop assembles all the content that has been tagged with that term or phrase and displays those content items in a list, as shown in Figure 4-2.

Home

Historical Buildings

Taj Mahal

Submitted by admin on Tue, 02/09/2016 - 6:40am

The **Taj Mahal** (/ˌtɑːdʒ məˈhɑːl/, more often /ˈtɑːʒ/;[3] Persian for "Crown of Palaces", pronounced [ˈtɑːdʒ mɛˈɦɛl]) is an ivory-white marble mausoleum on the so

Tags:

Historical Buildings   India   India Architecture
Tourist attractions

Read more   Log in or register to post comments

The Parthenon

Submitted by Anonymous (not verified) on Sun, 02/07/2016 - 5:44pm

The Parthenon (/ˈpɑːrθəˌnɒn, -nən/; Ancient Greek: Παρθενών; Modern Greek: Παρθενώνας) is a former temple on the Athenian Acropolis, Greece, dedicated to the goddess Athena, whom the people of Athens considered their patron. The template is located in central Athens. Construction began in 447 BC when the Athenian Empire was at the peak of its power. It was completed in 438 BC although decoration of the building continued until 432 BC. It is the most important surviving building of Classical Greece, generally considered the zenith of the Doric order.

Tags:

Parthenon   Greek architecture   **Historical Buildings**

Read more   1 comment   Log in or register to post comments

Figure 4-2. *A listing of tagged content*

Tagging is freeform, meaning it's up to you to define what words you want to use to classify your content. A common issue with using tagging as an approach to categorize content is that different people use different words to refer to the same concept. For example, a post about rain might be tagged with the word *rain* by one author, *precipitation* by another author, and *drizzle* by a third. Site visitors trying to find articles about the general concept of rain would have a difficult time finding the posts tagged with words other than *rain*. Another common problem is misspellings. If an author tags a post about rain with *reign*, then site visitors are going to have a hard time using taxonomy to find that article using the word *rain*.

Using Structured Taxonomy

The second approach for using taxonomy to categorize content in Backdrop is *structured taxonomy*. In this approach, a site administrator creates all the words that can be used to categorize content, and content authors simply select from the predefined list of words to categorize their content. This ensures that terms used to categorize content are consistent across the site and limits the list of available terms to those categories that were deemed important by the content editor.

Another benefit of structured taxonomy is that it can be hierarchical, meaning terms may be put into groups to categorize content. An example of a hierarchy could be taxonomy for sports. The first level of terms could be *team sports* and *individual sports*. Under *team sports*, you might see *football, basketball, baseball, hockey, volleyball*, and other team sports. Under *individual sports*, you might see *golf, swimming, track and field*, and *motor sports*. You could continue to build out the hierarchy of sports until you have a representation of every sport on the planet. As an author writing a post about a sporting event, I could choose one or more predefined terms to categorize my article.

A big benefit of structured and hierarchical taxonomy over simplified tagging is the ability to select articles by individual terms or by categories of terms. In the previous example, you could look for articles specifically about football, or you could take a more generalized approach and look for all articles in the category of team sports.

Determining whether to use tagging or structured taxonomy is a matter of deciding how rigid you want the categorization of content to appear on your site. The great news is that you can use both approaches simultaneously to provide authors with a high level of flexibility.

Implementing Structured Taxonomy

Let's take a look at a real-world example. Let's say you are creating a web site that is focused on sports news. Your targeted audience is people who like to follow what is happening with their favorite teams. If you think about how people might want to search and navigate content on your site, you might decide to organize the content by the type of sport:

- Football

- Baseball

- Basketball

- Hockey

- Soccer

People may also want to find sports news by team:

- Ravens

- Trailblazers

- Lakers

- Raiders

- Yankees

In this case, you can follow the previous example and create a structured taxonomy. You first create a *vocabulary*, which is the highest level in a hierarchical structure. For this example, you can create a vocabulary called *type of sport*. The terms you create in that vocabulary are *football, baseball, basketball, hockey*, and *soccer*. You then create a second level in the hierarchy where you assign the terms for the team names; for example, beneath the term *football* you assign the terms *Ravens* and *Raiders*. Beneath the term *basketball*, you assign the terms *Trailblazers* and *Lakers*. Beneath the *baseball* term, you assign the term *Yankees*. You can continue adding team names until every team in every sport is assigned to their appropriate spot. For the purposes of this demonstration, let's stick with the simplified list.

Creating Vocabularies

The first step in using taxonomy is to identify and create the vocabularies you use to categorize content on your web site. Depending on the focus of your site and the breadth of subjects you cover, you may need only a single vocabulary, or you may need several vocabularies. There isn't a correct answer, nor is there a formula you can use to determine how many vocabularies your site needs. The best approach is to think about the content you include and the subjects the content covers. If the subjects are all related (for example, types of sports), then a single vocabulary is likely all that you need. If the subjects are not related (for example, a book-related web site where books may be categorized by author, subject, publisher, and targeted audience), then the use of several vocabularies may be necessary. It's up to you, the site creator, to define the structure that best suits the purpose of your site, how you want content structured, and how you want visitors to access that content.

Once you've identified at least one vocabulary, navigate to Structure ➤ Taxonomy. The Taxonomy page lists all the vocabularies that have already been defined for your site. By default, Backdrop creates a vocabulary called Tags as a default generic container for terms. See Figure 4-3.

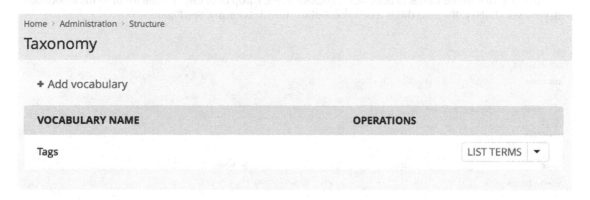

Figure 4-3. *The Taxonomy page*

To add a new vocabulary, click the Add Vocabulary link at the top of the list, revealing the form shown in Figure 4-4. In the Name field, enter **Type of sport**, and enter a brief description in the Description field. The Description field is an optional field and by default is not displayed on the administrative interface for taxonomy. However, you may want to use this field when rendering lists of content as a description about the content contained in the list. You may also restrict what user roles are able to edit and delete terms in this vocabulary. For this example, leave the administrator as the only one who can edit and delete terms from this vocabulary.

Home › Administration › Structure › Taxonomy
Taxonomy

Name *

Description

Permissions Administrator	PERMISSION	ANONYMOUS	AUTHENTICATED	ADMINISTRATOR	COMPANY USER	RESTRICTED USER
URL pattern [term:vocabulary]/[term:name]	Edit terms	☐	☐	☑	☐	☐
	Delete terms	☐	☐	☑	☐	☐

SAVE

Figure 4-4. *Creating a new vocabulary*

Once you've entered values in both fields, click Save. Backdrop then displays the list of terms associated with your vocabulary. Because this is a new vocabulary, the list is empty. See Figure 4-5.

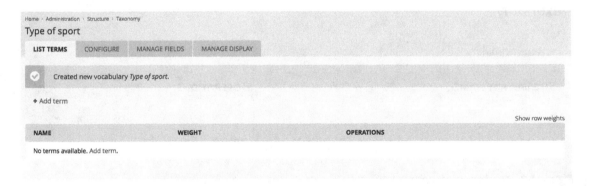

Home › Administration › Structure › Taxonomy

Type of sport

LIST TERMS   CONFIGURE   MANAGE FIELDS   MANAGE DISPLAY

✓ Created new vocabulary *Type of sport.*

✦ Add term

Show row weights

NAME	WEIGHT	OPERATIONS

No terms available. Add term.

Figure 4-5. *Your newly created vocabulary*

The next step is to create a list of terms that are associated with the Type Of Sport vocabulary. To create terms, click the Add Term button for the vocabulary you created. You see the form shown in Figure 4-6. Enter **Basketball** as the name of the term, and enter a brief description that expands on the meaning behind the term.

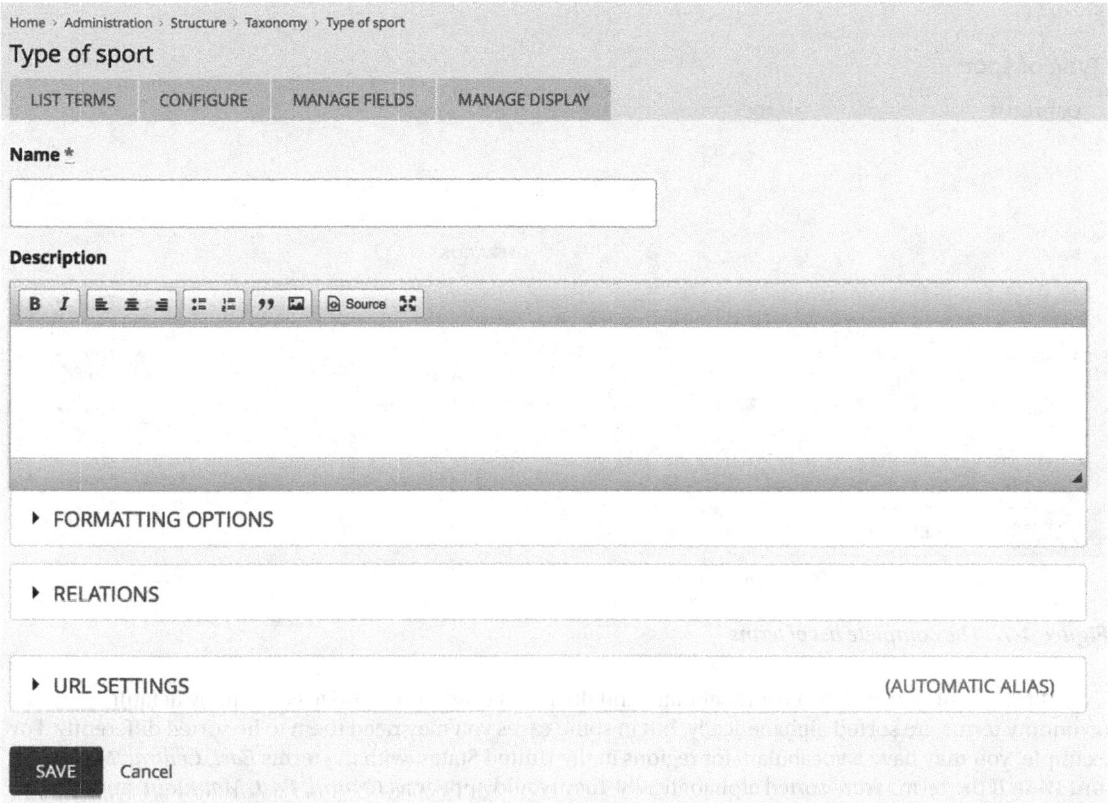

Home › Administration › Structure › Taxonomy › Type of sport

Type of sport

| LIST TERMS | CONFIGURE | MANAGE FIELDS | MANAGE DISPLAY |

Name *

Description

| B | *I* | ≡ ≡ ≡ | ≔ ≔ | 99 | ▢ | ⊠ Source | ⤢ |

▶ FORMATTING OPTIONS

▶ RELATIONS

▶ URL SETTINGS   (AUTOMATIC ALIAS)

SAVE   Cancel

Figure 4-6. Adding terms

After entering the term and a description, click Save. Backdrop then redisplays the form to enable you to enter another term. To practice, create terms for other sports, such as baseball, football, and soccer. Once you've completed the process of entering the terms associated with your vocabulary, click Type Of Sport in the breadcrumb to return to the Edit Vocabulary page, and then click the List Terms tab at the top of the page to see the complete list of terms for the vocabulary, shown in Figure 4-7.

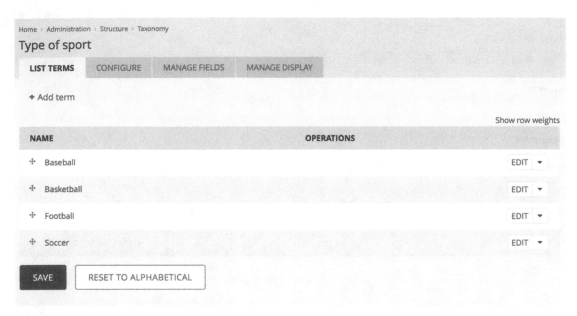

Figure 4-7. *The complete list of terms*

At this point, you've created a vocabulary and the terms used to categorize content. By default, taxonomy terms are sorted alphabetically, but in some cases you may need them to be sorted differently. For example, you may have a vocabulary for regions in the United States, with the terms *East*, *Central*, *Mountain*, and *West*. If the terms were sorted alphabetically, they would appear as *Central*, *East*, *Mountain*, and *West*. You may want the terms sorted in an east-to-west fashion, meaning the order should be *East*, *Central*, *Mountain*, and *West*, in which case you want the order to differ from the default order. You may reorder the terms by simply clicking and holding the arrow icon to the left of a term and dragging that item to the position in the list where you want it to appear. Remember to click the Save button after reordering, because the order is not permanent until you save the list.

You now have to identify which content types will use this vocabulary as a method for categorizing content, and configure your vocabulary so that it will appear on the content-creation screens for those content types.

Assigning a Taxonomy Vocabulary to a Content Type

Enabling content authors to assign one of the terms to a new piece of content requires that a site administrator make changes to the content types. The first step is to identify all the content types that you want to associate with the new vocabulary. You may decide that all content types will use the vocabulary to categorize the content created on your site, or you may decide the vocabulary is only appropriate for one or a few content types. For example, if you had a vocabulary that listed terms for event venues (such as *cafeteria*, *gym*, *courtyard*, *soccer field*, and so on), you might want to restrict which content types could be used. That vocabulary might only be appropriate for a Calendar event content type and not your Page content type.

As an example, let's update the Post content type on the test site to incorporate the ability to tag content with the type of sport vocabulary. The first step is to navigate to Structure ➤ Content Types to visit the page that lists the available content types (shown in Figure 4-8).

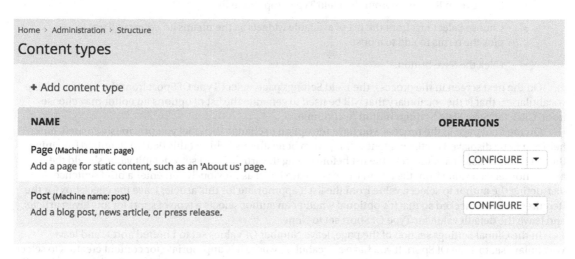

Figure 4-8. *Available content types*

To the right of each content type, in the Operations list, clicking the down arrow reveals a list of options, including a Manage Fields button for managing the fields associated with that content type. Chapter 5 explains how to add several types of fields to a content type (for example, you may wish to add a file-upload field, an additional text box to collect specific information, check boxes, radio buttons, or a select list to expand the content collected when someone uses that content type). For now, you concentrate on adding the taxonomy vocabulary to your content type so that an author can select one of the types of sports terms.

Click Manage Fields for the Post content type to show the form used to add your vocabulary to the list of available fields (see Figure 4-9).

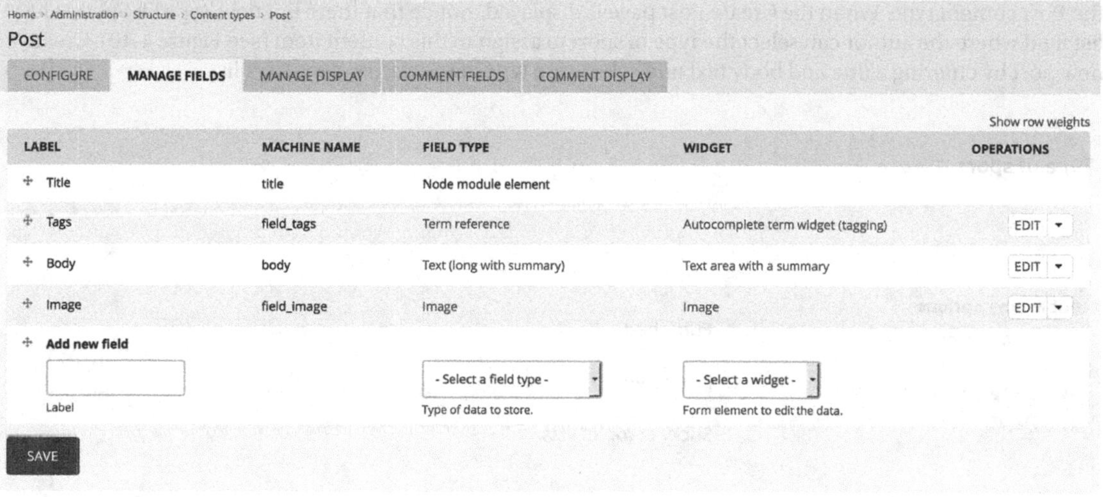

Figure 4-9. *Managing a content type's fields*

In the Add New Field section on this page, do the following:

- Enter **Type of sport** in the Label field.

- Select Term Reference from the Field Type drop-down list.

- Choose Select List from the list of available widgets as the means an editor will use to pick the terms to add to a post.

- Click the Save button.

On the next screen in the process, the Field Settings page, select Type Of Sport from the list of available vocabularies; that is the vocabulary that will be used to generate the list of options an editor may choose from. Click the Save Field Settings button to continue.

On the final page in the process, you have the option to change the label you previously created, enter help text to be displayed on the content-editing form beneath this field, set this field to Required (meaning the author must select a value from the list before saving the article), and set a default value should the author not select a value from the list. In this case, leave Label as previously set; enter a brief sentence instructing the author to select a value from the list if appropriate for this article; leave the check box for the Required field unchecked so that it's optional whether an author selects a type of sport for any given article; and leave the default value for Type Of Sport set to None.

In the Global Settings section of the page, leave Number Of Values set to Limited and 1, and leave Vocabulary set to Type Of Sport. If you have a vocabulary where it is appropriate for content creators to select more than one term from a vocabulary, you may change Number Of Values to Unlimited, or you may leave it as Limited but increase the number of values that may be selected.

After reviewing the values on this page, click the Save Settings button, which returns you to the list of fields for the Post content type. To complete the process, click Save at the bottom of the page. The Type Of Sport field is now enabled and ready for authors to use when creating or updating posts.

Selecting a Taxonomy Term When Creating Content

Based on your actions in the previous section, creating a new content item using the Post content type now presents the author with a list of values they can select from to categorize the content they are authoring. To test this feature, click any of the Create Content links described previously. In the list of content types, click the Post content type. When the Create Post page is displayed, notice that there is a new Type Of Sport select list field where the author can select the type of sport to assign to this content item (see Figure 4-10). Create a new post by entering a title and body text and selecting a type of sport from the select list.

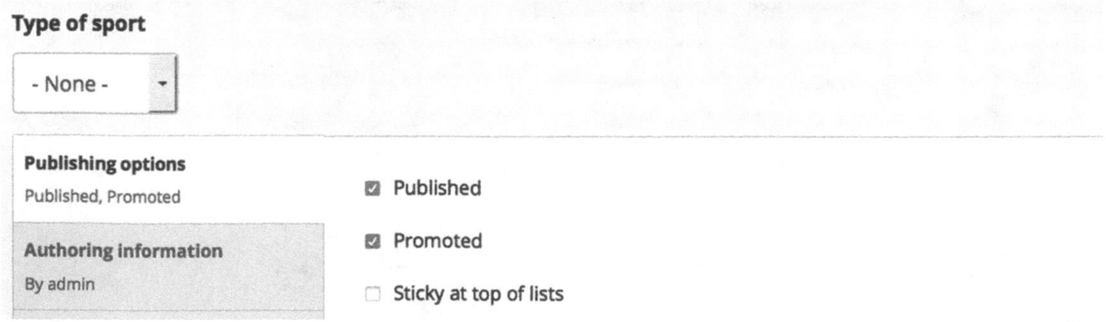

Type of sport

- None -

Publishing options
Published, Promoted

☑ Published

Authoring information
By admin

☑ Promoted

☐ Sticky at top of lists

Figure 4-10. *Creating a post and assigning a type of sport*

Clicking Save results in Backdrop displaying your new post with a new field, Associated Sport, with the value you selected in the Type Of Sport field listed.

To demonstrate the power of taxonomy, create two additional posts using the same taxonomy term you selected in the first example. Once you have saved the final content item, click the term you used. In Figure 4-9, you would click Football.

2017 Superbowl Top Picks

| View | Edit |

Submitted by admin on Tue, 02/09/2016 - 7:58am

With the 2016 Superbowl behind us it's time to look forward to the 2016-2017 football season and Superbowl 51. The top favorites for next year's Superbowl are the Patriots, Seahawks, and Steelers.

Type of sport:
Football

Figure 4-11. *A new content item assigned to the Football taxonomy term*

The result of clicking the term is a page that lists all other pages that were created and assigned to the Football taxonomy term (see Figure 4-12).

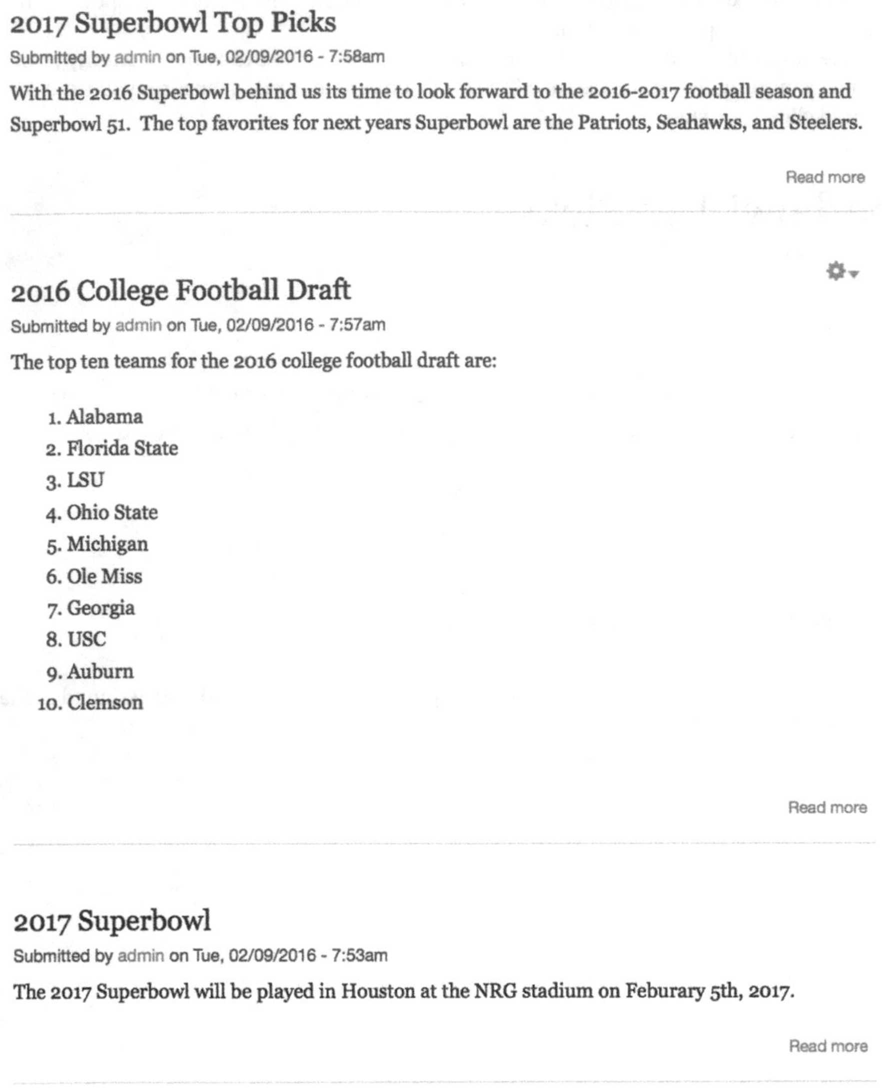

2017 Superbowl Top Picks

Submitted by admin on Tue, 02/09/2016 - 7:58am

With the 2016 Superbowl behind us its time to look forward to the 2016-2017 football season and Superbowl 51. The top favorites for next years Superbowl are the Patriots, Seahawks, and Steelers.

Read more

2016 College Football Draft

Submitted by admin on Tue, 02/09/2016 - 7:57am

The top ten teams for the 2016 college football draft are:

1. Alabama
2. Florida State
3. LSU
4. Ohio State
5. Michigan
6. Ole Miss
7. Georgia
8. USC
9. Auburn
10. Clemson

Read more

2017 Superbowl

Submitted by admin on Tue, 02/09/2016 - 7:53am

The 2017 Superbowl will be played in Houston at the NRG stadium on Feburary 5th, 2017.

Read more

Figure 4-12. *All pages assigned to the term Football*

Backdrop automatically renders all the posts associated with the selected term. The list is sorted by default in date/time order, with the most recently added post at the top of the list. You may change the order in which the posts appear by modifying the default view. Chapter 10 covers views in detail.

Creating Human- and Search Engine–Friendly Lists

By default, Backdrop creates human- and search engine-friendly URLs for lists of content related to taxonomy terms. The structure of the URL that is automatically generated by Backdrop is vocabulary name/term name, which in most instances is appropriate for humans and search engines. There may be cases when you need to override the automatically generated URL for a given taxonomy term, and Backdrop provides a simple mechanism for doing so. Navigate to Structure ➤ Taxonomy ➤ List Vocabularies, and click the List Terms link in the Operations column of the vocabulary that contains the term you want to update. Click the Edit link in the Operations column for the term you wish to change; and in the URL Settings section, uncheck the Generate Automatic URL Alias check box and enter the URL alias that you wish to use (see Figure 4-13).

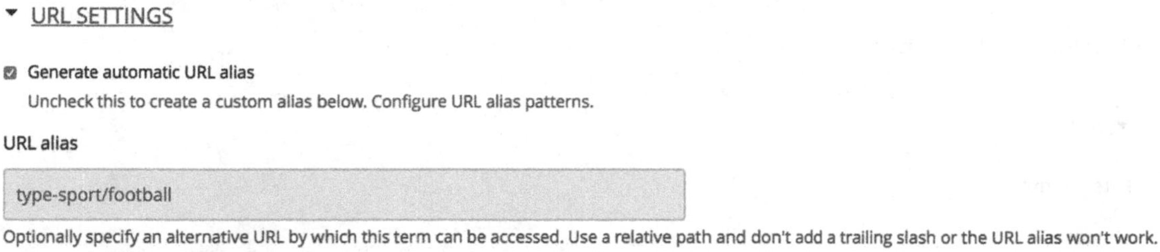

▼ URL SETTINGS

☑ Generate automatic URL alias
   Uncheck this to create a custom alias below. Configure URL alias patterns.

URL alias

type-sport/football

Optionally specify an alternative URL by which this term can be accessed. Use a relative path and don't add a trailing slash or the URL alias won't work.

Figure 4-13. *Backdrop-created URL*

Hierarchical Terms

What if you need to define a hierarchical structure of taxonomy terms—say, for basketball? You need the ability to further categorize basketball content as follows:

- Basketball

  - High School

  - College

  - Division 1

  - Division 2

  - Division 3

  - NBA

  - Central Conference

  - Eastern Conference

  - Western Conference

Fortunately, Backdrop provides a simple mechanism for creating a hierarchical structure of taxonomy terms. To update the example, navigate to Structure ➤ Taxonomy ➤ List Vocabularies, and click the List Terms link for the Type Of Sport vocabulary. Click the Add Term link, which reveals the Term Creation screen. Begin by adding the *High School* term. Enter **High School** as the Name, and then click the Relations link at the bottom of the form. In the Parent Terms list, select Basketball, and then click Save (see Figure 4-14).

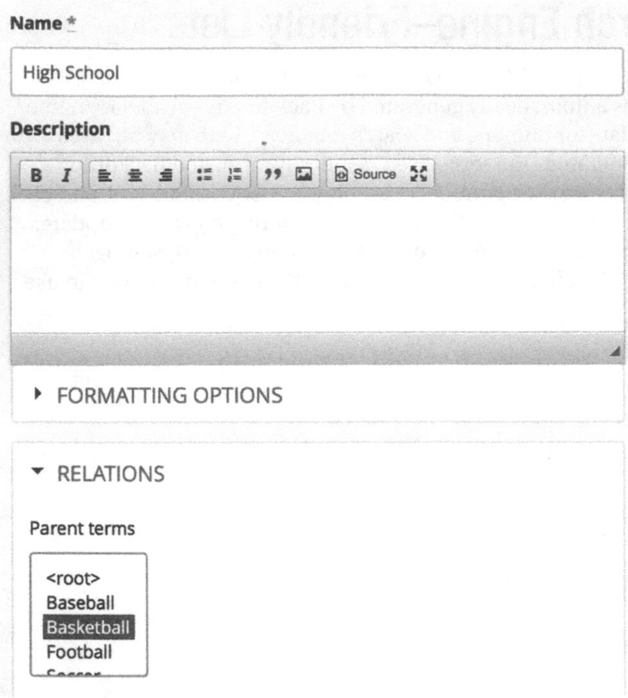

Name *

> High School

Description

| B | *I* | ≡ ≡ ≡ | ☷ ☷ | ,, 🖼 | 🔲 Source ⤢ |

▶ FORMATTING OPTIONS

▼ RELATIONS

Parent terms

```
<root>
Baseball
Basketball
Football
```

Figure 4-14. *Adding a child taxonomy term*

Continue the process by entering **College** and **NBA**, also selecting Basketball as the parent term. To create the third level of the hierarchy, enter **Division 1** as the term name and, for the relationship, select College as the parent. Continue until you've created all the terms in the preceding list. The resulting structure should look something like that shown in Figure 4-15.

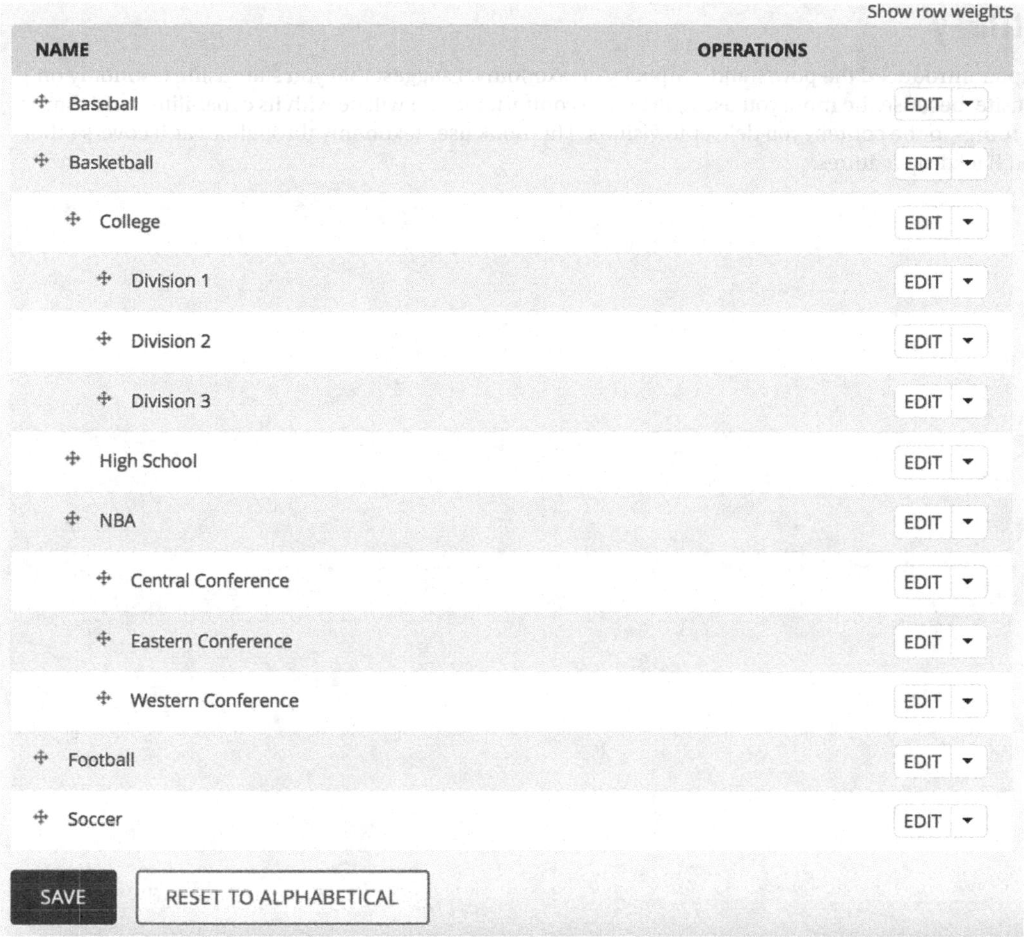

NAME	OPERATIONS	Show row weights
✛ Baseball		EDIT ▼
✛ Basketball		EDIT ▼
✛ College		EDIT ▼
✛ Division 1		EDIT ▼
✛ Division 2		EDIT ▼
✛ Division 3		EDIT ▼
✛ High School		EDIT ▼
✛ NBA		EDIT ▼
✛ Central Conference		EDIT ▼
✛ Eastern Conference		EDIT ▼
✛ Western Conference		EDIT ▼
✛ Football		EDIT ▼
✛ Soccer		EDIT ▼

SAVE   RESET TO ALPHABETICAL

Figure 4-15. *The resulting list*

If you forget to select a parent term before saving, you can always position a term by clicking the arrows icon to the left of the term, holding down the button, and dragging the term to the position in the hierarchy where it should reside. You may also assign the term to the appropriate parent term by clicking the Edit button and modifying the value in the Relations section.

You now have the ability to assign taxonomy terms to content items at the child level as well as at the parent level.

Assigning More Than One Vocabulary

There may come a time when categorizing content by a single vocabulary represents a constraint that you must overcome to address a complex requirement for content categorization. Fortunately, Backdrop does not constrain the number of vocabularies you can assign to a content type. Simply follow the steps you performed earlier in this chapter to add a second field to the content type. Select a different vocabulary as the source for the values you wish to present to the author.

Summary

This chapter introduced the power and simplicity of taxonomy. I suggest that you start using taxonomy on your first site, because the more you use it, the more comfortable you will be with its capabilities and the power it brings to the content you deliver to visitors. This book uses taxonomy throughout as it covers other advanced Backdrop features.

CHAPTER 5

■ ■ ■

Content Types

If you ask Backdrop developers what the most powerful feature of Backdrop is, many will say it's Backdrop's ability to create custom content types. What is a content type? Think of a content type as a template that you provide to users who author content on your site. You may decide the standard content types that come with Backdrop out of the box, Page and Post, provide all the features you need for your site. But you're likely to encounter situations where you want more control over how users enter information and how that information is displayed on your site, and that's where custom content types come into play. This chapter shows you how simple it is to create a new content type from scratch. Hold on to your tickets: we're about to take off!

The Page and Post Content Types

When you install Backdrop, you automatically receive two content types defined by the team that maintains Backdrop core: Page and Post. If you author a piece of content using the Page content type, it provides two basic fields: a title and a body.

An author using the Page content type simply enters a title (a required field, as indicated by the red asterisk) and the text of the content in the Body field. The Body field is flexible and can contain whatever the author feels like writing about. The author can

- Write an entire book in the Body field, including HTML markup (headings, tables, CSS, and so on).

- Insert pictures.

- Write a single sentence.

The Post content type is similar to Page, except it offers the ability to upload a picture as a stand-alone element, such as a banner image for the post (not embedded in the body text). The author can also enter one or more tags to categorize the content (see Chapter 4 for details on categorizing content).

Like a page, a post can be used to author content about any subject, and the body area allows for entering free-form text.

Although the Page and Post content types are perfect for general content, sometimes you want to provide a form of structure around the information that is captured. You may want to

- Require that certain information is entered before the author submits the content for publishing: for example, the start date and time for an event, the address of the venue where the event is being held, and a link to the event on a Google map.

- Have the ability to perform calculations based on the information captured in a content item.

- Be able to sort content items by specific fields.

© Todd Tomlinson 2016
T. Tomlinson, *Beginning Backdrop CMS*, DOI 10.1007/978-1-4842-1970-6_5

- Filter or restrict which content items are displayed on a page based on a value in a field on a content type.

- Enforce the structure of how a piece of content is rendered on a page: for example, you may want to display information about a book and want the title to be followed by the author, followed by the ISBN, followed by the price, followed by the description of the book.

You could publish all of this information in a page or a post, but providing the features for sorting, filtering, making values required, calculating, and structuring how a content item is rendered on a page would be extremely difficult. Fortunately, Backdrop's ability to define custom content types makes all this possible and provides many more features you will find invaluable over time.

Defining a Custom Content Type

A custom content type is defined by you, the Backdrop administrator, over and above the Page and Post content types. The ability to create custom content types is included in Backdrop core.

To demonstrate the power and flexibility of custom content types, let's create a new custom content type for capturing information about upcoming events. An event could be a concert, a play, a class, a game, or any other activity that is scheduled in advance.

When authoring information about an event, you may want to include the following details:

- The name or title of the event

- The date and time when the event begins

- The date and time when the event ends

- The venue or address where the event will be held

- A description of the event

- The price for attending the event

- The types of seating

- The types of assistance available at the venue

- The type of event

- The ability to provide a file that can be downloaded by the site visitor (such as a program)

As you see in a few moments, Backdrop provides a simple-to-use administrator's interface for creating and modifying custom content types. As soon as you define a custom content type, it is immediately available to users who have the proper privileges to author, edit, publish, and delete that specific content type (Backdrop lets you restrict access to custom content types by user role).

Creating a Custom Content Type

Creating a custom content type takes two basic steps: listing the types of information you want to collect, and building the custom content type using Backdrop's custom content type administration screens. For this example, let's create a custom content type for an event that includes the types of information listed in the previous section.

To get started, navigate to Structure ➤ Content Types. The Content Types page (shown in Figure 5-1) lists all the existing content types, which in this case are the Post and Page content types included with Backdrop core. The Content Types page also provides a link to create a new content type. Click the Add Content Type link to start the process of creating an Event content type.

Home › Administration › Structure

Content types

+ Add content type

NAME	OPERATIONS
Page (Machine name: page) Add a page for static content, such as an 'About us' page.	CONFIGURE ▼
Post (Machine name: post) Add a blog post, news article, or press release.	CONFIGURE ▼

Figure 5-1. *The Content Types page*

The first screen that appears when you click the Add Content Type button is a form that defines the general characteristics of your new content type (see Figure 5-2). There is a field for the name of the content type, a field for a description (the description is displayed on the author's screen when they create new content), a field for the label of the title field, an explanation and submission guidelines field, and several other configuration options that this section walks through in detail.

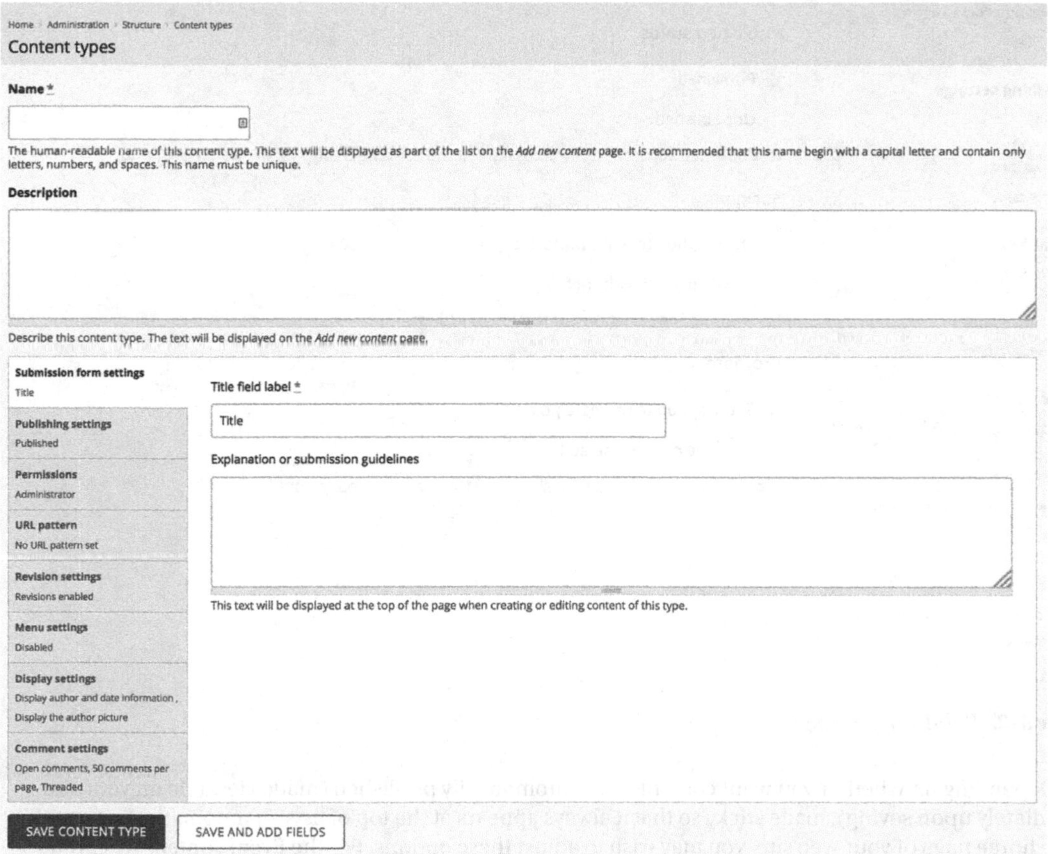

Home › Administration › Structure › Content types

Content types

Name *

The human-readable name of this content type. This text will be displayed as part of the list on the *Add new content* page. It is recommended that this name begin with a capital letter and contain only letters, numbers, and spaces. This name must be unique.

Description

Describe this content type. The text will be displayed on the *Add new content* page.

Submission form settings Title	**Title field label** * `Title`
Publishing settings Published	**Explanation or submission guidelines**
Permissions Administrator	
URL pattern No URL pattern set	
Revision settings Revisions enabled	This text will be displayed at the top of the page when creating or editing content of this type.
Menu settings Disabled	
Display settings Display author and date information , Display the author picture	
Comment settings Open comments, 50 comments per page, Threaded	

SAVE CONTENT TYPE   **SAVE AND ADD FIELDS**

Figure 5-2. *The content type creation form*

To begin the process, do the following:

- Fill in the name of the content type, in this case **Event**. The text below the Name field provides a set of guidelines you should follow when creating a name for a new content type.

- Provide a description of how this content type should be used, such as "A content type used to capture the details about upcoming events."

- Change the Title field label from just Title to **Event Title**, making it more descriptive and intuitive to the author who will be using this template for authoring event information.

- Provide a brief explanation of the submission guidelines for this content type. This is an optional value and may not apply to your content type. For the Event content type, enter **Please fill out all required fields before submitting the event** as the submission guidelines. You can choose to use or ignore this field when creating new content types.

There are other optional settings that you should consider carefully when creating a new content type. First are the publishing options. In the left vertical menu, click the Publishing Settings tab (see Figure 5-3).

Submission form settings Event Title	Published status
Publishing settings Published	◉ Published ○ Unpublished Unpublished content is only accessible to the content creator or site administrators.
Permissions Administrator	Sticky
URL pattern No URL pattern set	☑ Show option to make posts sticky ☐ Make posts sticky by default
Revision settings Revisions enabled	Sticky posts may be shown at the top of listings. Promote
Menu settings Disabled	☑ Show option to promote posts ☐ Promote posts by default
Display settings Display author and date information , Display the author picture	Promoted posts will often be shown on the main homepage or blog.
Comment settings Open comments, 50 comments per page, Threaded	

Figure 5-3. *Publishing settings*

Depending on whether you want content to be automatically published (made viewable on your site immediately upon saving), made sticky so that it always appears at the top of lists, or automatically appear on the home page of your web site, you may wish to adjust these options. For the Event content type, you want an event to be automatically published when it's saved, but you don't want it to automatically be sticky and you don't want it to automatically show up on the home page. So, ensure that the Make Posts Sticky By Default and Promote Posts By Default options are unchecked. Check the boxes for Show Option To Make Posts Sticky and Show Option To Promote Posts to enable a content author to make the choice to as whether the event will be sticky or promoted to the home page.

The next set of settings is for permissions (see Figure 5-4). Building on the roles you set up in Chapter 2, this section allows you to define who has the ability to create, edit, and delete events. For this example, leave all the permissions set to their default values.

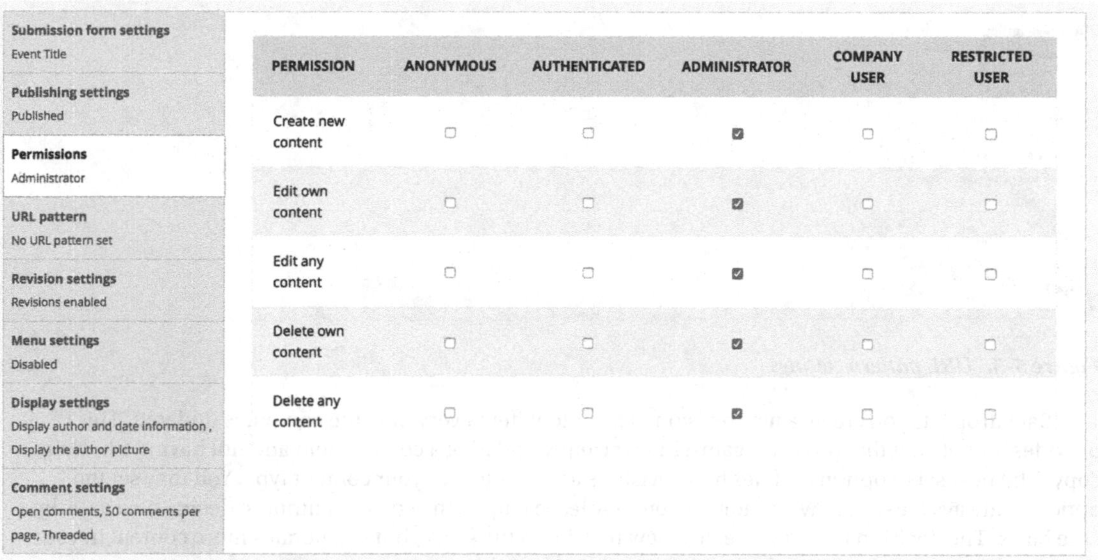

	PERMISSION	ANONYMOUS	AUTHENTICATED	ADMINISTRATOR	COMPANY USER	RESTRICTED USER
Submission form settings Event Title						
Publishing settings Published	Create new content	☐	☐	☑	☐	☐
Permissions Administrator	Edit own content	☐	☐	☑	☐	☐
URL pattern No URL pattern set	Edit any content	☐	☐	☑	☐	☐
Revision settings Revisions enabled	Delete own content	☐	☐	☑	☐	☐
Menu settings Disabled	Delete any content	☐	☐	☑	☐	☐
Display settings Display author and date information , Display the author picture						
Comment settings Open comments, 50 comments per page, Threaded						

Figure 5-4. *Permissions settings*

The next set of options, URL Pattern, lets you define the URL that is generated when an event is saved (see Figure 5-5). For readability and site structure, set the URL structure for events to **events/[node:title]**, where [node:title] is a token that will be replaced with the actual value of the title the author enters when they create an event. You may browse and use other tokens by clicking the Browse Available Tokens link.

Submission form settings Event Title	Default URL pattern
Publishing settings Published	
Permissions Administrator	New pages will have URLs that match a pattern based on wildcards called *tokens*. For example the URL "blog/my-first-post" could be created using the pattern "blog/[node:title]" if the title of the blog post was "My first post".
URL pattern No URL pattern set	Browse available tokens.
Revision settings Revisions enabled	
Menu settings Disabled	
Display settings Display author and date information , Display the author picture	
Comment settings Open comments, 50 comments per page, Threaded	

Figure 5-5. *URL pattern settings*

Backdrop lets you create a new revision of a content item every time the content is updated. This provides a safety net that protects against inadvertently updating a content item and not having a backup copy. The next set of options defines how revisions are handled for your content type. You may set the option to always create a new revision, or you may leave it up to the content author to decide on a case-by-case basis. The decision to always create a new revision is the safest, but it generates more content in your database because each revision is stored. Figure 5-6 shows the revision options.

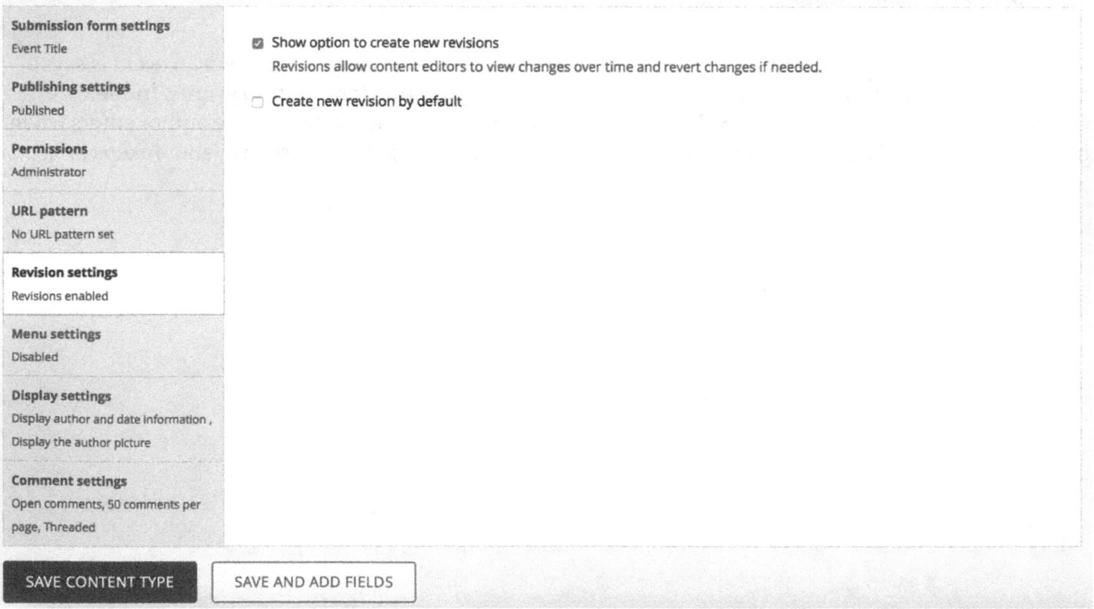

Submission form settings Event Title	☑ Show option to create new revisions Revisions allow content editors to view changes over time and revert changes if needed.
Publishing settings Published	☐ Create new revision by default
Permissions Administrator	
URL pattern No URL pattern set	
Revision settings Revisions enabled	
Menu settings Disabled	
Display settings Display author and date information , Display the author picture	
Comment settings Open comments, 50 comments per page, Threaded	

`SAVE CONTENT TYPE` `SAVE AND ADD FIELDS`

Figure 5-6. *Revision settings*

The Menu Settings tab displays a list of the menus enabled on your site (see Figure 5-7). If you check one or more of the boxes, a content item may be added to one of the site's menus during the content-authoring process, simplifying the process of linking content to menu items. You may select one or more menus that will be presented to the content author, given them the option to add the item being created to one of the selected menus.

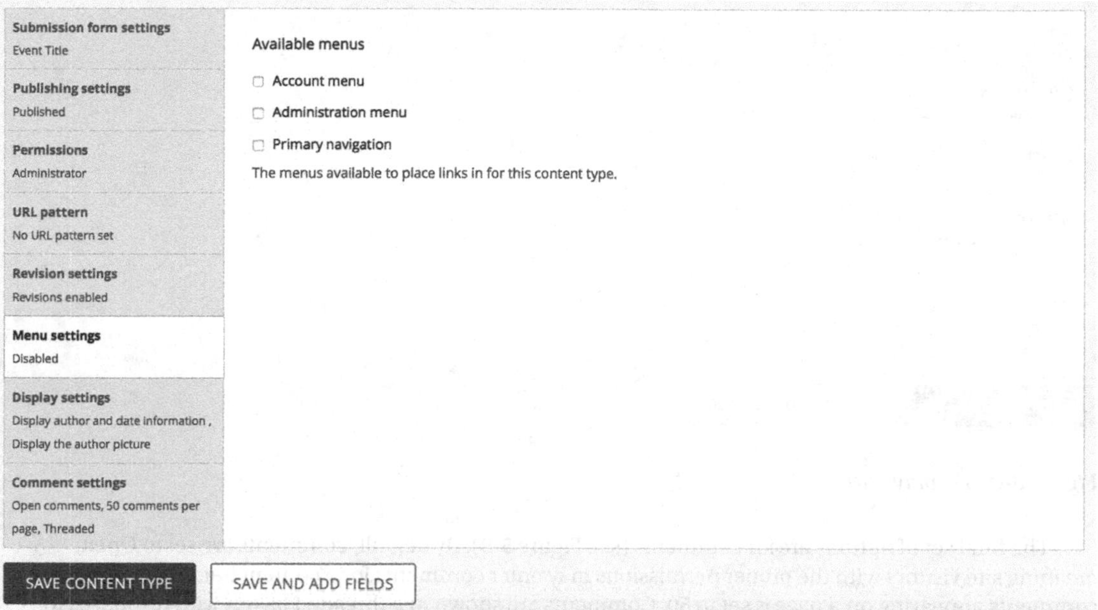

Figure 5-7. *Menu settings*

The next set of options is for display settings. Click the Display Settings tab in the left column to reveal the option that is available with this configuration parameter (see Figure 5-8). You can set whether Backdrop should display the name of the author who created the event content item and the date the item was authored, and the author's profile picture if they've uploaded one. Let's say in this case you don't feel that having the author, date published, and author's picture is relevant: uncheck the boxes for both options. You may, depending on the type of content being authored, decide that it is important to display the author's name, date that the content was published, and author picture. If so, leave the boxes checked.

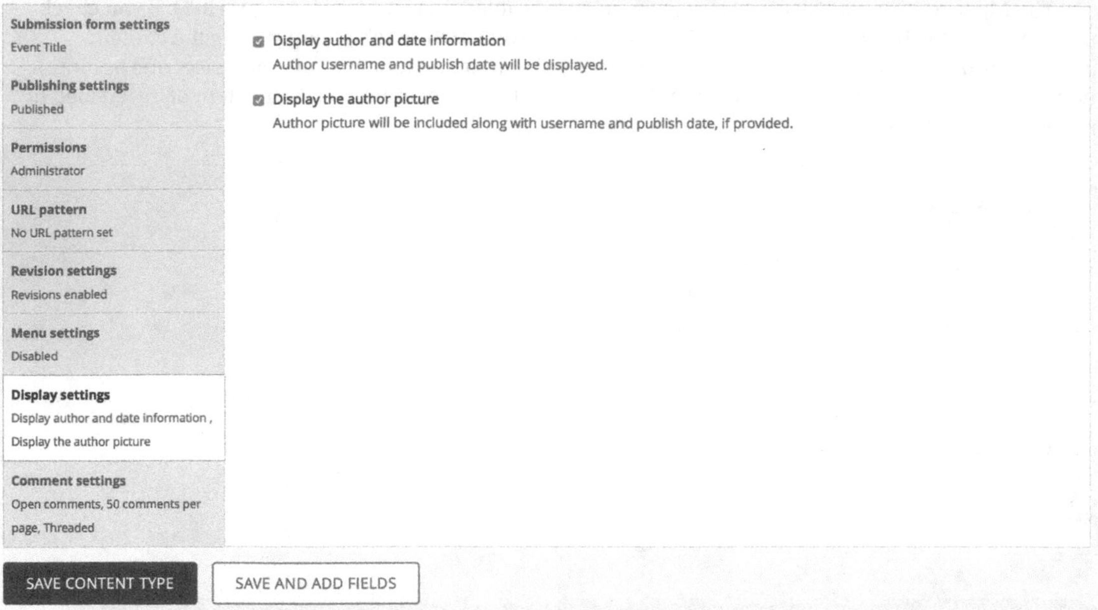

Submission form settings Event Title	☑ Display author and date information Author username and publish date will be displayed. ☑ Display the author picture Author picture will be included along with username and publish date, if provided.
Publishing settings Published	
Permissions Administrator	
URL pattern No URL pattern set	
Revision settings Revisions enabled	
Menu settings Disabled	
Display settings Display author and date information , Display the author picture	
Comment settings Open comments, 50 comments per page, Threaded	

SAVE CONTENT TYPE   SAVE AND ADD FIELDS

Figure 5-8. *Display settings*

The final set of options are for comments (see Figure 5-9). By default, comments are set to Open, meaning site visitors with the proper permissions may enter comments for a content item. The number of comments appearing on a page is set to 50. Comments are shown in a threaded layout with responses to comments directly beneath the comment being responded to, as opposed to in chronological order; this is also the default. There are options for determining whether a comment has a title, whether users' pictures are shown next to their comments, whether the form to submit comments is displayed on the same page as the comments, as well as the options to enable and disable previewing comments before they are posted. For the Event content type, user comments will remain enabled so that site visitors can discuss the events your organization hosts.

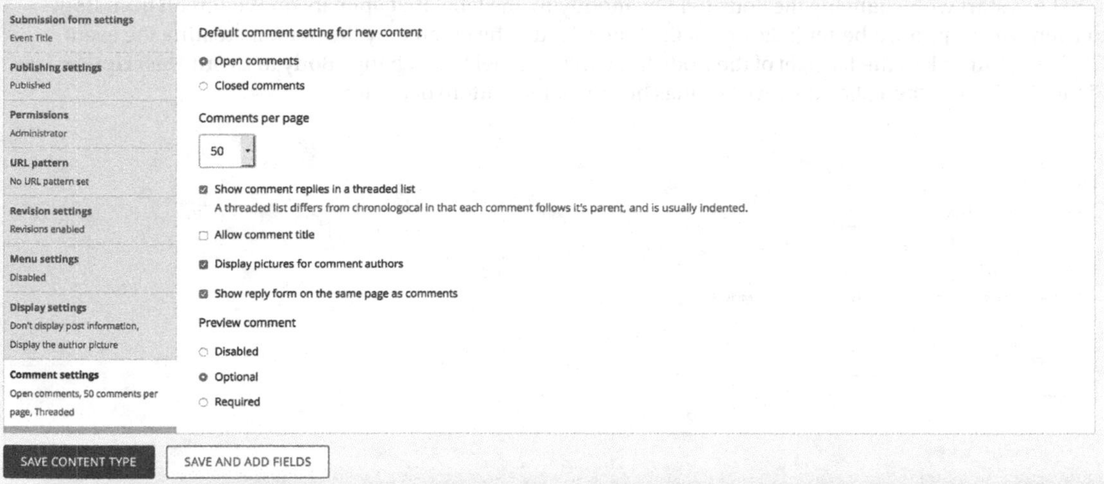

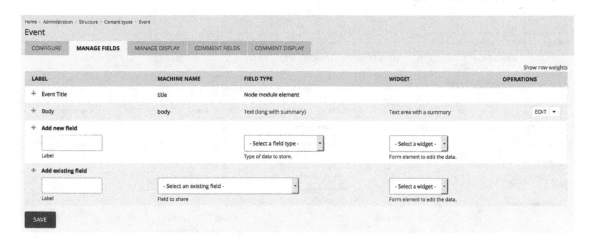

Figure 5-9. *Comment settings*

With all the values for the various settings in place, it's now time to create the fields associated with the Event content type. Click the Save And Add Fields button to continue. Backdrop now displays the Manage Fields page (see Figure 5-10).

Figure 5-10. *The Manage Fields page for the Event content type*

Customizing Your Content Type

At this point, you could create a new content item using the Event content type. However, the Event content type has only two fields: Event Title and Body. Your requirements call for an event description, start date, end date, venue/address, type of seating, assistance available at the venue, type of event, and the ability to provide a file that can be downloaded by the site visitor (such as a program). As you can see in Figure 5-10, Backdrop automatically creates a Body field, which you can use for the event description.

Let's start with changing the Body field by modifying the label that appears on the screen from Body to Event Description, a better indicator of the type of text to be entered by the person creating the event. Click the Edit link to the far right of the Body field. In the Label field, change Body to **Event Description** (see Figure 5-11), and then click the Save Settings button at the bottom of the form.

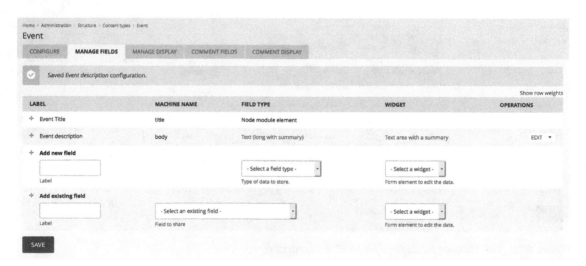

Figure 5-11. *Changing the Label field*

After saving the update to the Body label, Backdrop returns you to the Manage Fields page with the updated label, as shown in Figure 5-12.

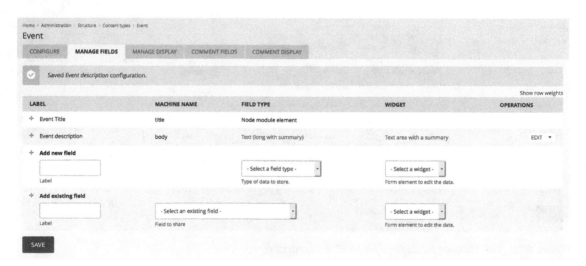

Figure 5-12. *Revised field label*

The next step is to add the Event Date field. To create the field, do the following:

- Enter **Event date** in the Add New Field Label text field.
- Select Date from the Field Type select list.
- Select Pop-up Calendar from the widget.

Click the Save button to continue to the settings page for the date widget (see Figure 5-13).

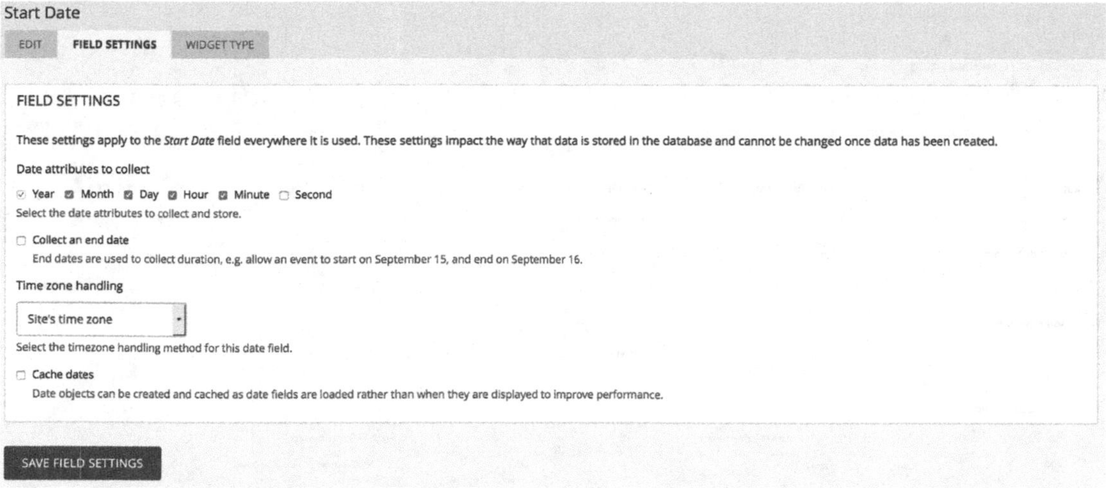

Figure 5-13. *Start date field settings*

For this example, leave Date Attributes To Collect set to Year, Month, Day, Hour, and Minute. Click the Collect An End Date check box to also let a content author specify an end date and time. Leave Time Zone Handling set to Site's Time Zone, because all of your events are held at your organization. If you host online events, you may want to set Time Zone Handling to the user's time zone so that the start and end time are calculated in the visitors time zone. Next, click the Save Field Settings button.

The next form provides additional details about the date field, such as these:

- The ability to change the label you previously defined for this field. Unless you made a mistake or changed your mind, you can leave the value as it is shown.

- Enter content in the Help text field to be displayed beneath the text field on the screen. This is a great place to describe requirements for data entered in this field, such as requesting that authors enter dates as mm/dd/yyyy. This is an optional field.

- Define whether this field is required. A required field is displayed with a red asterisk, and Backdrop forces the user to enter a value in this field before the content item can be saved. Because your content type is about an event and dates are important attributes of an event, you want a date to be required, so check the Required Field check box.

- The settings for the Date pop-up that appears when creating a new date, such as the format of the date that is collected, the span of years that may be selected from when creating a new date, and the increments for selecting the time (1-minute intervals, 15-minute intervals, and so on).

- Define whether a default value is assigned to the field before the content-creation screen is displayed to the author. Because your field deals with dates in the future, providing a default value doesn't make sense. There may be cases where a default value makes sense for other fields, such as selecting a seating preference for the event: for example, you may wish to set a default value of Best Available.

Click the Save Settings button to complete the configuration of the Start Date field. Backdrop then redisplays the general Manage Fields page with the new Start Date field added to the Event content type (see Figure 5-14).

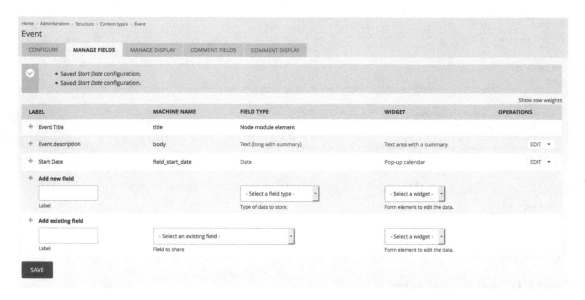

Figure 5-14. *A list of fields for the Event content type, including the Start Date field*

You are now ready to add the other fields defined earlier: event venue/address, a file upload for brochures and documents, a field for the price to attend the event, seating preferences, and special services available at the venue.

Start with the Event Venue/Address field. You follow the same general steps that you did to add the Start Date field, with the primary difference being the type of widget you use based on the content of the field. When creating the Event Venue/Address field, select Text (Long) for the field type instead of Date, because the values entered for the venue will be a paragraph or two of text. Then, click Save and continue through the configuration options for the new field. Review the list of required fields and add the remaining fields. When you're finished, the list of fields should look similar to Figure 5-15.

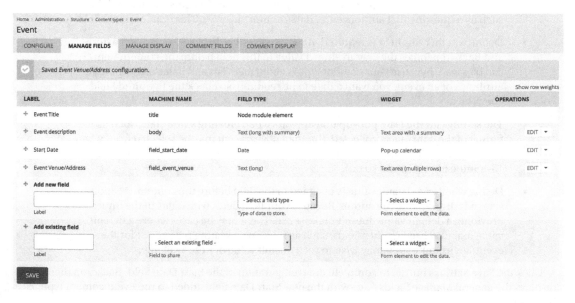

Figure 5-15. *The Event Venue/Address field added to the Event content type*

You can check the progress of the Event content type by navigating to Content ➤ Add Content, where you see that Event is now in the list of available content types. Click Event to reveal the content-creation page for the Event content type (see Figure 5-16). The page shows the Event Title, Event Description, Start Date, and Event Venue/Address fields.

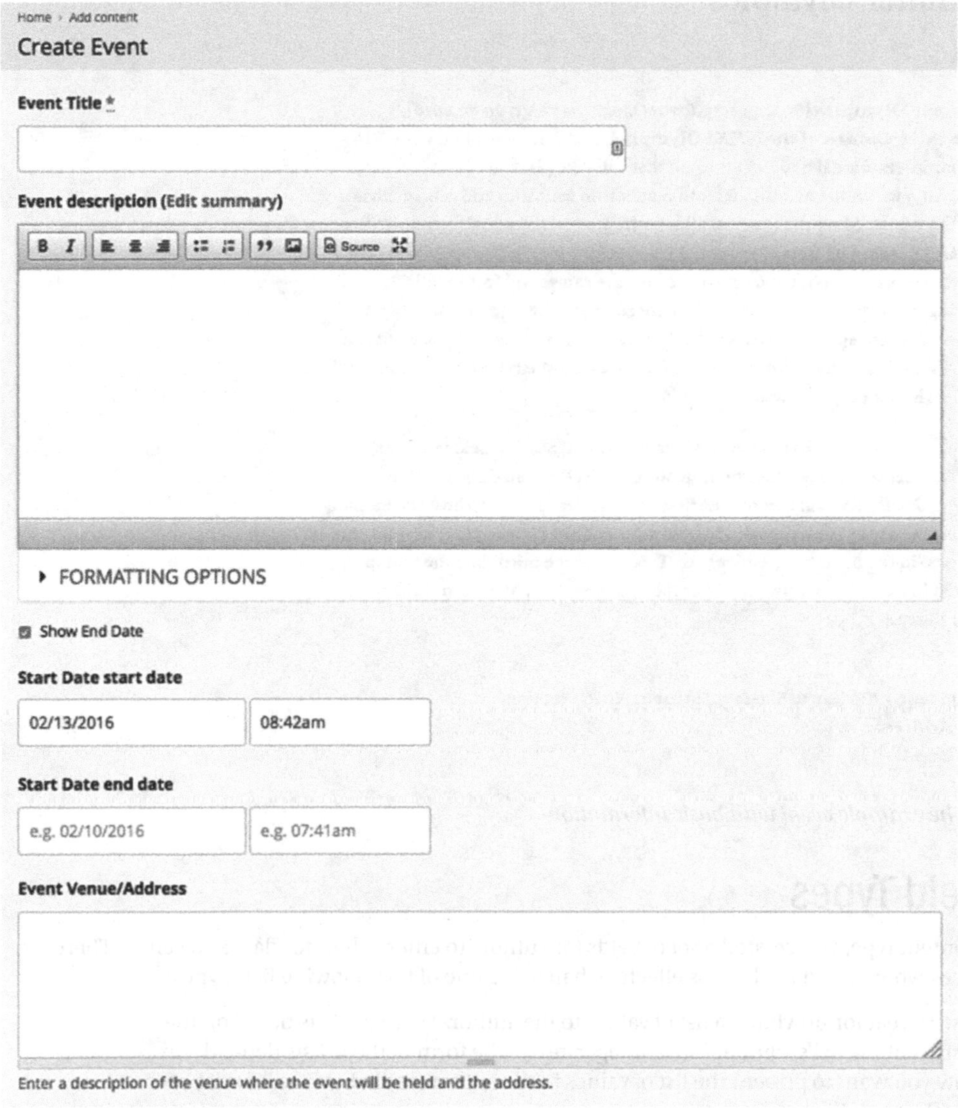

Figure 5-16. *Creating a new event*

Create a sample event using the event-creation form. When you've finished entering values, click Save And Publish. Backdrop renders your new event content item using the values you specified. The example event entered on the form in Figure 5-16 appears as a new event in Figure 5-17.

Home

 Event *2016 Summer Olympics* has been created.

2016 Summer Olympics

View | Edit

The **2016 Summer Olympics** (Portuguese: *Jogos Olímpicos de Verão de 2016*),[1]
officially known as the **Games of the XXXI Olympiad,** and commonly known as **Rio
2016,** are a major international multi-sport event that will take place in Rio de Janeiro,
Brazil, from August 5 to August 21, 2016. Record numbers of countries and sets of medals
are awaiting in the games. More than 10,500 athletes from 206 National Olympic
Committees (NOCs), including from Kosovo and South Sudan for the first time, will take
part in this sporting event.[2] With 306 sets of medals, the games will feature 28 Olympic
sports — including rugby sevens and golf, which were added by the International Olympic
Committee in 2009. These sporting events will take place on 33 venues in the host city and
additionally on 5 venues in the cities of São Paulo (Brazil's largest city), Belo Horizonte,
Salvador, Brasília (Brazil's capital), and Manaus.[2]

The host city of Rio de Janeiro was announced at the 121st IOC Session held in Copenhagen,
Denmark, on 2 October 2009. The other finalists were Madrid, Spain; Chicago, United
States; and Tokyo, Japan. Rio will become the first South American city to host the Summer
Olympics, the second city in Latin America to host the event after Mexico City in 1968, and
the first since 2000 in the Southern Hemisphere. This will be the third time the Summer
Olympics are held in a developing country, after the 1968 Games in Mexico and the 1988
Games in South Korea.

Start Date:
Friday, August 5, 2016 - 8:00am to Sunday, August 21, 2016 - 6:00pm
Event Venue/Address:
Rio de Janeiro, Brazil

Figure 5-17. *The example event with basic information*

Other Field Types

In the Event content type, you created a set of fields for authors to enter values for date and venue. There
may be instances where a text field is less effective than using one of the following field types:

- *Lists*: Great for providing a list of values to the author. There are lists based on the
  format of the list's content (float, integer, text). The form of those lists depends on
  how you want to present the list of values to the author (radio buttons, check boxes,
  or select lists).

- *File upload*: The right field to use when you want to provide the ability to upload and
  attach a file to a piece of content.

- *Image upload*: The field type to use when you want to upload and display an image.

- *Text area*: The field to use when the author is expected to enter paragraphs of
  content. It provides a box with multiple lines, whereas a text field has only a single
  line of text.

- *Numeric field*: Perfect when you want the author to enter numbers only.

- *Link fields*: It's the field to use when you insert either a hyperlink to an page on your site or an external URL to a page on another web site.

- *Term reference field*: When you want to include taxonomy terms as part of your content item, this is the field to use.

The field types listed here are part of Backdrop core. Other custom field types are available as contributed modules. For a list of those modules, please visit www.backdropcms.org/project/modules, enter **Fields** in the search box, and click the magnifying glass. You see a list of add-on modules that provide value-added capabilities, such as other field types. You can install additional modules by following the process described in Chapter 12. One module you will likely want to install and use is the References module, which lets you link an existing piece of content or user to the content item being created or edited. An example of using References would be when you want to link an author to a book. For more information on the capabilities of the References module, visit https://backdropcms.org/project/references.

You will probably need to use one of the other field types as you create new content types. Let's expand the Event content type by adding several other types of fields.

List Fields

List fields are useful when you want to present the author with a list of values from which they can select only a single item (radio button) or more than one value (check boxes or list boxes). Let's expand the Event content type to include the ability to select the type of seating available at the event: reserved seating or general admission. To start the process, navigate to Structure ➤ Content Types, and click the Manage Fields link from the Operations drop-down list. Enter **Type of Seating** in the Label field under Add New Field, select List (Text) from the list of available field types, and select Check Boxes/Radio Buttons as the widget type (see Figure 5-18). Click Save to continue the process of adding the new field.

Figure 5-18. *Adding a list field*

The next step is to provide the values that will appear in the list (see Figure 5-19). On this screen, you have to specify the Allowed Values List, which is the list of options presented to the author. Backdrop requires that options be listed as a *key|label* pair, where *key* is a value representing which option was selected (the key value is stored in the database), followed by the pipe character (press the Shift key and \ to enter a pipe character, |); and *label* is the value displayed on the screen. In Figure 5-18, entering **reserved|Reserved** and **general|General Admission** results in the values *reserved* and *general* being stored in the database. If you set the Allowed Number Of Values field to Limited and 1, Backdrop renders this list as radio buttons, because the user is restricted to selecting a single value. If the number is greater than 1, Backdrop renders this list as check boxes. After entering the values, click the Save Field Settings button to continue.

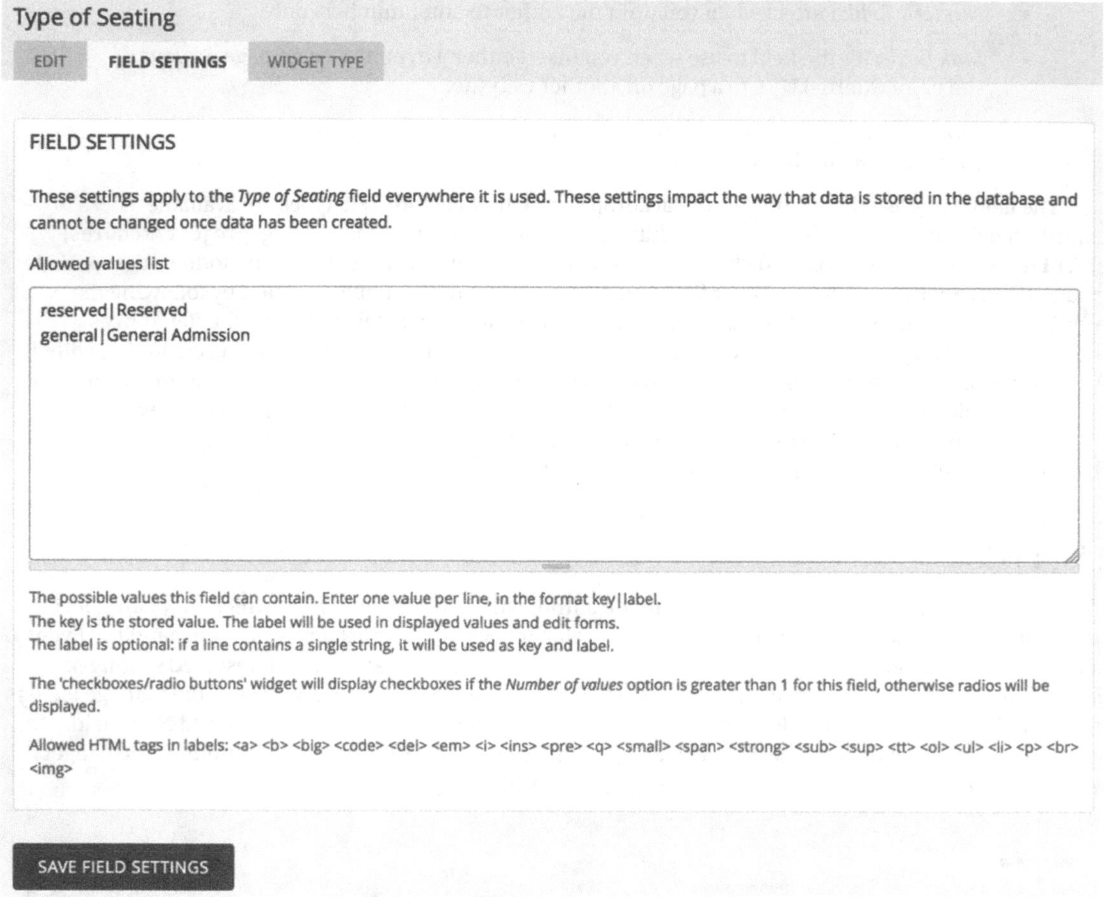

Type of Seating

EDIT | **FIELD SETTINGS** | WIDGET TYPE

FIELD SETTINGS

These settings apply to the *Type of Seating* field everywhere it is used. These settings impact the way that data is stored in the database and cannot be changed once data has been created.

Allowed values list

```
reserved|Reserved
general|General Admission
```

The possible values this field can contain. Enter one value per line, in the format key|label.
The key is the stored value. The label will be used in displayed values and edit forms.
The label is optional: if a line contains a single string, it will be used as key and label.

The 'checkboxes/radio buttons' widget will display checkboxes if the *Number of values* option is greater than 1 for this field, otherwise radios will be displayed.

Allowed HTML tags in labels: <a> <b> <big> <code> <del> <em> <i> <ins> <pre> <q> <small> <span> <strong> <sub> <sup> <tt> <ol> <ul> <li> <p>
 <img>

SAVE FIELD SETTINGS

Figure 5-19. *Creating the options*

The next step in the configuration process for this field is shown in Figure 5-20. On this form you can

- Change the label.

- Create help text. Enter help text that will help the author understand what this field is about.

- Mark the field as required.

- Set the option that will be selected by default when the page is rendered.

- Set the number of values. If you selected Check Boxes/Radio Buttons as the widget type, setting the number of values to 1 results in the values listed as radio buttons, or as check boxes if you allow more than one value. If you chose a select list as the widget type, setting the value to 1 results in the values listed as a drop-down list; if you set the value to greater than one, the widget is rendered as a scrollable select list.

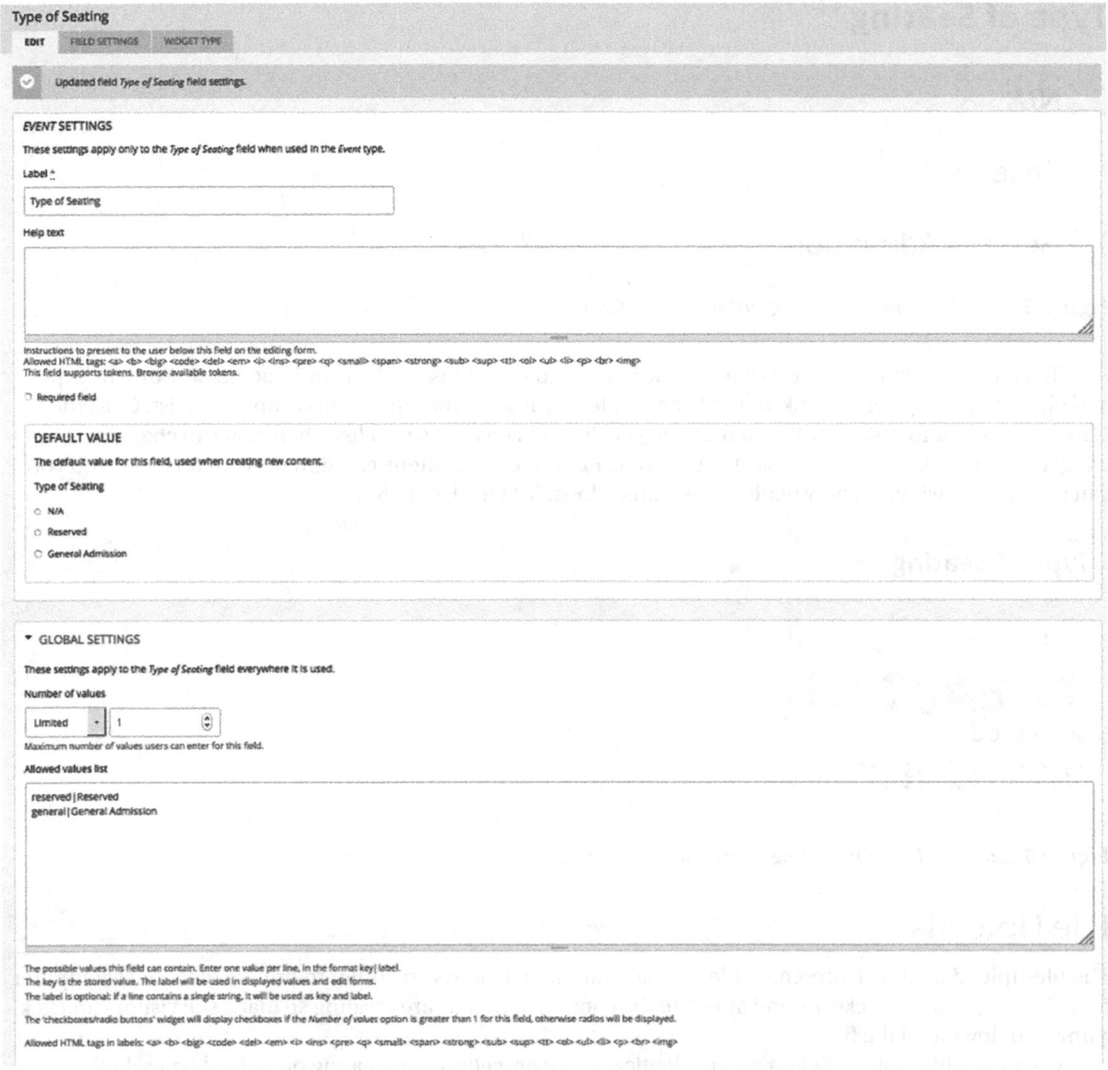

Type of Seating

EDIT   FIELD SETTINGS   WIDGET TYPE

✅ Updated field *Type of Seating* field settings.

EVENT SETTINGS

These settings apply only to the *Type of Seating* field when used in the *Event* type.

Label *

Type of Seating

Help text

Instructions to present to the user below this field on the editing form.
Allowed HTML tags: `<a> <b> <big> <code> <del> <em> <i> <ins> <pre> <q> <small> <span> <strong> <sub> <sup> <tt> <ol> <ul> <li> <p> <br> <img>`
This field supports tokens. Browse available tokens.

○ Required field

DEFAULT VALUE

The default value for this field, used when creating new content.

Type of Seating

○ N/A

○ Reserved

○ General Admission

▼ **GLOBAL SETTINGS**

These settings apply to the *Type of Seating* field everywhere it is used.

Number of values

Limited   ▾   1 ⊕

Maximum number of values users can enter for this field.

Allowed values list

reserved | Reserved
general | General Admission

The possible values this field can contain. Enter one value per line, in the format key | label.
The key is the stored value. The label will be used in displayed values and edit forms.
The label is optional: if a line contains a single string, it will be used as key and label.

The 'checkboxes/radio buttons' widget will display checkboxes if the *Number of values* option is greater than 1 for this field, otherwise radios will be displayed.

Allowed HTML tags in labels: `<a> <b> <big> <code> <del> <em> <i> <ins> <pre> <q> <small> <span> <strong> <sub> <sup> <tt> <ol> <ul> <li> <p> <br> <img>`

Figure 5-20. *Configuring a list field*

Update the values as desired, and click Save Settings to continue.

The new field is ready for use, as shown in Figure 5-21. Note that Backdrop added a third option to your list: N/A. Because you did not check the Required Field check box for this field (see Figure 5-19), Backdrop automatically inserts the N/A option because a visitor may wish to not select an option. If you want to remove the N/A option, check the Required Field check box; Backdrop will remove that option from the list shown to the content editor.

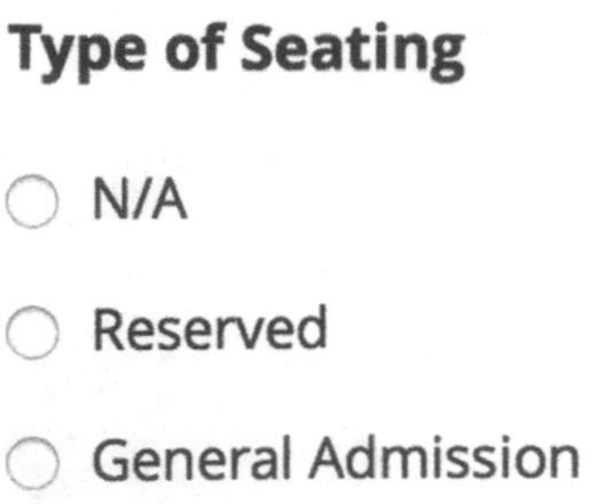

Type of Seating
N/A
Reserved
General Admission

Figure 5-21. *The Type Of Seating radio buttons field*

To change the type of widget from Check Boxes/Radio Buttons, navigate to Structure ➤ Content Types, and click the Manage Fields link for the Event content type from the Operations drop-down list. Click the Check Boxes/Radio Buttons value in the Widget column to reveal a select list where you can change the widget to Select List. Then, click Save to continue. Return to the content-creation page for an event and you can see that the widget is now rendered as a drop-down list (see Figure 5-22).

Type of Seating
- None -
- None -
Reserved
General Admission

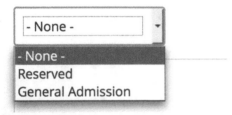

Figure 5-22. *The Type Of Seating select list*

File Uploads

The file-upload field type presents a file browser button that allows an author to browse their local computer for a file to upload to Backdrop and attach to the content item they are creating so that a site visitor can click a link and download the file.

Creating a file-upload field is nearly identical to the procedure for creating other field types. Let's expand the Event content type to include the ability to attach a program for the event. As with previous fields, navigate to the Event content type's Manage Fields page. Enter **Event Program** in the Label field, and select File as the field type. The only widget option is File (see Figure 5-23). Click the Save button to continue.

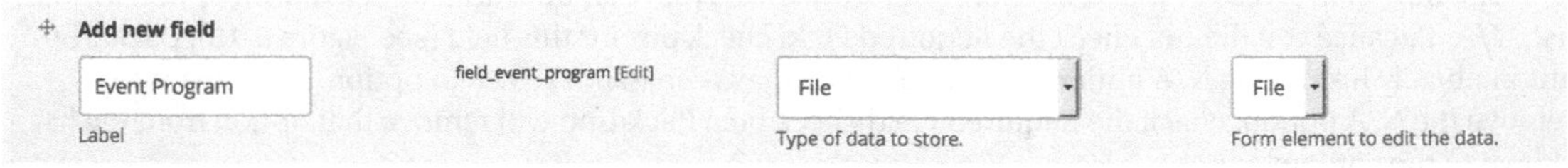

Add new field
Event Program
Label
field_event_program [Edit]
File
Type of data to store.
File
Form element to edit the data.

Figure 5-23. *Setting the file-upload parameters*

On the Field Settings form (see Figure 5-24) are options that define whether the file will be displayed when a site visitor views an event, and where the file should be stored. Click the Enable Display Field check box so that the editor can choose whether to display the file when creating a new event, and check the Files Displayed By Default check box to automatically display files when one is attached to an event. The only place files can be stored in is the public directory; other options may be enabled, as discussed in Chapter 16. Click the Save Field Settings button to continue.

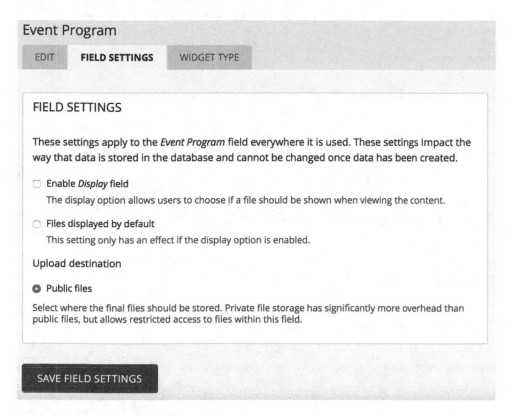

Figure 5-24. *File-upload field settings*

The final step in the configuration of a file-upload field is setting other important attributes of the field (see Figure 5-25):

- *Help Text:* Provides additional instructions to editors when uploading files.

- *Allowed File Extensions:* The default setting is .txt, but you may wish to allow other file types, such as `.pdf`, `.xls`, `.xlsx`, `.doc`, `.docx`, `.ppt`, and `.pptx`; or one of the typical image formats, `.png`, `.gif`, `.jpeg`, and `.jpg`.

- *File Directory:* You may specify a subdirectory of the files directory where files uploaded through this field will be stored. You may leave it blank and all files uploaded will be stored in the default files directory.

- *Maximum Upload Size:* If space is a consideration, you may limit the size of files that are uploaded using this field. The structure of the value you enter is explained in the help text: for example, 5 MB or 500 KB.

- *Enable Description Field:* If you check the box, the author can enter a description for the uploaded file and display that description to site visitors.

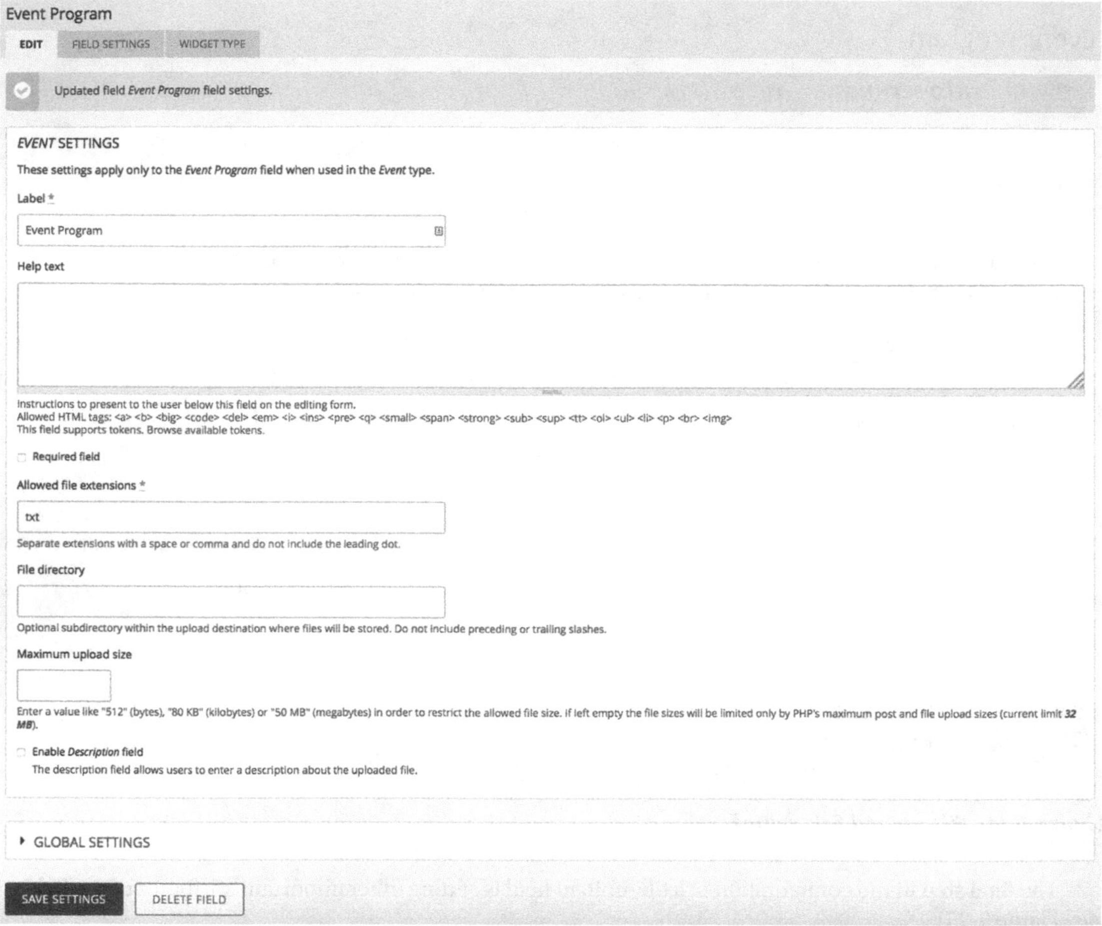

Figure 5-25. *File-upload attributes*

There are also global settings you can configure for file-upload fields. Clicking Global Settings displays several additional settings, as shown in Figure 5-26. You can set how many files may be uploaded, a useful capability when you have scenarios where you want to let authors upload several files instead of having a separate field for each file uploaded. The other values are settings that were previously collected but may be updated here. Click the Save Settings button to finish the process of creating the file-upload field.

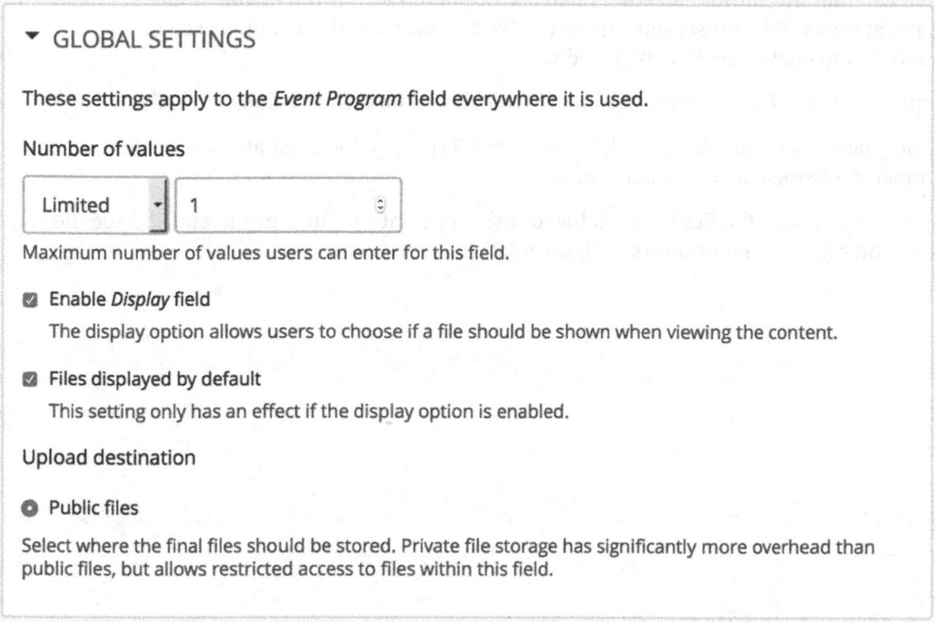

▼ GLOBAL SETTINGS

These settings apply to the *Event Program* field everywhere it is used.

Number of values

| Limited ▾ | 1 ⏳ |

Maximum number of values users can enter for this field.

☑ Enable *Display* field

The display option allows users to choose if a file should be shown when viewing the content.

☑ Files displayed by default

This setting only has an effect if the display option is enabled.

Upload destination

◉ Public files

Select where the final files should be stored. Private file storage has significantly more overhead than public files, but allows restricted access to files within this field.

Figure 5-26. File-upload global settings

Return to Content ➤ Add Content ➤ Event, and note that the file-upload field is now present on the content-editing form for an event (see Figure 5-27).

Event Program

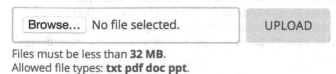

Files must be less than **32 MB**.
Allowed file types: **txt pdf doc ppt**.

Figure 5-27. The file-upload field

Text Area

There will likely be scenarios where you want to provide a field on a content-creation form that enables an author to enter a paragraph or more of text. Although you could provide this capability through a text field (a single-line text-entry box), the more acceptable and standard way is to provide a text area. Extending the event example, let's add a new field that will capture driving directions to the venue. To create a text area, follow the same steps you used to create other fields in the previous sections.

Enter **Driving directions** in the Label field, select Text (Long) for the field type, and choose Text Area (Multiple Rows) for the widget type. Click Save to continue to the settings page, where you may

- Enter help text.

- Set the field to Required.

- Specify the number of rows to be displayed in the text area.

- Define whether the author can enter plain text or filtered text. If you enable filtered text, the author will be presented with a WYSIWYG editor. For this example, select Filtered Text to enable the WYSIWYG editor.

- Specify a default value. For text areas, there typically isn't a default value.

- Set how many values to allow (in Global Settings). Typically, for a text area the value is 1, meaning a single text area per event.

After you click Save Settings, the field is available for use. Try creating a new event, and you see the text area where you can enter driving directions (see Figure 5-28).

Figure 5-28. *The new text area for driving directions*

Numeric Fields and Other Field Types

By walking through the various field types listed previously, you can see that there is a pattern and a common set of parameters for nearly every field type you've created. A numeric field is essentially a text field, but it's restricted automatically by Backdrop so that it only accepts numeric characters (0–9). As you expand on the types of fields you can create by downloading and enabling contributed field modules, you will find slight variations in the process due to the structure of the fields you are creating. However, the overall process is the same. If you haven't done so, now is the perfect time to browse the list of field modules that are available to extend the capabilities of what is available in Backdrop core. Visit http://www.backdropcms.org/project/modules, enter **Fields** in the search field, and click the magnifying glass to see the list of available modules.

Formatting the Input Form for a Custom Content Type

Sometimes the visual representation of your new content-creation form may not fit with how you would like it to appear. You may want to change the order of fields on the form, the type of widget used to create content in a field, or the format of the widget itself. To change how the form is displayed, edit a content type following the steps you've performed previously, and then navigate to Structure ➤ Content Types ➤ Event ➤ Manage Fields. The Manage Fields form lists all the fields created for the Event content type (see Figure 5-29).

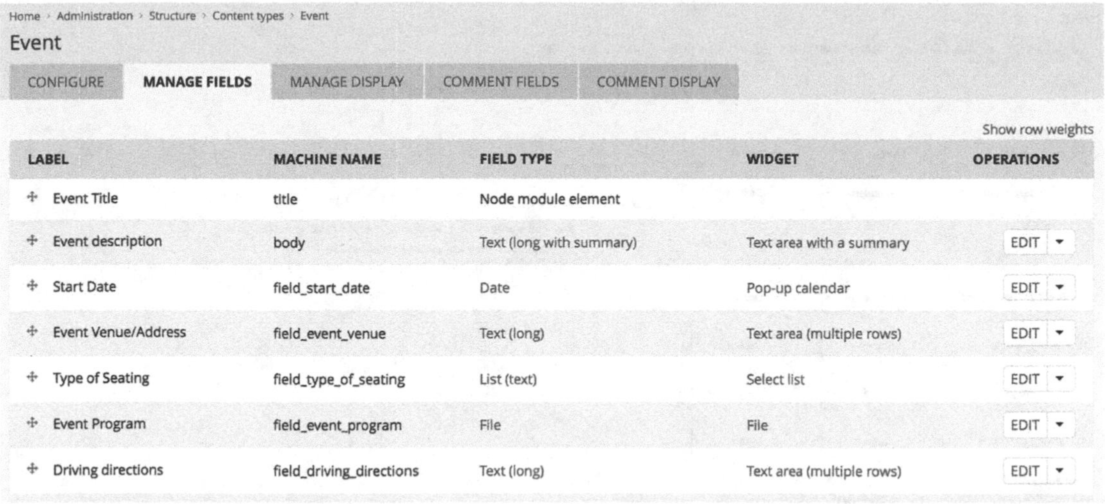

Home › Administration › Structure › Content types › Event

Event

CONFIGURE · **MANAGE FIELDS** · MANAGE DISPLAY · COMMENT FIELDS · COMMENT DISPLAY

Show row weights

LABEL	MACHINE NAME	FIELD TYPE	WIDGET	OPERATIONS
✛ Event Title	title	Node module element		
✛ Event description	body	Text (long with summary)	Text area with a summary	EDIT ▾
✛ Start Date	field_start_date	Date	Pop-up calendar	EDIT ▾
✛ Event Venue/Address	field_event_venue	Text (long)	Text area (multiple rows)	EDIT ▾
✛ Type of Seating	field_type_of_seating	List (text)	Select list	EDIT ▾
✛ Event Program	field_event_program	File	File	EDIT ▾
✛ Driving directions	field_driving_directions	Text (long)	Text area (multiple rows)	EDIT ▾

Figure 5-29. *The Manage Fields tab*

To rearrange the order of the fields on the form, click and hold the arrows icon next to the field you wish to move, drag the field to the position where you want it to appear, and release the mouse button. To change the widget type, simply click the existing widget type and, on the Widget Type screen, select a new value.

To change the settings for a field, click the Edit link in the Operations column. To delete a field, click the arrow next to Edit, and select Delete.

Formatting the Output of a Custom Content Type

Sometimes the visual representation of your new content type, as displayed to the site's end user, doesn't fit with how you want the content to be rendered on the screen. In the previous section, you looked at rearranging the fields on the form used by content authors to create an event; in this case, you are rearranging the content as it appears when an event is rendered to an end user.

Adjusting the order and positioning of the labels in relation to the field can be accomplished by clicking the Manage Display tab on the custom content type edit form. Let's use the Event content type to demonstrate. Clicking the Manage Display tab reveals the page shown in Figure 5-30.

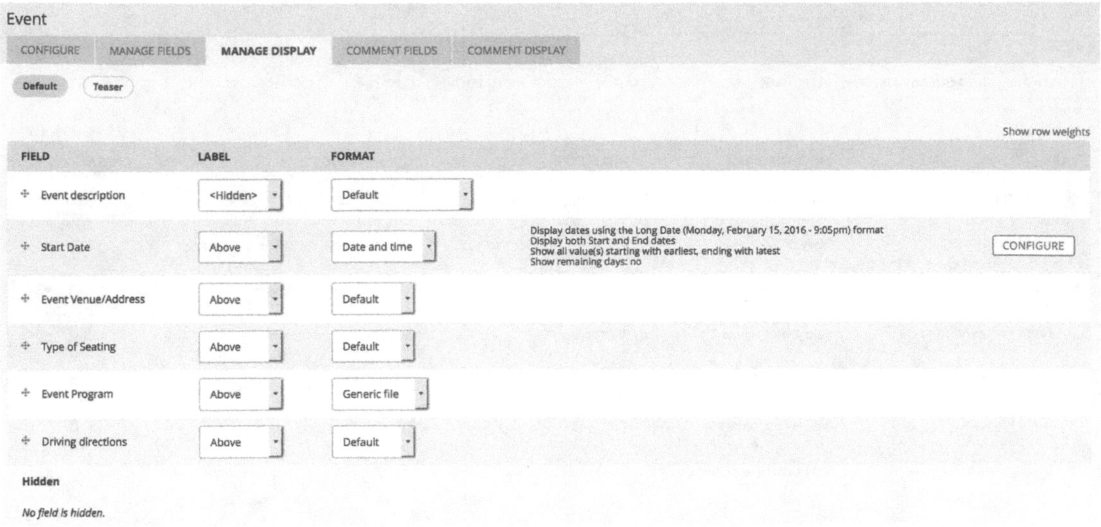

Figure 5-30. *Manage Display page*

This page lists all the fields associated with your content type. For field labels, you may specify where the label appears:

- *Above (the default):* The label appears above the value that is displayed.

- *Inline:* The label appears immediately before the value.

- *Hidden:* The label is not displayed.

If you click the Format select list of each field, you find a selection of options depending on the field type. For text-related fields, the options are as follows:

- *Default*: The content is rendered on the screen as you specified when you created the field.

- *Summary or Trimmed*: If the field type has a summary value and a body value, the summary value is displayed. If there isn't a summary, the body value is trimmed to a specified length.

- *Trimmed*: The content is trimmed to a specified number of characters. If the content is longer than the specified number of characters, a Read More link is displayed.

- *Hidden*: The content does not appear on the screen.

For other field types, the options depend on the type of content being displayed.

Some fields provide advanced configuration options. Those settings may be viewed and set by clicking the Configure button.

To reposition a field, click and hold the arrows icon next to the field label of the item you wish to move, drag the field to the position where you want it to appear, and release the mouse button. Remember to click the Save button after you have moved all the fields to their proper position.

You can also define how the content is displayed for modes other than the default and Teaser, such as RSS, Search Index, and Search Result Highlighting Input. To enable those modes, simply click the Custom Display Settings link at the bottom of the Manage Display page to expand the list. With the additional modes enabled, you can define how your content is displayed when, for example, an event is displayed on the Search Results page.

Summary

Content types are one of the "killer app" aspects of Backdrop, and this an important concept to understand. You could construct a Backdrop site with just the Page and Post content types, but you are likely to want to use the features and functions provided through the use of custom content types. This chapter demonstrated just one of the custom content types that I create for nearly every site I build for my clients. Other custom content types that I frequently use include Customers, Products, Departments, FAQs, Locations, and Employees. As you design and develop a new site, I'm sure you'll identify one or more custom content types you can use.

Another powerful feature of custom content types is the ability to develop custom reports or views of data from the custom content type that is stored in the Backdrop database. If you think about the Event content type you created in this chapter, it might be valuable to generate a list of events sorted by the start date, or a list sorted by venue.

The next chapter provides an overview of Backdrop themes. Now that you have content, let's make it look good!

CHAPTER 6

■ ■ ■

Creating Layouts

One of the powerful features of Backdrop is the Layout module. The Layout module provides the ability to create, manage, and control page structure on your Backdrop site. This chapter describes what layouts are, how to use them, the default layouts provided with Backdrop core, and how to create your own custom layouts.

Default Layouts

The Layout manager is included in Backdrop core and is enabled by default during the installation process. To access the Layouts administrative user interface, navigate to Structure ➤ Layouts.

During the installation process, the Layout module creates two layouts: a default layout used for all non-administrative pages on the site and a default administrative layout (see Figure 6-1).

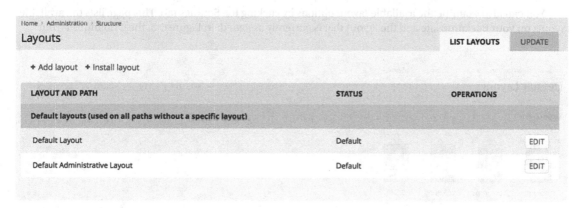

Figure 6-1. The default layouts

There are three basic areas to focus on when looking at layouts:

- What determines when a specific layout is used

- What structure the layout provides, such as one column, two columns, and so on

- What appears in each areas on the page

Let's examine the default layout to see how it is constructed, as an example for creating additional layouts. Clicking the Edit link to the right of Default Layout in the Layout module displays a page that shows each of the regions in the layout and the elements enabled in each of those regions, as shown in Figure 6-2.

© Todd Tomlinson 2016
T. Tomlinson, *Beginning Backdrop CMS*, DOI 10.1007/978-1-4842-1970-6_6

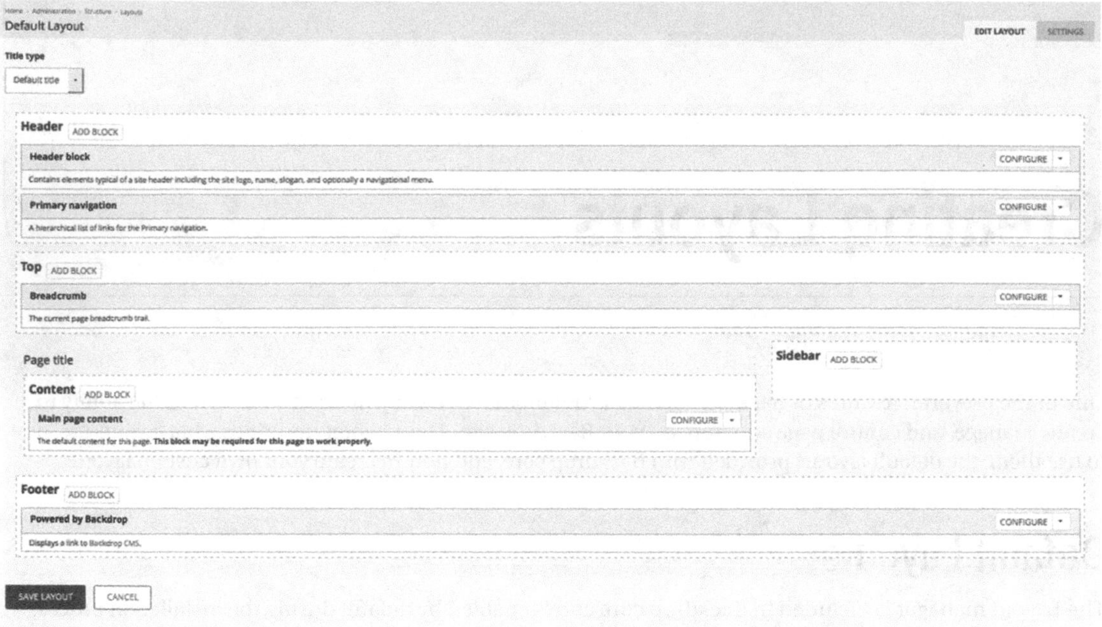

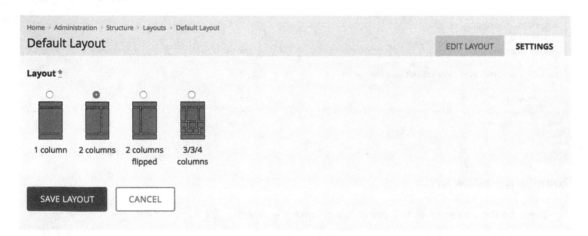

Figure 6-2. *The default layout*

You can also examine the available layout options by clicking the Settings tab. This page lists the available layouts on your Backdrop site and the layout that is currently assigned: in Figure 6-3, the 2 Columns layout.

Figure 6-3. *The available layouts*

At this juncture, you could add new blocks to the standard layout or change the physical structure of the layout using the screens shown in this section. Instead of changing the defaults, let's create a custom layout.

Creating Custom Layouts

The default layout is automatically applied to every page of the site. You may have pages on your site where the default layout does not fulfill the needs of those pages and a different layout is needed. This section demonstrates by creating a new layout that uses the pages on the site that display an individual node.

You start the process of creating a new custom layout by clicking the Add Layout link at the top of the Layouts administration page, as shown in Figure 6-1. The first form in the process lets you specify a name for the new layout, the structural layout of the page, and the path structure that determines when this layout is used (see Figure 6-4).

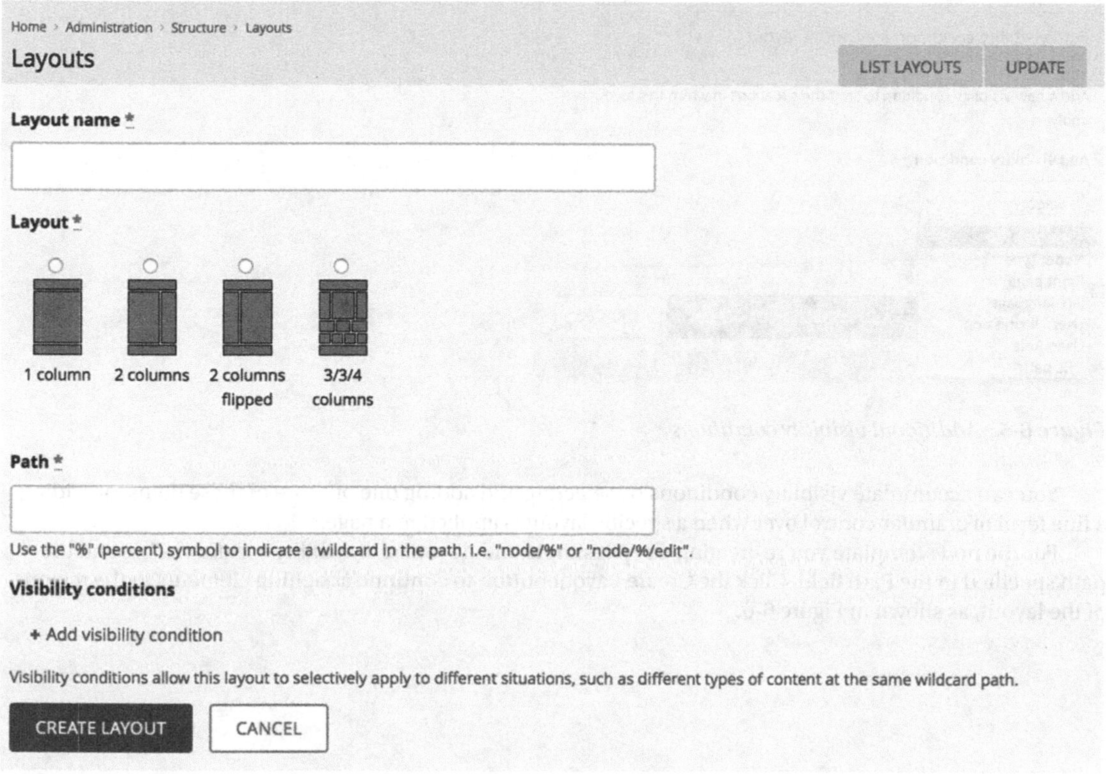

Figure 6-4. *Creating a custom layout*

Use **node** as the layout name, the single-column layout, and a path of **node/%** to control when this template will be used. After entering the path, you can click the Add Visibility Condition link to specify additional criteria to further refine when the template will be used by. Clicking the link opens a list of visibility options (see Figure 6-5):

- *Node: Type*: Displays a checklist with all the content types enabled on the site, allowing you to define a specific layout by content type.

- *Front Page*: Displays a list of two conditions that let you choose whether to use the template only if the visitor is on the front page of the site or only if the visitor is *not* on the front page. In the case of a node-specific template, the only viable option is if the user is not on the front page.

- *Site Language*: Shows a list of enabled languages on the site, allowing you to control when this layout is used based on activated language.

- *User: Permission*: Shows a list of all the site's permissions, enabling restriction based on a visitor's enabled permissions.

- *User: Role*: Performs a function similar to User: Permission. Displays all the roles enabled on the system, allowing restriction based on the visitor's assigned roles.

- *URL Path*: Provides an interface to specify additional URL details including paths to include and paths to exclude.

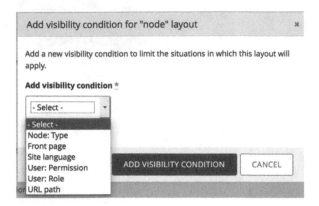

Figure 6-5. *Additional visibility conditions*

You can accumulate visibility conditions by selecting and adding one or more of these items, providing a fine level of granular control over when a specific layout is applied to a page.

For the node template you're creating, keep it simple and do not add visibility conditions beyond the path specified in the Path field. Click the Create Layout button to continue assigning elements to the regions of the layout, as shown in Figure 6-6.

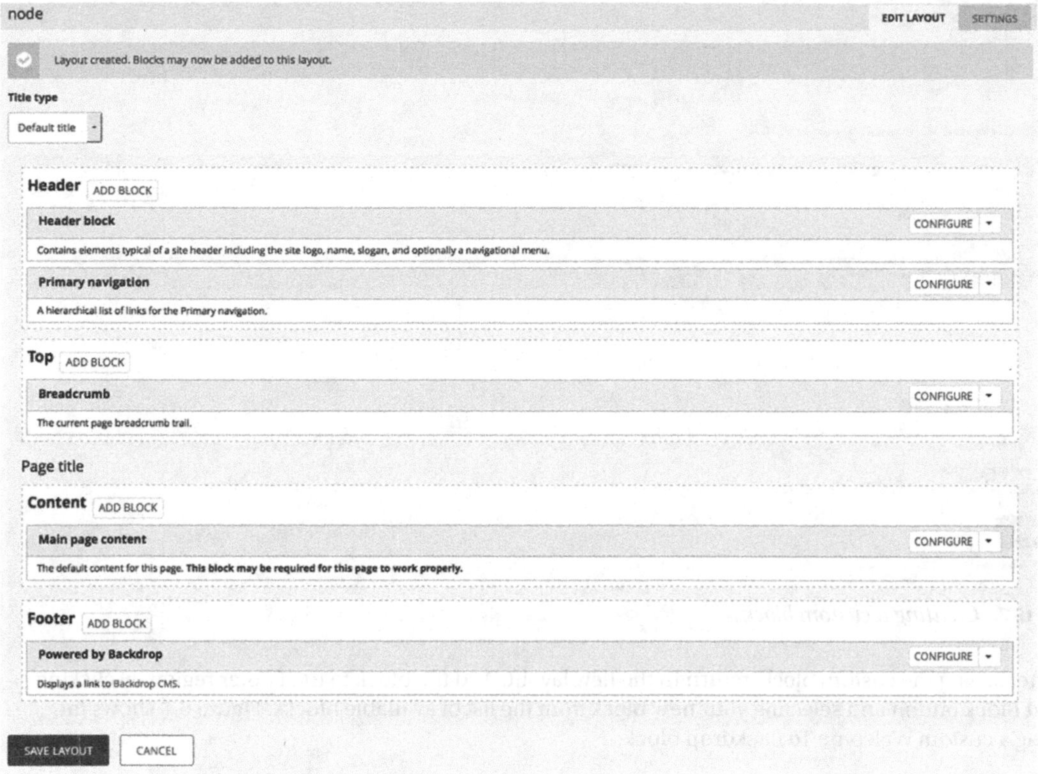

Figure 6-6. *Assigning elements to regions*

When the Layout module creates the new layout, it automatically copies all the elements assigned to regions in the default layout to the new custom layout. At this point, you can rearrange the elements by dragging and dropping them on different regions of the layout, you can remove elements from the layout, or you can add new elements that do not appear in the standard layout. To demonstrate these capabilities, let's do the following:

1. Remove the Powered By Backdrop block from the footer.

2. Create a new custom block to insert into the footer.

To remove the Powered By Backdrop block, click the arrow next to the Configure link, and select the Remove option. To create a new custom block, open a new tab in your browser, navigate to Structure ➤ Custom Blocks, and select the Add Block link. The rest of the process is relatively easy: enter a name, title, and body content, as shown in Figure 6-7.

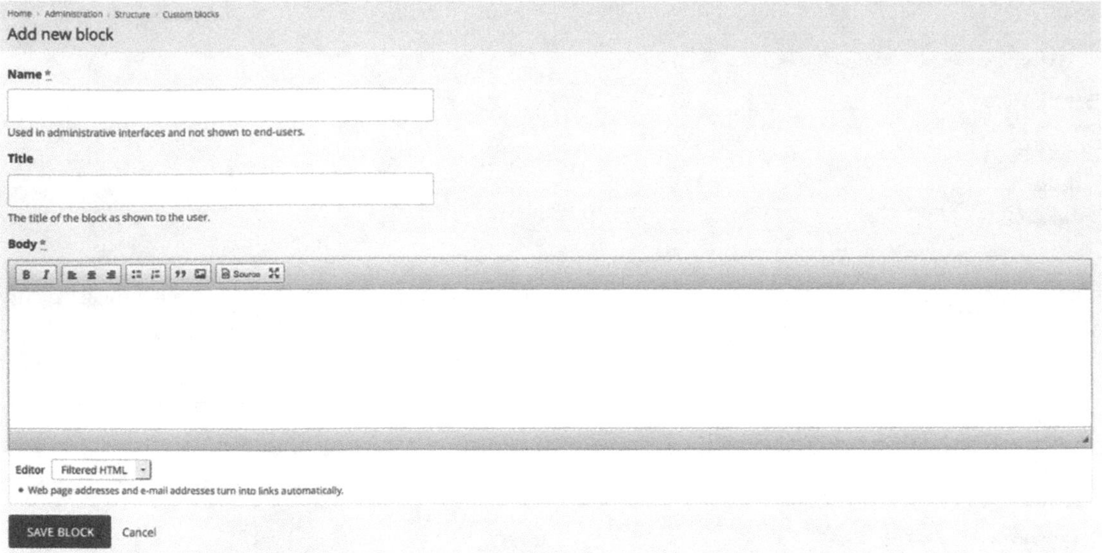

Figure 6-7. *Creating a custom block*

After saving the custom block, return to the new layout. Add the block to the Footer region by clicking the Add Block button and selecting your new block from the list of available blocks. Figure 6-8 shows me selecting a custom Welcome To Backdrop block.

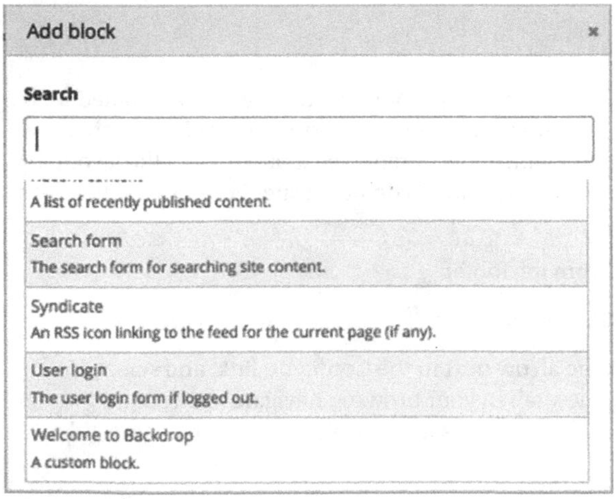

Figure 6-8. *The list of available blocks*

You then see a list of options to configure the block for this specific layout, including modifying the title, body, style settings, and block visibility parameters (see Figure 6-9). Chapter 9 covers blocks in detail.

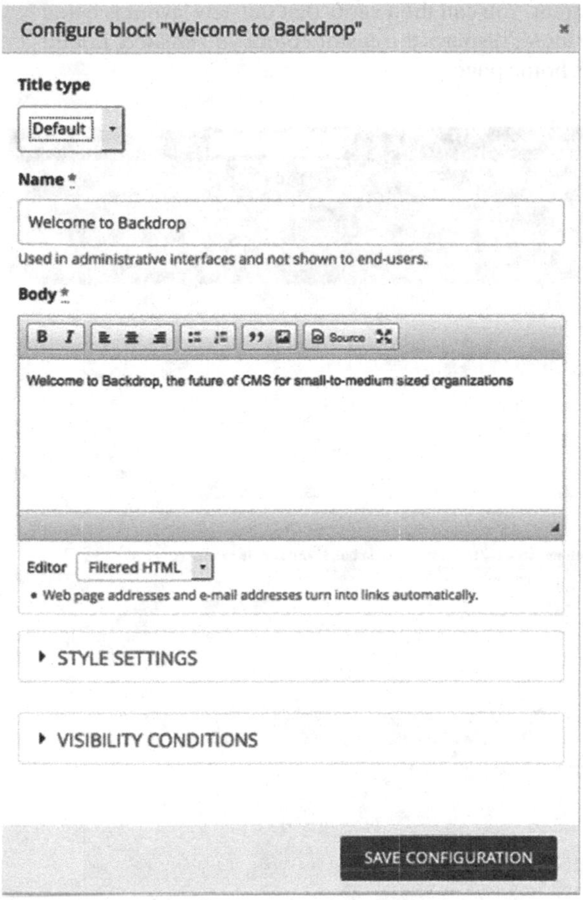

Figure 6-9. Configuring a block for placement on a layout

With the layout complete, you're ready to test it by creating a new post and viewing that post to validate that the new layout is being used. Click the Save Configuration button at the bottom of the page, which returns you to the list of available layouts. You see the new layout you just created listed as a custom layout (see Figure 6-10).

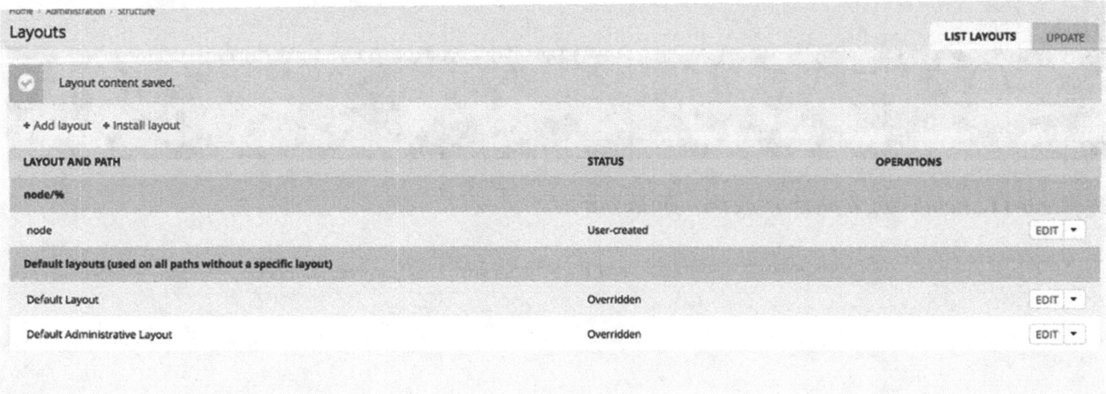

Figure 6-10. The revised list of available layouts

Create a new Post content item and view the content. You can then verify that the new layout is being used to render the page, as shown in Figure 6-11: the footer displays the custom block you created, not the Powered By Backdrop block that appears on the site's home page.

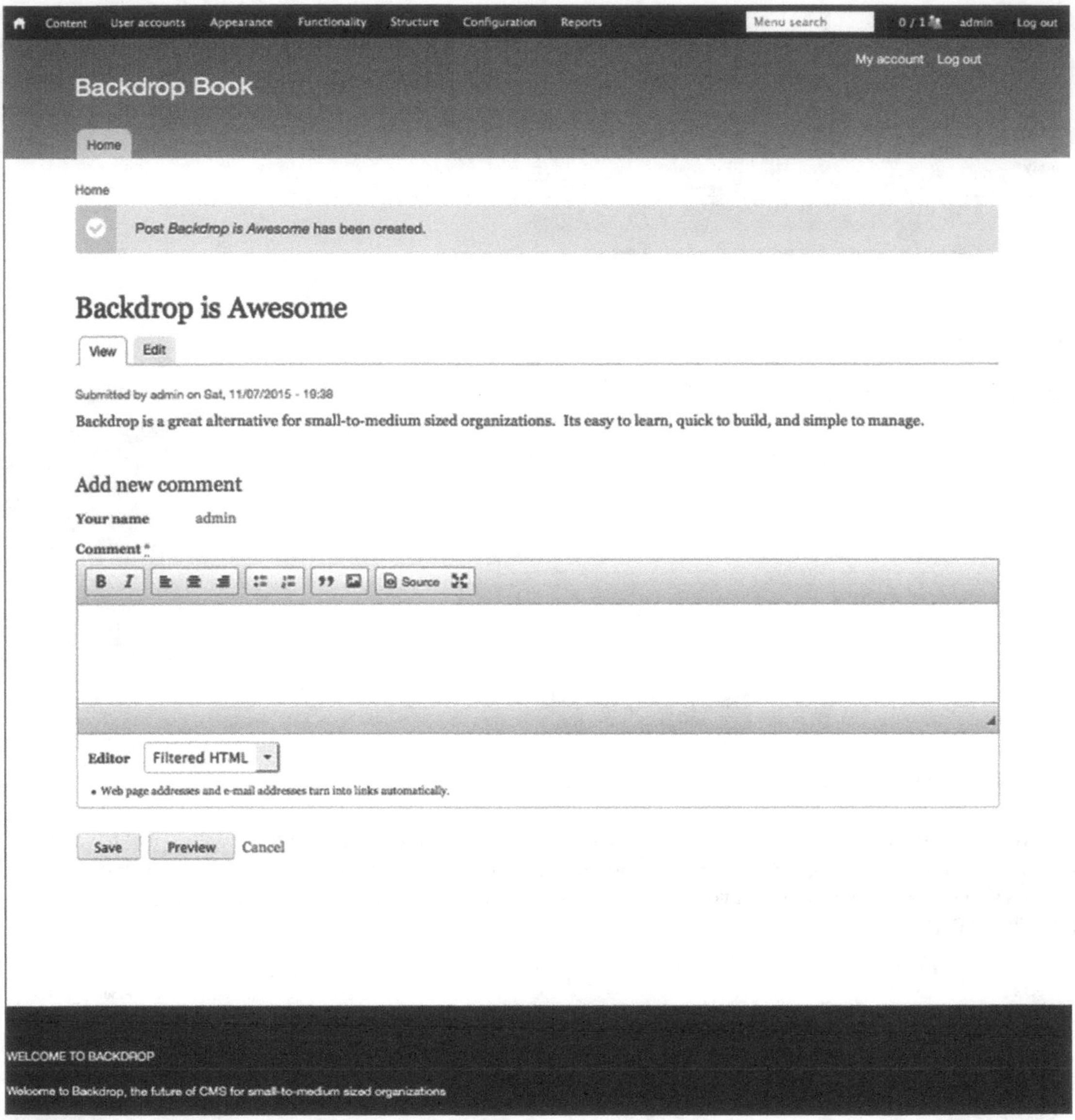

Figure 6-11. *Rendering a node using the new layout*

Installing Other Layouts

Although the basic layouts that come with Backdrop core may suffice for your site, a growing number of contributed layouts are available that you can install. You can find the additional layouts by visiting https://backdropcms.org/layouts or http://github.com/backdrop-contrib?utf8=√&query=Layout. I'm a fan of the Radix layouts and have used them on a majority of my sites over the past year. Let's add those layouts to your Backdrop site to provide several structural layouts in addition to the four standard structural layouts that come with Backdrop's Layout module.

The Radix layouts are found on Backdrop's GitHub site at http://github.com/backdrop-contrib/radix_layouts. Use Git to clone the Radix layouts in the site's layouts directory, which is in the root directory of the Backdrop site. Clone the layouts into layouts/radix, clear the cache, and click the Add Layout link on the Layouts administration page to see all the additional layouts Radix provides for you to enable and use, as shown in Figure 6-12.

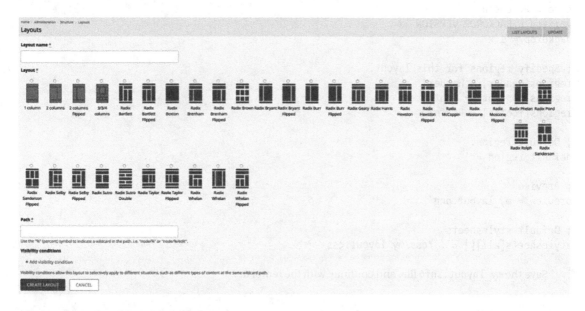

Figure 6-12. *The additional Radix layouts*

Creating a Custom Layout Template

The combination of the off-the-shelf layouts provided by the Layout module and the Radix layouts give you a wide variety of structural layout options, but there may be cases where you need a template that doesn't exist. Creating a template is relatively straightforward.

A custom structural layout has five basic elements:

- A directory in the layouts directory named to match the custom layout: for example, my_layout

- A .info file in the layouts directory with the same name as the directory it resides in: for example, my_layout.info

- A .png file that represents the structure of the physical layout: for example, my_layout.png

- A template file: for example, my_layout.tpl.php

- A style sheet with the associated CSS for the layout: for example, my_layout.css, stored in a css subdirectory

Creating the Layout's .info File

The content of the .info file is relatively short and simple. As an example, following is the .info file for my_layout. *Regions* are the areas on the layout where you place elements like blocks, menus, and content. In the case of my_layout there are three regions, Header, Content, and Footer:

```
name = My Layout
version = BACKDROP_VERSION
backdrop = 1.x

; Specify regions for this layout.
regions[header] = Header
regions[content] = Content
regions[footer] = Footer

; Default region.
default region = ''

; Preview
preview = my_layout.png

; Default stylesheets
stylesheets[all][] = ../css/my_layout.css
```

Save the my_layout.info file, and continue with the template.

Creating the Layout's .tpl.php File

The .tpl.php file is a template that is managed by the Layout module. It is constructed using a combination of HTML markup and PHP snippets and tells the templating engine what to place in that specific spot in the layout. For example, <?php print $content['header']; ?> tells the template engine to place any content assigned to the header region in that spot, in a div that has a class of container. If you are not familiar with HTML or PHP, now would be a great time to pick up a reference book on the subject.

The content of my_layout.tpl.php, is as follows:

```
<?php
/**
 * @file
 * Template for My Layout.
 */
?>
<div class="my-layout <?php print implode(' ', $classes); ?>"
<?php print backdrop_attributes($attributes); ?>>
```

```php
<?php if (!empty($content['header'])): ?>
  <header id="header" class="header" role="header">
    <div class="container">
      <?php print $content['header']; ?>
    </div>
  </header>
<?php endif; ?>

<?php if ($messages): ?>
  <section class="messages container">
    <?php print $messages; ?>
  </section>
<?php endif; ?>

<main class="main container" role="main">
  <div class="page-header">
    <a id="main-content"></a>
    <?php print render($title_prefix); ?>
    <?php if ($title): ?>
      <h1 class="title" id="page-title">
        <?php print $title; ?>
      </h1>
    <?php endif; ?>
    <?php print render($title_suffix); ?>
  </div>

  <?php if ($tabs): ?>
    <div class="tabs">
      <?php print $tabs; ?>
    </div>
  <?php endif; ?>

  <?php print $action_links; ?>
  <div class="container-fluid">
    <div class="row">
      <div class="col-md-12 my-layout-layouts-contentmain">
        <?php print $content['content']; ?>
      </div>
    </div>
  </div>
</main>

<?php if ($content['footer']): ?>
  <footer id="footer" class="footer" role="footer">
    <div class="container">
      <?php print $content['footer']; ?>
    </div>
  </footer>
<?php endif; ?>
</div><!-- /.my_layout -->
```

Creating the Layout's .css File

Using standard CSS, you create the layout's .css file to specify how you wish the layout to render and behave through the various breakpoints, thus making the layout responsive. The .css file for My Layout has nearly 1,000 lines; for brevity, it isn't included here. However, there is nothing unique about a layout's .css file; it is what you would typically implement for any HTML-based web site.

After saving all the files and clearing the cache, you can now use the custom layout. It appears in the list of available layouts, as shown in Figure 6-13.

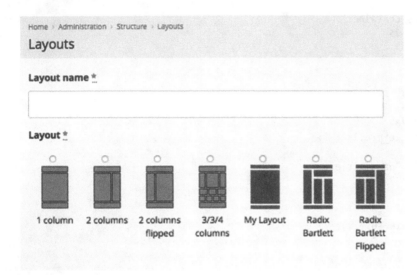

Figure 6-13. *My Layout, available for use*

Changing Layouts

Over time, you may have a page assigned to a specific layout and need to change the physical structure of that page. You can do so by navigating to Structure ➤ Layouts and clicking the Edit link for the layout you wish to change. On the layout's configuration page, click the Settings tab, select a different layout, and click the Save Layout button. On the Edit Layout tab, you can then rearrange the blocks into regions, add new blocks, or remove existing blocks.

Summary

The Layout module provides a simple-to-use interface for managing the structure of the pages rendered on your site. Using layouts gives you fine-grained control and is a powerful solution for creating beautifully structured pages across a Backdrop site, with little to no programming required. The Layout module also gives you the flexibility to integrate contributed layouts, such as Radix, and create your own custom layouts.

The next chapter walks you step by step through the process of installing a theme to customize the look and feel of your Backdrop web site.

■ ■ ■

## CHAPTER 7

Using Backdrop Themes

The look of your Backdrop web site is governed by the theme you have installed and enabled. A Backdrop theme provides all the detailed parameters that are used by Backdrop core to define

- The colors used on the page

- The fonts used for text, headings, links, and other elements

- The placement of images and graphics that are present on every page of the site (images and graphics associated with the page itself rather than a content item)

A theme can be as simple as a plain white canvas or as complex and visually energizing as your imagination can conjure up. This chapter explains the process of changing the overall look and feel of your site by installing a new theme. You've added some neat things to your site in previous chapters, and you've seen some exciting features of Backdrop; but this chapter will have you exclaiming, "Wow!"

You have already worked with a Backdrop theme; the basic Backdrop site you installed as part of the earlier chapters in this book uses Backdrop's default theme, named Bartik. Bartik by itself is a great theme and is highly configurable through administrative settings, and for many sites it has all the features required. However, not everyone wants their site to look like a standard off-the-shelf Backdrop site, so let's look at the options you have to choose from: installing a contributed theme from the http://backdropcms.org web site, or constructing a theme from scratch.

The quickest and easiest path is to pick a contributed theme and either use that theme as is or customize it to meet the specific visual design you are trying to achieve on your site. You can find the list of contributed themes at http://backdropcms.org/themes. Themes listed on the Backdrop web site include a detailed description, and most provide a preview of what the theme looks like once it has been installed (see Figure 7-1).

© Todd Tomlinson 2016

T. Tomlinson, *Beginning Backdrop CMS*, DOI 10.1007/978-1-4842-1970-6_7

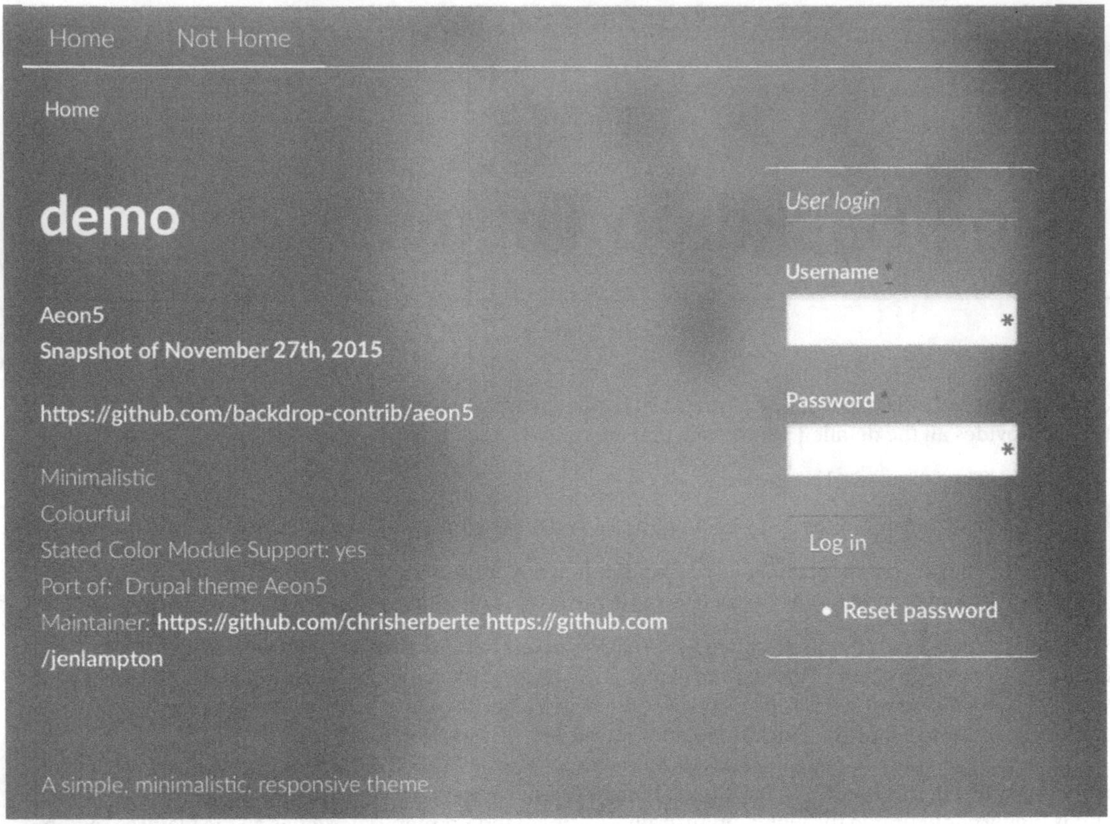

Figure 7-1. *The Afterlight Tribute theme*

You'll find as you browse through various Backdrop themes that many of them follow this same generic layout, which for many people is a negative because they feel as though every Backdrop site looks nearly identical. The truth is that, yes, many off-the-shelf themes follow this same design pattern. However, you can create a design that significantly deviates from the standard. Figure 7-2 shows how I used a PHP template to create a site for the University of Oregon; high school students use this site to manage their electronic portfolio of learning assets and track their progress toward graduation. The area at the top of the page with the brown background is the header, the area in the middle of the page with the green background is the content area, and the brown area at the bottom is the footer.

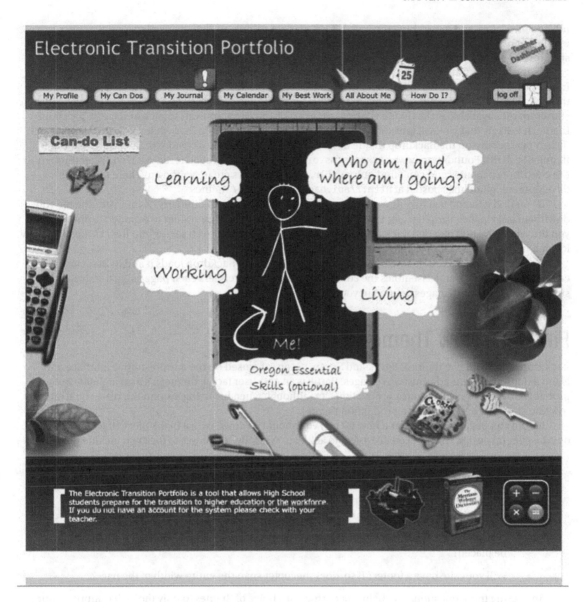

Figure 7-2. A creative, nontraditional Backdrop theme

How a Backdrop Theme Works

Understanding some of the basics of how a Backdrop theme works will help lay the foundation for topics covered in later chapters. The fundamentals of how a theme works can be distilled into a few basic concepts, explained here.

A Backdrop theme's primary purpose is to define the look and feel a Backdrop site. It performs that function through a relatively simple combination of HTML markup, PHP, and CSS. The CSS is responsible for defining attributes such as color, font size, font family, spacing between elements, and padding. The PHP code within a theme is focused on processing elements that appear on a page, defining variables that can be

91

utilized on a page, and in combination with HTML markup, templates that are used to render entities such as content types, menus, blocks, and comments on the site. Other elements of a page, such as the physical structure of the page and the rendering of content is handled by the Layout system.

As the administrator, you can pick which theme your site will use. You can download a stock theme from http://backdropcms.org/theme, you can purchase a commercial theme from various providers that sell HTML-based themes and convert it to Backdrop, you can create your own theme using one of the starter themes available on http://backdropcms.org/, or you can start from scratch and create a custom theme. It is likely that you will find something that matches or closely matches what you want from a visual design perspective on the Backdrop theme download site or by creating a custom theme using a starter theme like ZURB Foundation (www.backdropcms.org/project/zurb_foundation_6). If you scan through the contributed themes and can't find one you like, you can always create your own. There are theme-development .guidelines posted at http://api.backdropcms.org/ themes.

If you find a theme you like, download it, and save it in the /themes directory of your site. The file you download is a zip file; unzip it using the tools provided by your operating system to expand zip files (just as you did when you downloaded Backdrop), and copy the theme to your web server into the /themes directory located in the root directory of your site.

Once the theme has been downloaded, copied, and enabled, Backdrop loads it and its associated cascading style sheets and assembles the content. Backdrop then renders each page using the structure, style, colors, fonts, and images defined in your theme.

Finding a New Theme

Backdrop ships with two themes: Bartik and Seven. Seven is focused on the administrative interface and is the default theme for administrative pages. Bartik is an end-user facing theme; it's a great theme but probably not one you will use on a production site (although when browsing around the Web, you'll often run into sites that uses Bartik as a production theme).

Before you begin searching for a new theme, you should sit down with a blank piece of paper and sketch out the general design concept you are trying to achieve. Typically, attributes to focus on include these:

- Do you want a responsive theme, meaning your theme handles the details of different screen widths on phones, tablets, laptops, desktops, and larger displays?

- Will your site have a header or banner area? If so, how tall will the header be, and will it span the entire width of your page?

- Will your site use horizontal menus? If so, how many will it have, and where will they be placed?

- Will your site have a footer? If so, does the footer span the entire width of the page?

Answering these questions will help you narrow the choice of themes to only those that support your general layout and design goals.

The best place to begin your search for a theme is the http://backdropcms.org/ web site. To view a list of the available Backdrop themes, visit http://backdropcms.org/themes (see Figure 7-3).

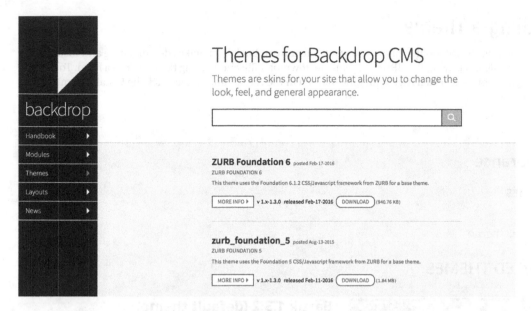

Figure 7-3. *Backdrop CMS contributed themes*

Most theme developers provide a sample screenshot of their design so you can see the general layout and design of their theme. As an example, select the Colihaut theme (`http://backdropcms.org/project/colihaut`). This theme provides a clean and simple layout, as you can see in Figure 7-4.

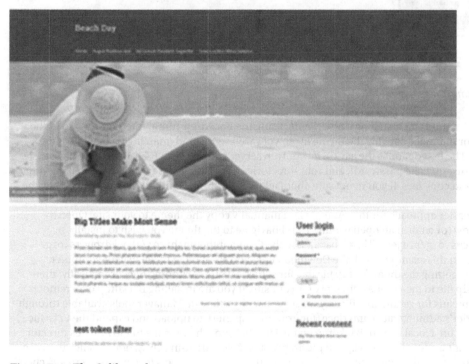

Figure 7-4. *The Colihaut theme*

Installing a Theme

The next step is to download the theme you want. A feature in Backdrop makes downloading and installing themes as simple as copying the URL for the theme download file and pasting the URL into a form. To get to this form, go to your site and navigate to Appearance. On the Appearance page, click the Install Theme link. See Figure 7-5.

Figure 7-5. *Installing a new theme*

There are two methods for installing a new theme: using the Backdrop admin interface to upload the file to your server, or manually copying the theme file to your web server and unarchiving that file in the /themes directory. The first option is the easiest if your web server is set up with FTP access, you have a valid FTP account (user ID and password), and your directories have the correct permissions to allow you to create directories and copy files. If you're not sure about all this, the simple method is to manually copy the theme file.

Let's take the easier approach for this example and manually copy the theme to your site. Open a new browser window (or a tab in an open window), and navigate to the theme you wish to install (http://backdropcms.org/project/theme_name). Use the Colihaut theme (http://backdropcms.org/project/colihaut) in this example. Click the Download link, and save the .zip file to your computer.

The next step is getting the theme's .zip file to your server. If you are running Backdrop locally, then simply copy the .zip file to the /themes directory for your site. If you are installing Backdrop on a remote server, you need a means for getting that file to your server, such as the File Manager tools available through your hosting provider's administrative interface (for example, Cpanel), to upload and expand the .zip file. Because I'm working on a local copy of Backdrop on my laptop, I copy the .zip file to the /themes directory and, using my operating system's tools, expand the archive file. If you are using OS X, double-click the .zip file to expand the archive. Other operating systems may require third-party tools to expand a .zip file; check your operating system vendor's documentation for details.

If your web server is set up with FTP access and you have an FTP account with access to your site's directory, you may follow the first approach—using the admin interface—to install the theme. To do so, click the Appearance link on the administrator's menu. At the top of the page, click the Install Theme button. The interface for installing themes is displayed, as shown in Figure 7-6.

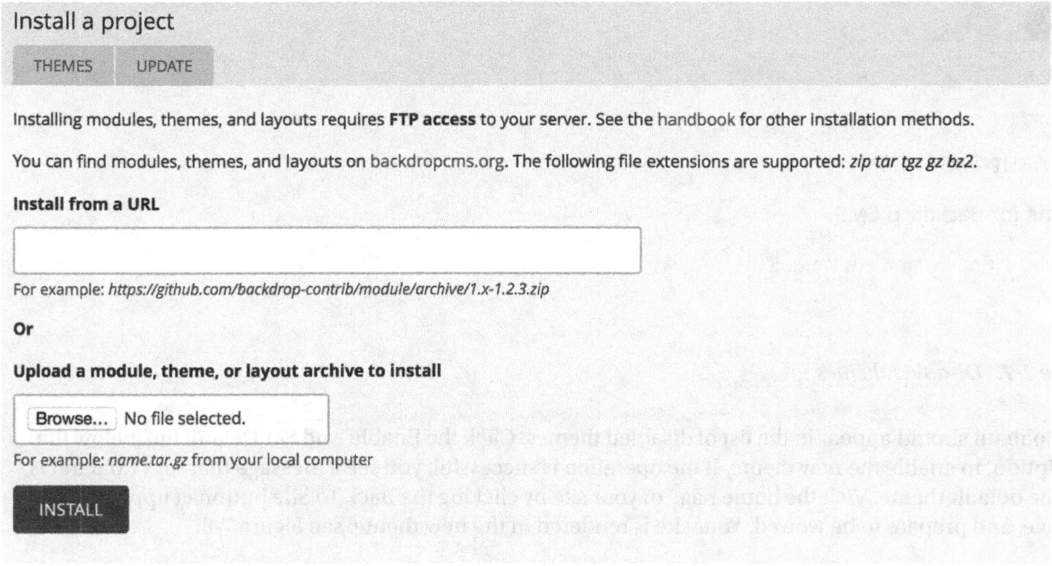

Install a project

THEMES   UPDATE

Installing modules, themes, and layouts requires **FTP access** to your server. See the handbook for other installation methods.

You can find modules, themes, and layouts on backdropcms.org. The following file extensions are supported: *zip tar tgz gz bz2*.

Install from a URL

For example: *https://github.com/backdrop-contrib/module/archive/1.x-1.2.3.zip*

Or

Upload a module, theme, or layout archive to install

Browse...   No file selected.

For example: *name.tar.gz* from your local computer

INSTALL

Figure 7-6. *The install A Project form*

On this form are two fields, providing two ways to install the new theme:

- *Install From A URL*: This option enables you to paste (or type) the URL of the theme's distribution file that you wish to install. Visit the theme's home page on http://backdropcms.org, and right-click the Download link. Copy the URL from the link, paste it into the Install From A URL text box, and click the Install button.

- *Upload A Module, Theme, Or Layout Archive To Install*: This method requires that you first download the .zip file to your local computer. Visit the theme's home page on http://backdropcms.org, click the Download link, and save the .zip file locally. Then, click the Browse button, locate the file using the file browser window and the standard approach for your operating system, select the file, and click the appropriate button (such as Save).

Once you have either pasted the URL or located the .zip file locally, click the Install button. The next page in the process asks you for the FTP information for your site (username and password). Enter valid credentials, and click the Continue button. Backdrop copies the .zip file to your server and expands the file, ready for you to enable and set as the default as outlined next.

With the theme file expanded in the /themes directory, return to your site, and click the Appearance link in the admin menu. Scroll down the page, and you should see a section titled Disabled Themes (see Figure 7-7).

DISABLED THEMES

Colihaut 1.x-1.0.1

Theme for Backdrop CMS.

Enable | Enable and set default

Figure 7-7. Disabled themes

Colihaut should appear in the list of disabled themes. Click the Enable And Set Default link below the description, to enable the new theme. If the operation is successful, you see a message that says Colihaut is now the default theme. Visit the home page of your site by clicking the Back To Site button at upper left on the page, and prepare to be wowed. Your site is rendered in the new theme; see Figure 7-8.

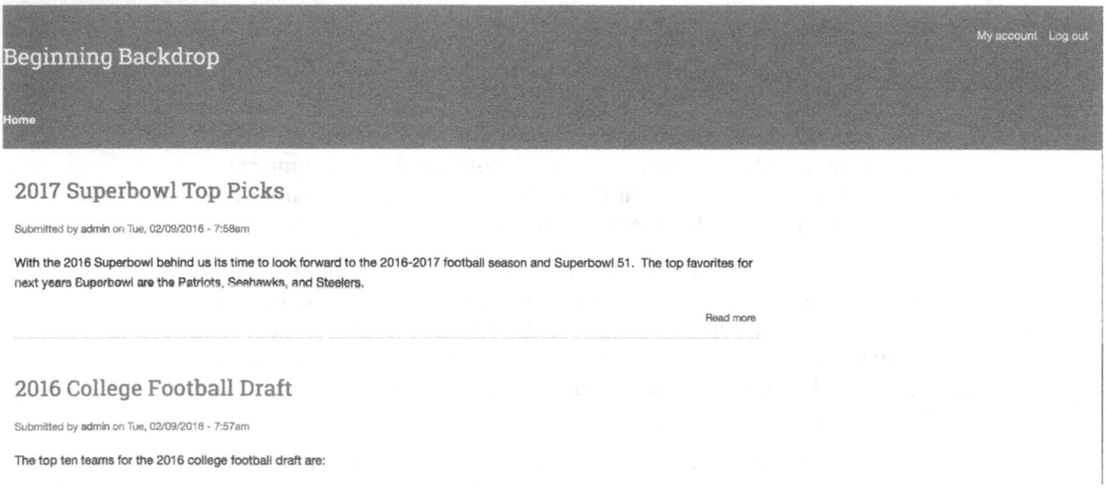

Beginning Backdrop

My account Log out

Home

2017 Superbowl Top Picks

Submitted by admin on Tue, 02/09/2016 - 7:58am

With the 2016 Superbowl behind us its time to look forward to the 2016-2017 football season and Superbowl 51. The top favorites for next years Superbowl are the Patriots, Seahawks, and Steelers.

Read more

2016 College Football Draft

Submitted by admin on Tue, 02/09/2016 - 7:57am

The top ten teams for the 2016 college football draft are:

Figure 7-8. The site rendered in the new theme

The Administration Theme

Administration forms tend to be wide and long, and sometimes they don't fit well within the confines of the content area defined for a given theme. To address this problem, Backdrop lets you specify a theme that should be used for administrative functions. You can try your new theme to see if it works for administration screens, or you can pick a different theme to use whenever a site administrator is performing site-administration tasks. Typically, a simple, clean theme that is at least 960 pixels wide works best as the admin theme.

To change the administration theme, click the Appearance menu item at the top of the page, and scroll down to the Administration Theme section. By default, Backdrop enables Seven as the administration theme, because it accommodates administration screens. You can change the administration theme to any other theme listed in the drop-down list that you know will work with administration forms. If you change the value, make sure you click the Save Configuration button.

Configuration Options

Some Backdrop themes let you adjust certain attributes of the theme through the administrative interface. The color scheme used for various elements on the site involves a common set of attributes that may be changed through the administrative interface. Click the Settings link for your enabled theme, and experiment with adjusting the colors; see Figure 7-9.

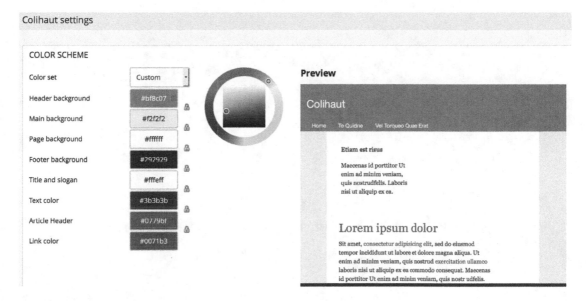

Figure 7-9. *Appearance configuration options*

Explore the various themes on the http://backdropcms.org web site, and try a few of them. You can probably find something that closely matches what you are trying to achieve. For more details on modifying the CSS associated with a theme, visit http://api.backdropcms.org/developing-themes.

Summary

This chapter stepped into the "Wow!" part of building a Backdrop-based site: themes. In a matter of minutes, you changed the entire look and feel of your site through a few simple steps. Spend some time browsing through the themes on Backdropcms.org. You'll be amazed at the breadth of options—you are just a few clicks away from changing the entire look of your site.

CHAPTER 8

■■■

Creating Menus

A key factor in defining the success or failure of your new web site is whether visitors can find information—particularly the information you want them to find. There are three basic mechanisms in Backdrop to provide navigational capabilities to your site:

- Text links embedded in content that direct the user to a new page
- Images and buttons that direct the user to a new page when clicked
- Menus, which are horizontal or vertical lists of text or image links

In this chapter, you learn how to use Backdrop's administrator's interface to create and manage menus.

Ordering from the Menu

A menu, in its simplest form, is a horizontal or vertical list of links that directs a user to a new page or pages. Menus help a visitor to a site understand (and access) the content, features, and functions that the site provides. If you examine the home page of your new web site, you see that there are three menus (see Figure 8-1).

Figure 8-1. *Menus on a site*

From top to bottom, the menus are as follows:

- The administrative menu, starting with Content
- The user account menu (top of the header), with My Account and Log Out
- The main navigation menu, starting with Home

T. Tomlinson, *Beginning Backdrop CMS*, DOI 10.1007/978-1-4842-1970-6_8

On the example site you're creating in this book, the menus shown on the page are all text links. Backdrop also provides mechanisms for creating menus that are button- and/or image-based.

Creating menus is facilitated through a set of screens that are part of Backdrop core. There are two basic activities for creating menus and items that appear on menus:

- *Adding an item to an existing menu:* Backdrop comes with several menus already created. All you need to do is to add items to those menus.

- *Creating a new menu:* If you need more menus than come with Backdrop, you can create a new one.

Adding an Item to a Menu

There are two general items you can add to a page as menu items: a link to an existing element on your site (a page, a content item, list of content associated with a taxonomy term, and so on) or a link to a page that is external to your site (for example, www.backdropcms.org).

Adding a Content Item to a Menu

There are two approaches for adding items to menus:

- The best practice is to use the content-creation form (see Figure 8-3). It simplifies the process by letting you create a menu link with a single step on the content-editing form.

- You can also use the menu administration form (see Figure 8-6) to create a new menu item, or you can create a menu link from the content item you wish to reference from within the form used to create or edit that content item.

To add a content item to a menu, you must first ensure that the content type is configured to allow editors to add a content item. Using the Post content type as an example, navigate to Structure ➤ Content Types, and click the Configure link for the Post content type. Click the Menu Settings tab, and ensure that the menu where you want editors to add links for Post content items is checked and Default Parent Item is selected. Click the Save button to commit your changes (see Figure 8-2).

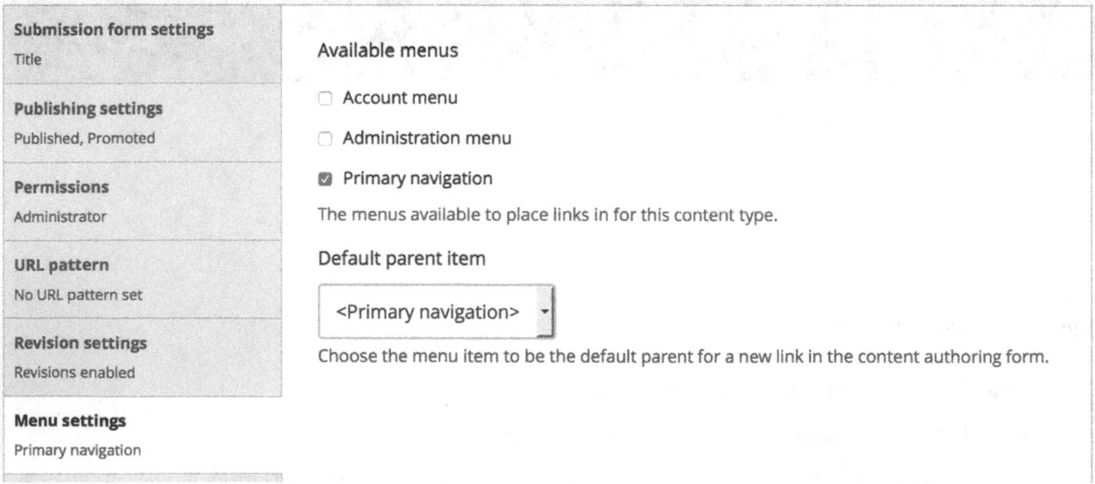

Figure 8-2. Content type menu settings

With the content type correctly configured to enable an author to place a post on the primary navigation menu, navigate to Content ➤ Add Content ➤ Post. Enter a title and some body text, and click the Menu Settings tab. Select the Provide A Menu Link check box, and Backdrop will display the form shown in Figure 8-3. Enter a menu link title and a brief description, leave Parent Item set to Primary Navigation and Weight set to 0, and click Save.

Publishing options	☑ Provide a menu link
Published, Promoted	
Authoring information	Menu link title
By admin	My first Backdrop post
URL settings	Description
No alias	This is my first post in Backdrop!
Menu settings	
My first Backdrop post	Shown when hovering over the menu link.
Comment settings	Parent item
Open	<Primary navigation> ▾
	Weight
	0 ▾
	Menu links with smaller weights are displayed before links with larger weights.

Figure 8-3. Adding a content item to a menu

After you click Save, note the new menu item added to the primary navigation menu (see Figure 8-4). Clicking that link takes you directly to the page you just created, regardless of where you are on the web site.

Home

✓ Post *Test* has been created.

Figure 8-4. A new menu item

Adding a Menu Item Through the Administrative Interface

You can also add menu links through the menu administration interface. Navigate to Structure ➤ Menus, locate the menu that is to receive the new link, and click the Edit Links item in the Operations column for that menu. Backdrop displays the list of existing links for that menu, as shown in Figure 8-5.

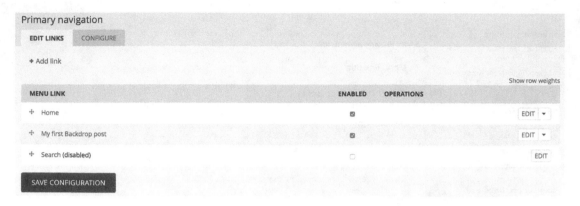

Figure 8-5. *The list of links for a menu*

Click Add Link to create a new menu item. The form for creating a new menu item is displayed, as shown in Figure 8-6. On this form, enter the following:

- *Menu Link Title*: The text that appears as the link in the menu.

- *Path*: The URL to the content, page, or web site where you want to direct the user. If the link is to an existing content item, it is in the form of node/NN, where NN is the node ID of the content item to be displayed. To find the node ID, hover over the Edit link for that content item and examine the link in the footer of your browser. For external links, enter the full URL for the site or page you wish to send users to: for example, http://apress.com.

- *Description*: Text displayed when the user hovers over the menu item.

- *Enables*: If selected, the menu item appears in the menu. If not selected, the menu item does not appear.

- *Show As Expanded*: If the menu item has children (hierarchical menu), selecting this check box instructs Backdrop to always render the children for this parent menu item.

- *Parent Link*: You may leave the selection as the parent of the menu (Primary Navigation) or select another menu item to create a hierarchical menu structure of parent menu links with children.

- *Weight*: Backdrop sorts menu items based on weight. The lower the number, the higher it appears in the list. A value of 0 instructs Backdrop to sort the menu alphabetically.

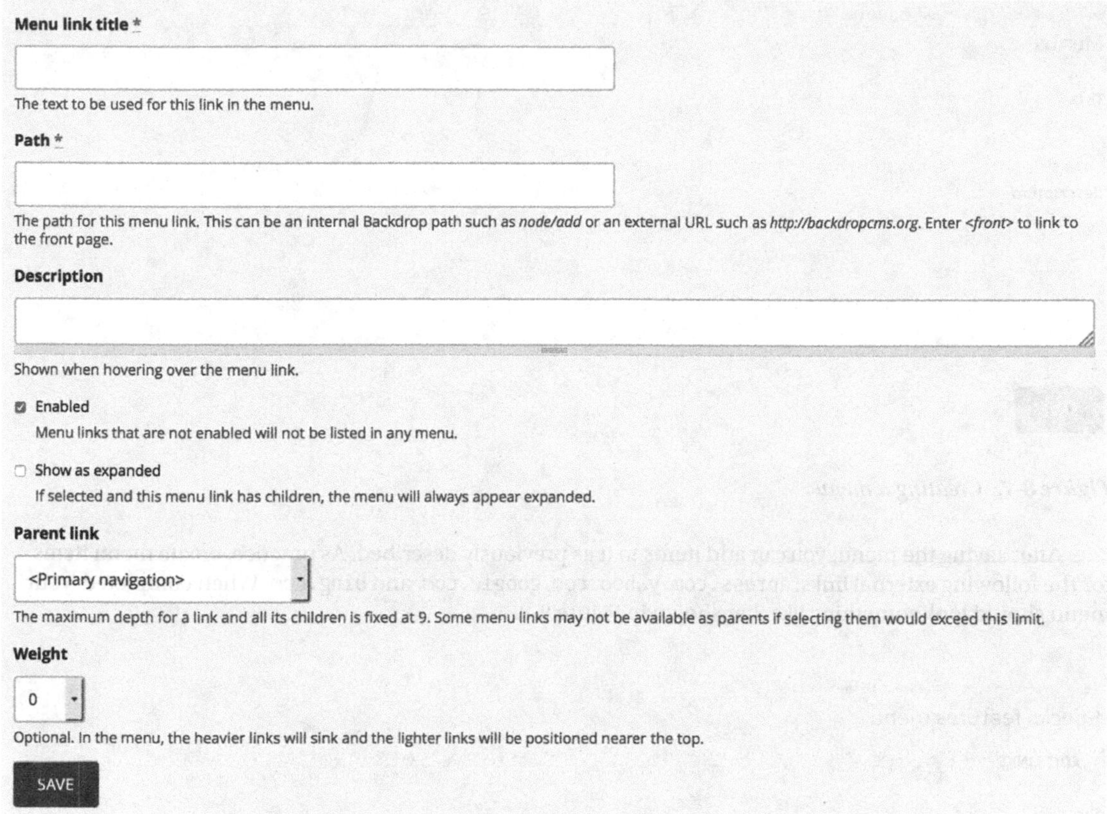

Menu link title *

[   ]

The text to be used for this link in the menu.

Path *

[   ]

The path for this menu link. This can be an internal Backdrop path such as *node/add* or an external URL such as *http://backdropcms.org*. Enter *<front>* to link to the front page.

Description

[   ]

Shown when hovering over the menu link.

☑ Enabled
  Menu links that are not enabled will not be listed in any menu.

☐ Show as expanded
  If selected and this menu link has children, the menu will always appear expanded.

Parent link

[<Primary navigation>   ▾]

The maximum depth for a link and all its children is fixed at 9. Some menu links may not be available as parents if selecting them would exceed this limit.

Weight

[0   ▾]

Optional. In the menu, the heavier links will sink and the lighter links will be positioned nearer the top.

[SAVE]

Figure 8-6. Creating a menu item

Once you've entered all the values, click the Save button at the bottom of the page (you may need to scroll down to see it). Backdrop then displays the complete list of items assigned to the menu, including the new item you just created.

Navigate back to the home page of your site by clicking the Home link in the breadcrumb. You should see the new menu item you just added. Clicking that menu item takes you to the link you entered when you created the menu item.

Creating a New Menu

There may be situations where you need to create menus beyond the standard menus created and enabled with Backdrop. As an example, when creating Backdrop-based web sites for public libraries, I am often asked to build a unique menu for each department in the library (a menu each for Adult Services, Youth Services, Teen Services, Circulation, and so on). In such a case, the basic menus shipped with Backdrop are not enough to fulfill the library's requirements. To create a new menu, navigate to Structure ➤ Menus ➤ Add Menus. A simple form is displayed, asking for the title of your menu as an optional description (see Figure 8-7).

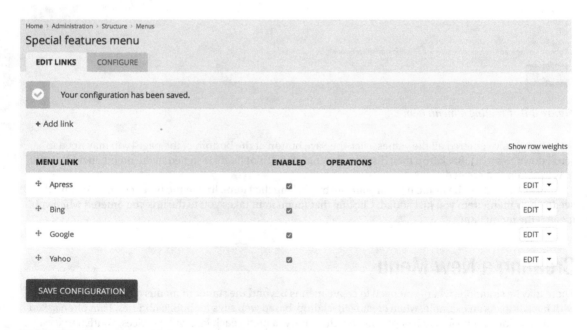

Figure 8-7. *Creating a menu*

After saving the menu, you can add items to it as previously described. As practice, create menu items for the following external links: apress.com, yahoo.com, google.com, and bing.com. When completed, your menu should look something like that shown in Figure 8-8.

Figure 8-8. *Your menu with items*

At this point the menu exists in Backdrop, but it isn't assigned to a position on a page and, therefore, isn't visible to site visitors. To make your new menu visible, navigate to Structure ➤ Layouts ➤ Default Layout ➤ Edit Layout. Scroll down until you find the Sidebar region on the layout, and click the Add Block button. Scroll down until you find your new menu, and click the title of the menu to add it. Leave the Block

Title Type, Style Settings, and Visibility Settings set to their default values, and click the Add Block button. Click the Save Layout button to complete the process. Navigate back to the home page, and voila! There's your new menu, as shown in Figure 8-9.

Figure 8-9. *The new menu on the home page*

Summary

This chapter covered the basics of adding links to a menu and creating a new menu. You learned about the process of adding content items to menus and adding links to external web sites. You also saw how to enable a new menu so that it appears on your site.

The next chapter dives into blocks: the foundation for placing a wide variety of content and images on your new Backdrop site.

CHAPTER 9

Backdrop Blocks

This chapter focuses on using blocks to assign content, along with using what are commonly called *widgets* (which include the user login form, latest blog posts, a list of who is currently logged in to your site, the current weather conditions, and the like) to specific positions on a layout. You learn about standard blocks that ship with Backdrop, blocks that come with contributed modules, and how to build a custom block from scratch. By the end of the chapter, you will be able to construct a page with some pretty exciting features.

Blocks, Blocks, and More Blocks

Block is a generic term applied to any self-contained piece of content, menu, or code. Several standard prebuilt blocks come with Backdrop: User Login, Search, Recent Comments, Recent Content, and more. There are also blocks that come with contributed modules, such as blocks that share the latest weather report, your recent Twitter posts, or your current Facebook status. As a site administrator, you can construct custom blocks, such as a list of upcoming events.

Making Blocks Appear on Layouts

Chapter 6 covered the structure of layouts and how layouts define regions on a page. Figure 6-2 showed how the default layout is divided into Header, Top, Content, Sidebar, and Footer regions. This section covers how to assign from one to dozens of blocks to the various regions on your layout, and how doing so increases visitor interest in your site by providing interesting, high-value features.

Figure 9-1 shows the blocks assigned to various regions on the default layout. Five blocks appear on this page.

© Todd Tomlinson 2016
T. Tomlinson, *Beginning Backdrop CMS*, DOI 10.1007/978-1-4842-1970-6_9

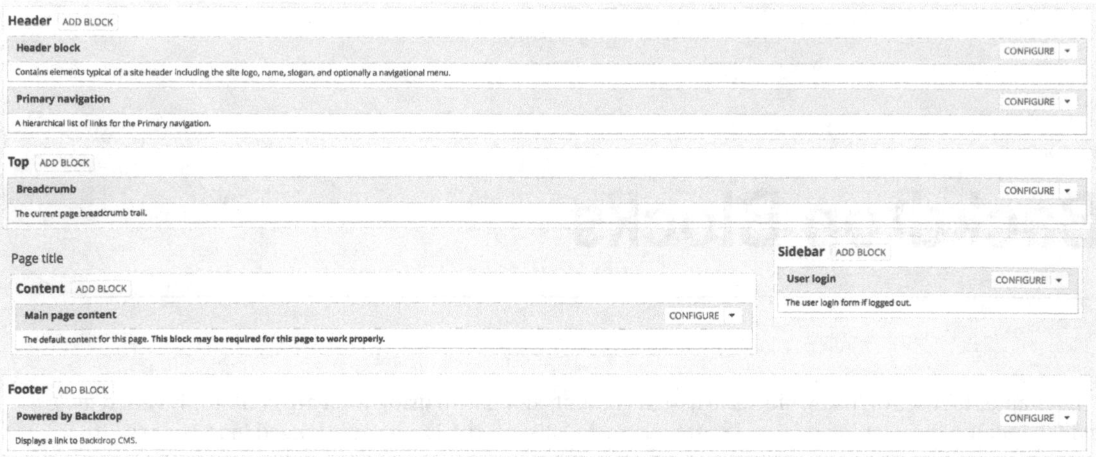

Figure 9-1. *See if you can spot the blocks*

This example includes a Header block, the Primary Navigation block, a Breadcrumb block, a User Login block, and the Powered By Backdrop block.

Let's take a look at the blocks that come with Backdrop and assign a few of them to regions on the default layout. You next install a module that provides a social media block you can add to your site, and then you create a custom block from scratch.

Finding the List of Available Blocks

To find the list of blocks available for you to use on your new web site, navigate to Structure ➤ Layouts ➤ Default Layout ➤ Edit Layout, and click any of the Add Block buttons. You see a scrollable list of blocks that may be placed on your layout (see Figure 9-2).

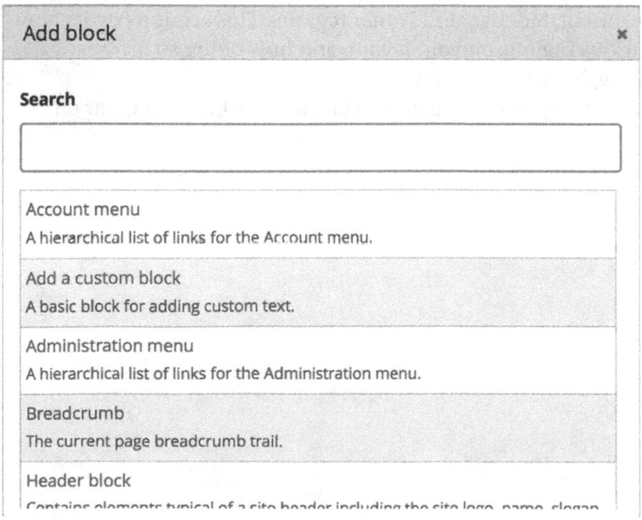

Figure 9-2. *The list of available blocks*

Backdrop provides a number of prebuilt blocks that can be placed on layouts on your site. Pick a few by selecting from the list of blocks in the Add Block box. When placing a block, you have the option of overriding the block title, assigning CSS classes to the block, and defining visibility conditions for when the block is to appear. I cover configuring blocks in a moment; in the meantime, go ahead and assign a few blocks and visit the home page to see the result of your efforts.

Rearranging Blocks

It is likely that at some point you're going to want to reorder how blocks appear on a page. In the example shown in Figure 9-1, you may want to move the User Login block to the footer. To move a block, click its title, hold, and drag the block to the region on the layout where you want it to appear. You can also rearrange blocks in a region using the same approach: click, drag, and drop.

Removing Blocks from a Region

You can remove a block from a region by clicking the down arrow to the right of Configure and then clicking Remove. Doing so removes the block from that region but does not delete the block from Backdrop. It is still available for placement in other regions on the current or other layouts.

Configuring Blocks

You can select various configuration settings for blocks by clicking the Configure link for any block on any layout. Clicking the link displays the Configure Block shown in Figure 9-3.

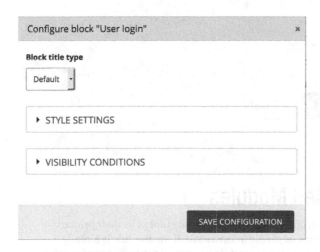

Figure 9-3. *The Configure Block form*

On the Configure Block form, you can specify the following:

- *Block Title Type*: The default renders the block title as defined in the block. Selecting Custom from the drop-down list allows you to override the default block title, and selecting None hides the title.

- *Style Settings*: Clicking this opens a Style drop-down list with two options: Default and Dynamic. Default allows you to enter additional CSS classes that are applied to the block when it is rendered. Dynamic reveals a number of CSS-related options, including setting wrapper tags, wrapper classes, how the heading (block title) is displayed, heading classes that can be assigned to the block heading, a content tag (wrapper), and classes that are assigned to the content area of the block.

- *Visibility Conditions*: Clicking this displays a list of preexisting conditions (if any have been assigned) that dictate when the block is rendered on a page. Clicking the Add Visibility Condition provides a number of options for controlling when the block is displayed, including only on the front page, when the site is being rendered in a particular language, when a user has a specific permission granted to their account, when a user is assigned to a specific role, or a specific URL path where the block will appear (see Figure 9-4). You can combine the visibility conditions by creating one to many conditions.

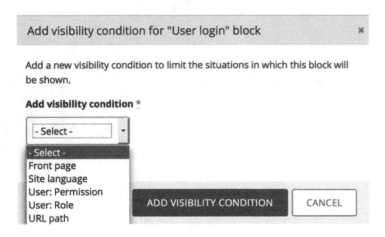

Figure 9-4. *Block visibility conditions*

Using Blocks from Contributed Modules

Several contributed modules are available for Backdrop. Some of them generate blocks as their primary means of displaying information to visitors, such as social media information. If the module is already installed and enabled on your site, the blocks generated by that module appear on the layout configuration page as an option when adding a block to a region. Simply place the desired block(s) in a region as previously described in this chapter. If you have not yet installed a module, follow the steps outlined in Chapter 12.

An example of a using a contributed module's block is the On The Web module, which displays icons that link to your social media accounts (see Figure 9-5).

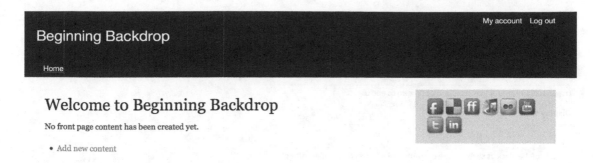

Figure 9-5. *On The Web social media icons block*

Several modules generate blocks. Visit http://backdropcms.org/modules and browse through the list.

Creating Custom Blocks

Sometimes you may need a block but, even after looking through the list of contributed modules, you can't find anything that meets your specific requirements. In that case, you have the opportunity to create a custom block. A custom block can contain any combination of static HTML and JavaScript and can be as simple as the example that follows or as complex as you would like to make it.

To demonstrate creating a custom block, let's create one that displays the static HTML text "Hello World!" Although it may not be exciting, it demonstrates the process of creating a new block. The first step is to navigate to Structure ➤ Custom Blocks ➤ Add Custom Block. The Admin Label field is the text that appears in the select list when you add a block to a region on a layout (see Figure 9-6). Enter **Hello World** in Admin Label, **Hello** in Display Title, and **Hello World!** in Block Content, and then click Save Block.

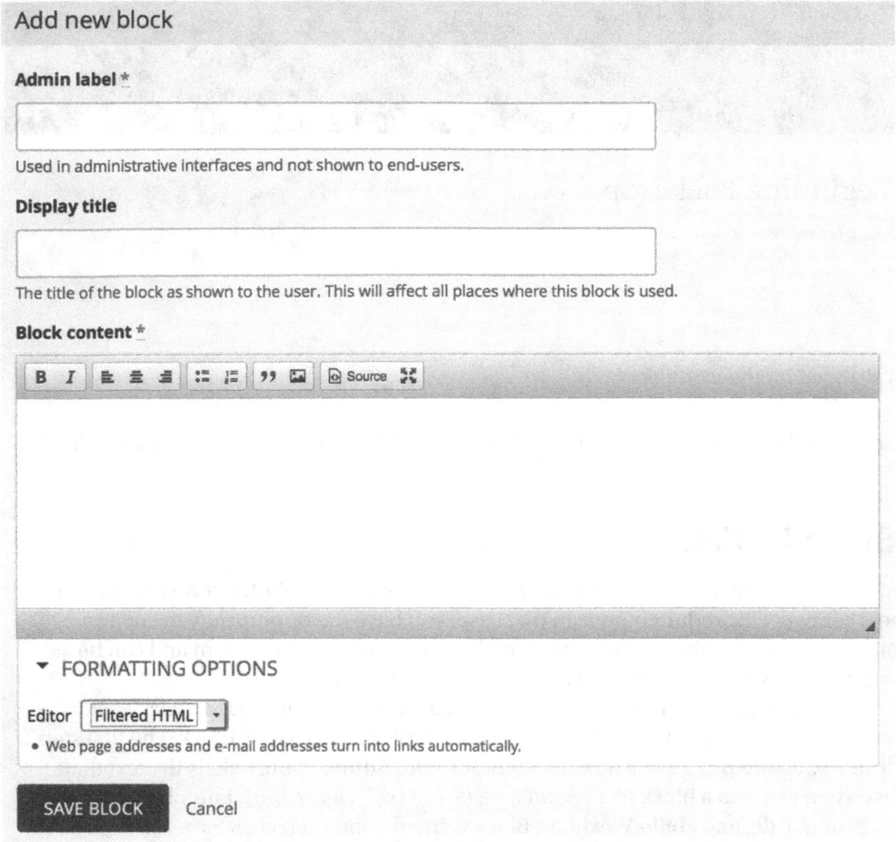

Figure 9-6. *Creating a custom block*

Backdrop displays a list of custom blocks that have been created on the site. Your Hello World block should be displayed in the list.

Place the block you created on the default layout by following the procedures described previously in this chapter. Place it in the Sidebar region, resulting in the block being displayed as shown in Figure 9-7.

Beginning Backdrop

My account   Log out

Home

Welcome to Beginning Backdrop

No front page content has been created yet.

• Add new content

Hello

Hello World!

Figure 9-7. *Your first custom block*

Summary

Blocks are powerful mechanisms for creating and displaying dynamic content and interactive features on your site. This chapter explored blocks that ship with Backdrop, using blocks from contributed modules, and how to create a custom block from scratch. Upcoming chapters continue to expand on the use of blocks.

CHAPTER 10

Views

If you ask anyone who has used Backdrop for a while what the "killer module" is, the answer will likely be Views, Layout, or custom content types. In that list, Views is usually mentioned first, and it's the module that many users say they can't live without. What does the Views module do that is so special? Simply stated, Views provides an easy-to-use interface for selecting and displaying lists of content on your web site. Examples of how you might use Views include

- Displaying the most recent news posts posted to your web site, sorted in descending order by the date of posting

- Displaying a list of company locations as a table that is sortable by clicking the titles for the location name, city, state, and country

- Displaying a photo gallery

- Displaying a slideshow

- Displaying a calendar

- Displaying a list of blog postings that is filterable by subject

- Creating an RSS feed that lists the most recent content posted on your web site

- Displaying just about any kind of list you can think of, created from the content stored on your web site, as a list, a table, or an RSS feed

This chapter uses the Post content type to demonstrate the power, capabilities, and flexibility of Views. However, you can use any content type, taxonomy, or user as the source of information.

The Views Module

The Views module is included in Backdrop core and is enabled by default during installation, because it is integral to the functionality of Backdrop. Backdrop core also includes the Views UI module, which provides the administrative interface used to create, modify, and delete a view. It too is enabled by default during the installation process. It is common to disable the Views UI module on production sites to minimize the chance of someone making an inadvertent change to a critical view. Disabling the Views UI module does not disable the views you have created with the module, only the administrative interface. Ensure that the module is enabled by clicking the Functionality link in the admin menu and entering **Views** in the search box (see Figure 10-1).

© Todd Tomlinson 2016
T. Tomlinson, *Beginning Backdrop CMS*, DOI 10.1007/978-1-4842-1970-6_10

Figure 10-1. *Verifying that Views UI is enabled*

You'll spend most of the rest of this chapter in Views UI.

Creating Your First View

With the Views UI module enabled, you can proceed. A view without content is, well, just a blank page, so the first step is to create some content. You've created several posts prior to this chapter, so let's use those as the basis for your first foray into views. If you skipped the previous exercises or have deleted the posts you created, then take a moment to create at least 12 posts.

You are now ready to create a view that displays a list of posts. Navigate to Structure ➤ Views to begin the process. Notice that there are already several views listed on this page. These are views that are part of Backdrop core and provide lists of items such as these:

- *Admin Content*: Shows all the content created on your site when you click the Content link in the administrator's menu

- *Administer Users*: Shows all user accounts on your site when you click the User Accounts link in the administrator's menu

- *Front Page*: Renders all content created on your site on the site's home page

- *Recent Comments*: Lists all the comments that have been posted on your site

- *Taxonomy Term*: Lists content tagged with a specific taxonomy term

To add a view, click the Add View link at the top of the page, which reveals the page for creating a new view (see Figure 10-2). On this page, define the following:

- *View Name*: You can assign any name you wish to a view, but it must be unique (a name that has not been used for another view on your site). It's a good idea to pick a descriptive name that conveys the purpose of the view so that others looking at the list can easily identify the right one to use. For the first view, use **Recent Posts** as the name.

- *Description*: This is another field you can use to provide additional information about the view. Check the box next to Description and enter **A list of recent posts published on the site**.

- The next set of options let you select what you want to render in this view: comments, files, content, content revisions, taxonomy terms, users, and module/theme/engine. For Show, select Content. The next option specifies what type of content you wish to render: select Post from the list. The Tagged With field lets you limit the content that appears in the view to only content that has a specific taxonomy term assigned to it. In this case, leave it blank to render all posts. And finally, the Sorted By field sorts the output of the view: Newest First, Oldest First, Title, or Unsorted. For the example view, select Newest First.

- *Create A Page*: A view may be embedded in a page as a block or as a stand-alone page accessed through a URL. To create a page, check the Create A Page check box. Then do the following:

  - Enter a page title, such as **Recent Posts**.

  - Enter a path that becomes the URL where the view may be accessed. In this case, enter **recent-posts**, making the view visible by visiting the web site and entering **recent-posts** at the end of the URL.

  - The first Display Format drop-down list specifies how the post is rendered in the list generated by the view:

    - *Grid:* Renders each item in a column in a row of results. The Grid format is great for photo galleries, where each photo is rendered in a column in a row of images.

    - *HTML List.* Renders the content wrapped in `<ul>` and `<li>` tags.

    - *Jump Menu:* A common use for this option is to render a drop-down list of links. This lets you create dynamic drop-down menus that are based on content, taxonomy terms, or users.

    - *Table:* Renders content in a spreadsheet-like fashion. Each field is contained in a column in the table. A table's columns may be sortable, providing a powerful tool for listing content.

    - *Unformatted List:* Similar to an HTML list, but in this case there is no HTML markup (`<ul>` and `<li>`) surrounding the items in the list. In this case, select the Unformatted List option.

  - The next Display Format drop-down list specifies how the content is rendered. The options are as follows:

    - *Teasers*: A shortened version of the entire content item, typically showing a Read More link to see the entire content item. You can specify the number of characters displayed as a teaser when you set up the content type and specify how teasers are rendered (see Chapter 5). Teasers are great when you want to give the visitor just enough information to entice them to click through to the full content item. Select Teasers as the option for this view.

    - *Full X*: X represents the name of the entity you are rendering, such as a post. Rendering a content item in a view as Full means the content item is displayed in its entirety in the list.

- *Titles*: Renders only the title of the content items contained in the view.

- *Titles (Linked)*: Renders the title of the content item linked to the full content item. This is a great option for a jump menu or other scenarios where you only want to render the title, but you also want to provide the visitor with the means to navigate to the full content item.

- *Fields*: Lets you render specific fields from the content item.

- The next set of options depends on the previous selection (Teaser, Full, Title, Fields). For Teaser and Full, the additional options let you specify whether links are displayed that allow visitors to add comments. The final Display Format option is whether comments are shown. In this case, select an unformatted list of teasers, without links and without comments:

  - *Items To Display*: Regulates how many items are displayed in your list. Setting the value to 0 renders all items regardless of how many exist. Any number greater than zero tells Views to display exactly that number of items. Here, select 10 as the number of items to display.

  - *Use A Pager*: If checked, renders a pager at the bottom of your list if the number of results exceeds the number of items to display. Each results page displays the number of items to display as set in the previous field. Check the Use A Pager check box.

  - *Create A Menu Link*: Lets you include the view as a link in the menu shown in the list of options that appears after clicking the Create A Menu Link check box.

  - *Include An RSS Feed*: Lets you create an RSS feed from the results of your view. Additional options appear that allow you to specify the URL where your RSS feed can be accessed and the feed row style (Content or Fields).

- *Create A Block*: You may want to embed the results of your view into a page on your site, such as a list of recent posts in the right sidebar of the site's home page. To create a block, select this check box. Then, specify the following:

  - *Enter A Block Title*: Enter **Recent Posts**.

  - Select the Display Format options Unformatted List and Titles (Linked), and display five items without a pager. This limits the list to the latest five posts.

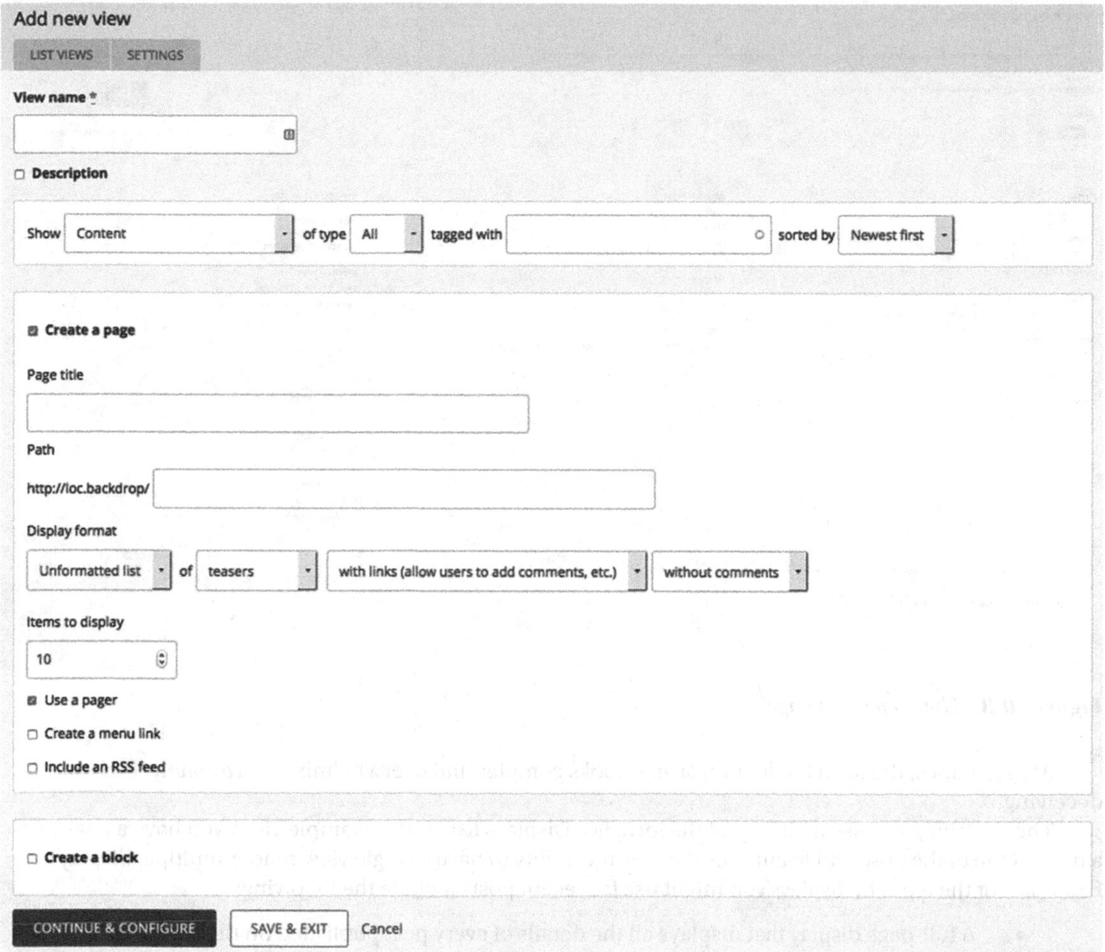

Add new view

LIST VIEWS   SETTINGS

View name *

☐ **Description**

Show   Content   ▾   of type   All   ▾   tagged with   ○   sorted by   Newest first   ▾

☑ **Create a page**

Page title

Path

http://loc.backdrop/

Display format

Unformatted list   ▾   of   teasers   ▾   with links (allow users to add comments, etc.)   ▾   without comments   ▾

Items to display

10   ⬍

☑ Use a pager

☐ Create a menu link

☐ Include an RSS feed

☐ **Create a block**

CONTINUE & CONFIGURE   SAVE & EXIT   Cancel

Figure 10-2. *Creating a new view*

Click the Continue & Configure button to proceed. The next step in the process is to configure your view, as shown in Figure 10-3.

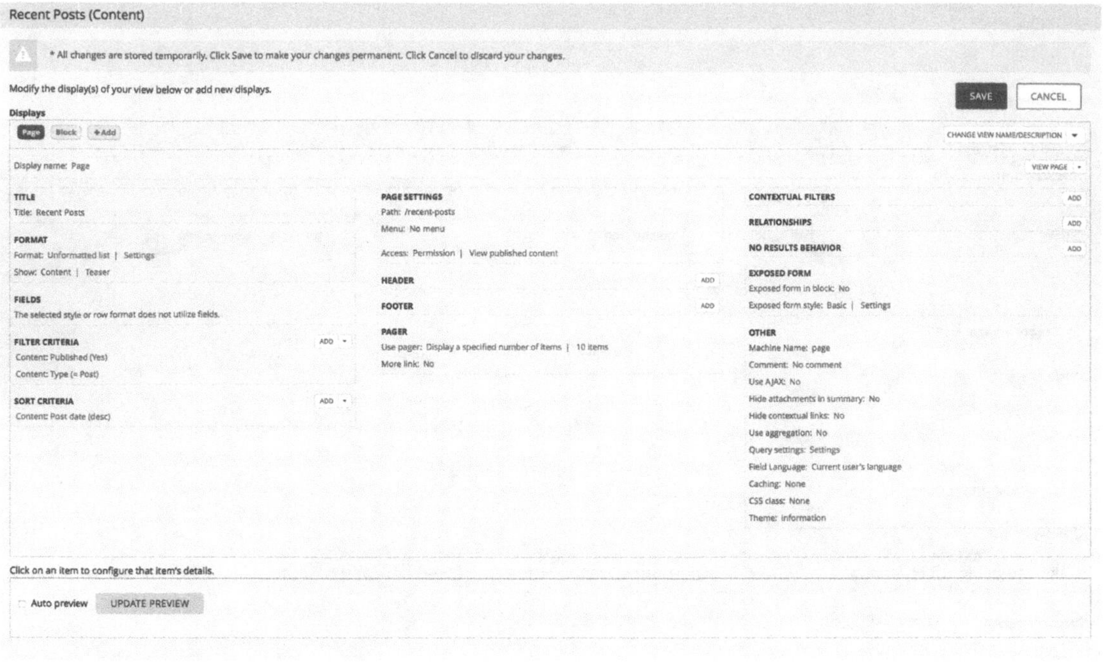

Figure 10-3. *The Views edit page*

At first glance, the form for defining a view looks complex and overwhelming. Fortunately, looks are deceiving.

The first thing you see at the top of the form is a Displays list. In the example view, you have a page and a block. One of the powerful features of Views is the ability to have a single view render multiple displays. Examples of the types of displays you might use for recent posts include the following:

- A full-page display that displays all the details of every post published on the site

- A block that lists the five most recent posts, displaying only the title for each article

- Another block that lists the five most recent posts, displaying the title and a shortened version of the post body

- Yet another block that lists the ten most recent posts, displaying the title, the date the post was published, the author who wrote the article, and a shortened version of the post body

This single view can be used to create several different types of displays that show posts in slightly different formats.

You start by defining the two displays, Page and Block, that were automatically created by Views when you selected the options on the first configuration screen (refer to Figure 10-2). You'll add to that list of displays after you have the first two working.

Page Display

Let's define the Page display first. Click the Page button that appears directly under Displays to configure the Page display. On this page, you display the complete post, which includes the title, body, author of the article, and date and time it was published. Let's work top to bottom, left to right through the configuration parameters you need to set to make this page display what you want it to:

1. Change Display Name from Page to something a little more descriptive, like **All Posts Page**. To change the value, click Page to the right of Display Name, and, in the pop-up form, enter the new value in the Name field. Click the Apply button. The new value is displayed both in the Displays area of the view edit form and in the Display Name field in the left column.

2. In the Title section, change the title of the view. This value is displayed at the top of the output generated by views for this display. Let's change it to **All Posts**. Click Recent Posts, and select This Page (Override) from the For select list. This means the changes you are making to this value will only be applied to this specific view display. If you leave the value set to All Displays, every display will show this new title. Because you're going to have different displays for different purposes, All Posts is likely a poor choice of titles for other displays. Click the Apply (This Display) button to continue.

3. In the Format section, you have the option to generate a list using different output formats. Click the Unformatted List value for Format to see a list of output options:

   - *Grid*: The output is displayed in rows and columns; in this example, each post would fill one column on a row in the grid. This is a great option for displaying photos in a photo gallery.

   - *HTML List*: The output is displayed as either an ordered list or an unordered list. In this example, each post would be listed as a <li> in a <ol></ol> or <ul></ul> tag. If you're not familiar with HTML tags, check out the tutorial at www.w3schools.com/html or pick up one of the great introductory books on HTML development at www.apress.com.

   - *Jump Menu*: The output is displayed as a select list of links. Typically used as a menu.

   - *Table*: The output is displayed as an HTML table, where each field is displayed in a column. A table is great when you want to let visitors sort the output of a view by the values in a column.

   - *Unformatted List*: The output is displayed as a list, but unlike the HTML list, there are no enclosing <ul>, <ol>, or <li> tags.

   For the example page, leave the value set to Unformatted List. If you click Settings to the right of Unformatted List, you see the configuration options available for that type of list. Each option has its own parameters you can set. To continue, click the Apply (This Display) button.

4. The Show parameter in the Format section defines how you want to handle the content you are going to display. The two options are Content and Fields:

- *Content*: Displays the complete entity that is being selected and displayed. In the case of posts, the complete post is displayed.

- *Fields*: Enables you to display specific fields from the entity you are rendering. In the example, you are selecting and displaying posts. You may have View Display where you only want to show the post title and the published date. Using the Fields option, you can specify which fields are to be displayed and the order in which those fields are displayed on the page.

For the example page, select Content and display the content as teasers, a shortened version of the article that shows the first 600 characters. When you defined the view, you set the page to display content in teaser mode, so the values for Show are already set. If you wanted the entire post to be rendered by the view, you would click the word Teaser and select Full Content from the list of view modes. In this case, leave the display mode set to Teaser.

5. In the example, the Fields Configuration parameters are not displayed because you are going to display the entire post. This chapter covers fields later, when you create block displays.

6. Filter Criteria is the next section to configure. You may restrict what content is rendered in the view by adding filter criteria to the view display. On the very first configuration screen when you created the view (refer to Figure 10-2), you selected the View Settings option to only display posts. By selecting Posts, you set a filter to only display Post content types. Additionally, Views creates a filter for content that is published (versus unpublished). You can add other filter criteria to your views; for example, in the case of posts, you might want a view display that only shows posts that have been published in the past 30 days. You can restrict the output of the view by adding filter criteria on any of the values stored on a content item. In this case, leave the filter criteria alone. This chapter covers adding filter criteria later, when you create block displays.

7. The Sort Criteria section lets you specify the order of the content in the list. Because you selected Sort By Newest First when you created the view, the sort criteria of Content: Post Date (Desc) is already set. If you don't specify any sort criteria when you create the view, the values rendered are sorted in ascending order by node ID (the unique identifier assigned to each content item by Backdrop). Typically, you want to set the sort criteria to Title for lists you want alphabetically ordered, or by the date in which the content was published with newest posts at the top of the list. To create a new sort order, click the Add button and select the field you want to sort by. Because your site is popular and your editors are busy creating new posts, add an additional sort criteria to be executed after items are sorted by publish date: a sort by title. Click the Add button to the right of the Sort Criteria label. You see a complete list of all fields defined for your site. To filter the list to only fields with *title* in their name, enter **title** in the Search field and select Content: Title from the list of fields. In the revised list of fields, scroll down until you find Content: Title. Check the box for that field, and change the value of the For select list at the top of the form to This Page (Override); then click the Add And Configure Sort Criteria button. The next screen allows you to

set the sort order—ascending or descending—as well as show this option to site visitors. Leave the Expose check box unchecked for the example page, and specify that you want titles to appear in ascending alphabetical order. Click the Apply (This Display) button to continue. Scroll to the bottom of the screen, and click the Update Preview button to see how the output will be rendered on the page.

In the second column of configuration options (refer to Figure 10-3), you begin by defining the Page Settings for the example.

8. Every View display defined as Page must have a unique URL specified in the Path field. For the example, when you created the view, you entered **recent-posts**. You can change the URL if you wish, but for this example leave it as is.

9. The Menu field gives you the option to add your View display page to a menu. In this case, add it to the primary navigation menu. Click the No Menu parameter, and click the Normal Menu Entry option. On the configuration page for adding the menu entry, enter a title and a description, and select Primary Navigation as the menu on which this item will be displayed. For sites you are building, you may want to add a View page to a menu other than the main navigation menu. Click the Apply button after entering the values on the form.

10. Views lets you restrict who can see the output generated by this View display. You can set the Access restrictions to

   • *None*: Anyone can see the output.

   • *Permission*: The visitor must be assigned to a role that has permissions to view the output.

   • *Role*: The visitor must be assigned to a specific role to see the output.

   By default, the value is set to Permission, where the default permission is that the visitor can view content on the site (see Figure 10-3). In most cases, the default values are appropriate. For the example page, leave them set to the defaults: only visitors who can view content can see the output of the view.

11. The Header setting enables you to add several things to the top of your view. For example, you can provide an introductory paragraph that describes the content rendered by the view, or a block you have defined on your site, the output of another view, or several other elements. Click the Add button, and select from the list of options. The most common option is to add an introductory paragraph; to do so, click the Global: Text Area option, select the This Page (Override) option in the For select list at the top of the options, and click the Add And Configure Header button. On the next form, enter a label that will be used for the administrative interface for this view and a value that describes what the text is about, and then enter the text you want to display at the top of the view. If you want the header text to display even when there are no results for your view, check the Display Even If View Has No Result box, followed by clicking the Apply (This Display) button.

12. The Footer setting, similar to Header, enables you to add a footer to the output of a view. Follow the same process as in step 11 to insert a footer at the bottom of the view.

13. If your view returns a long list of items, consider using a pager at the bottom of the view and restricting the number of results displayed at any given time. For example, a view may return 100 content items. Instead of showing all 100 in a long list, you can show 10 items at a time, with a pager at the bottom of the view to navigate through the list of content. The Pager Configuration option also lets you list a specific number of items (for example, three most recent articles) or list all items that fit the filter criteria set in the previous column. Because you set the values for Pager on the view creation page, the display is already set to a pager with ten items per page.

   In the third column (refer to Figure 10-3), there are several advanced configuration options, two of which you focus on here.

14. Contextual Filters is a powerful configuration option that allows you to use values passed in the URL to filter content returned by the view. For example, you may wish to limit the posts returned by your view to only those tagged for a specific category. If your Post content type has the Event taxonomy vocabulary as a field that editors can use to specify which category an post is associated with, you can then use values passed in the URL to filter which posts are displayed. By selecting a contextual filter of Has Taxonomy Term ID and setting the content type to Post, the vocabulary to Category, and Filter Value Type to Term Name Converted To Term ID, you can now update the Path value to `all-articles/%`, where % represents a value that is passed to the view through the URL. The benefit is that you can have one view that can display any post tagged by any category in your taxonomy vocabulary. This single view can render a list of posts about Backdrop by using a URL of `/all-articles/backdrop`, or all posts about dinosaurs by using `/all-articles/dinosaurs`, or any other term in your type of category vocabulary. Amazing! But for simplicity's sake, let's not use contextual filters in this example.

15. Relationships are used in cases where you need to pull content from two different content types in order to meet the requirements of a specific view. For example, you may have a Venue content type that lists the address, hours of operation, and accessibility options. Instead of typing that information for every event that happens at that venue, you can create a relationship between the Event content type and the Venue content type to combine the information stored in both content types. Once you have created the relationship, fields on both content types are then available to display in your view. Because you are keeping this example simple, leave off relationships for now.

At this point, you're ready to test your view. Make sure you click the Save button before proceeding. Then, return to the home page of your site, and you should see the Recent Posts link in the primary navigation menu. Click the Recent Posts link, and you see the fruits of your labor (see Figure 10-4).

Home

All Posts

Welcome to our site. This is a list of all the recent posts on our site.

Abbas Bene Populus Sagaciter

Submitted by admin on Mon, 03/14/2016 - 7:49pm

Plaga refoveo zelus. Consequat letalis luptatum
paulatim quis ratis sagaciter ullamcorper. Abluo
causa pneum probo quidne refoveo typicus. Aliquip
capto esse iusto luctus neo nibh quis suscipere
volutpat.

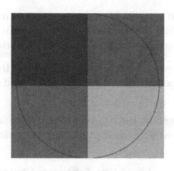

Amet neque nisl singularis. Acsi iusto nobis nulla
qui utrum velit.

Appellatio Defui Ludus Sed

Submitted by Anonymous (not verified) on Mon, 03/14/2016 - 7:49pm

Importunus ludus macto ulciscor virtus. Acsi at conventio humo iaceo in
probo refoveo tego. Abluo acsi neo odio turpis virtus volutpat. Capto
consectetuer enim lenis uxor volutpat. Commodo dolor dolore exputo
proprius quia. Abigo euismod nimis suscipere validus. Importunus patria
turpis.

Abbas comis ideo lenis mos nutus pala saluto si vulputate. Cogo fere ideo
inhibeo neo pala plaga rusticus turpis. Nibh nobis pertineo secundum.
Abdo consectetuer quae saepius vulpes.

Figure 10-4. *The All Posts view page*

Block Display

With the Recent Posts page under your belt, let's now revise the Block display. Return to the Views
administration page by navigating to Structure ➤ Views. Locate the Recent Posts view, and click the
Configure link in the Operations column. You should see the Recent Posts view configuration page
(see Figure 10-3).

The first step in the process is to click the Block button in the View display list, directly to the right of the All Posts Page button. Clicking the Block button displays all the configuration parameters for the block. Let's update the display to only show the three most recent post titles, sorted in date-published order, descending, so the most recent post appears at the top of the block. Start by updating the name of the display from Block to something more descriptive, followed by making the changes to the display:

1. In the first column, next to Display Name, click Block. Change the value of the Name field to **Recent Posts Block**.

2. Leave Title as Recent Posts, because it still applies to what you are going to display.

3. Leave Format as Unformatted List, because you still want the posts to appear as a list.

4. Leave the Show option set to Fields, because you only want to display the title of the posts in your list. You specified what you wanted the block to display when you created the view, so this value is already set properly.

5. In the Fields section, leave the item to be displayed as the title. If it doesn't say Content: Title, click the Add button for that section and search for **Title**, adding it to the display.

6. In the Filter Criteria section, leave Content Publishing Status and Content Type Criteria set as only showing published content (Yes) and only content that is of type Post.

7. The Sort Criteria section should already be set to Content: Post Date (Desc), because that is what you specified when you created the view. If it is not set, click the Add button and search for **Date**. You see Content: Post Date in the list of options. Check the box next to this field, change the For option to This Block (Override), and click the Add And Configure Sort Criteria button at the bottom of the form. On the next form that appears, select Sort Descending, because you want the most recent posts to appear at the top of the list and the oldest posts at the bottom. Select Second as the granularity, ensuring that you get the latest post down to the second. Apply that change as well.

8. The last change you need to make is to limit the number of posts that appear in the list to three. In the second column of configuration options, make sure the value for Use Pager is set to Display A Specified Number Of Items | 3 Items. If the number of items is not 3, click the link associated with the value, and change it.

Click the Save button. You're now ready to place the block you just created on a page on your site.

To place the block created by your view on a page, navigate to Structure ➤ Layouts, and click the Edit link for Default Layout. In the Sidebar region, click the Add Block button, and scroll down to find the block created by the Recent Posts view. Depending on the name assigned to your block, it should appear as something similar to View: Recent Posts: Recent Posts Block, where *Recent Posts* represents the view that generates the block and *Recent Posts Block* is the name assigned to the display that generates the block. Click the block to continue the configuration process.

The next page displays a list of options you can set when displaying the block. The first option specifies how the title is to be rendered. Because you set a title in the view, leave it set to Default. You can also override the default block title by selecting the Custom option, or hide the block title by selecting None. Style settings provides options to override how the block is displayed, as well as assign CSS classes to the block. If you select Dynamic from the list of options, you are presented with additional configuration parameters that specify how the block is wrapped (for example, DIV), additional wrapper classes (CSS), how the title is rendered (for example, H2), CSS classes for the heading (title), the wrapper tag for the content of the block (for example, DIV), and CSS classes that are applied to the content in the block. This is a powerful yet easy way to customize the output of a block. In this case, leave it set to Default.

Visibility conditions allow you to control when the block is rendered: for example, only on the home page. Click the Add Visibility Condition link, and you see a list of options:

- *Frontpage*: The block appears only on the front page of the site.

- *Site Language*: The block appears only when the site is being rendered in a specific language (English, German, or other languages you have set your site to display in).

- *User: Permission*: The block appears only when the user has the assigned permission.

- *User: Role*: The block appears only when the user is assigned to a specific role.

- *URL Path*: The block appears only when the URL matches a pattern you specify, such as only on a page that has a URL of about-us.

In this case, select Frontpage as the visibility option. This instructs Backdrop to display the block only on the front page of the site and on no other pages. Click the Save Configuration button to enable the block, and click the Save Layout button to complete the change to the layout.

Return to the home page of your site. You should be happy to see the list of posts you created displayed through the block you created using views (see Figure 10-5).

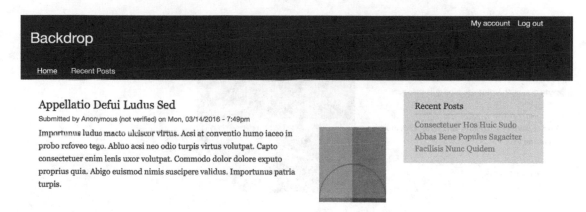

Figure 10-5. *The home page displaying the Recent Posts block*

Filtering

In the previous example, you filtered the output of your view based on content type and publishing status. Those are pretty typical filters on most views, but what if you want to restrict the output of the view beyond just content type and status? Let's use tagging as an example of the power of view filtering. In this section, you add a few tags to the example posts on your web site.

Edit several of your articles, and, in the Tags field, enter several keywords, separated by commas, that describe the content of each article. Use similar words in at least two posts so you can use those posts in upcoming examples. To find posts to update, click the Content link in the admin menu; from the list, click the Edit button to add tags to existing articles. After adding the tags, return to the Recent Posts page you built in the previous sections and note that the tags you added are now displayed beneath the teaser of each post (see Figure 10-6).

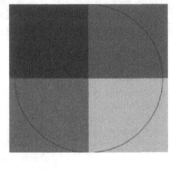

Figure 10-6. Rendering tags through views

As a quick demonstration of the power of taxonomy, tags, and views, click one of the tags you entered. Backdrop renders a list of all content tagged on your site with that term. Behind the scenes, Backdrop is using Views to generate this list. But let's take it one step further and allow users to filter content that is rendered from your Recent Posts view by entering a tag.

Return to the Views administration page by navigating to Structure ➤ Views. Locate the Recent Posts view you have been working on, and click the Configure button. Click the All Posts Page display button in the Displays area of the view configuration page. Add a new filter for tags by clicking the Add button in the Filter Criteria section. Search for the Tags field by entering **tags** in the Search box at the top of the Add Filter Criteria form, and check the box for the Content: Tags (field_tags) field. Change the For option to This Page (Override) so the filter is only applied to the All Posts Page display, and click the Add And Configure Filter Criteria button.

The next step in the process is to select the type of interface you wish to provide: a drop-down list of terms to select from, or an autocomplete field where the user types in the keyword to search for. A drop-down field shows the user what terms are available, whereas the autocomplete approach requires the user to know what terms they wish to search for. The choice depends on your desired user experience. In this case, select Dropdown and Show Hierarchy In Dropdown, and click the Apply And Continue button.

Now you need to configure the filter and how it works. You want to allow users to select which terms to filter on, so you'll show the filter to the user so they can control what content is displayed by the view. To do so, check the Expose This Filter To Visitors, To Allow Them To Change It check box, leave the Filter Type To Expose setting at Single Filter, and change Label to **Select one or more tags**. Leave Operator set to Is One Of, meaning the values you want the user to select from are only the tags that exist in the posts on the site. Also check the Allow Multiple Selections check box to allow visitors to select more than one tag to search for. Click the Apply (This Display) button to continue the process (see Figure 10-7), and then click Save to save the changes made to the view.

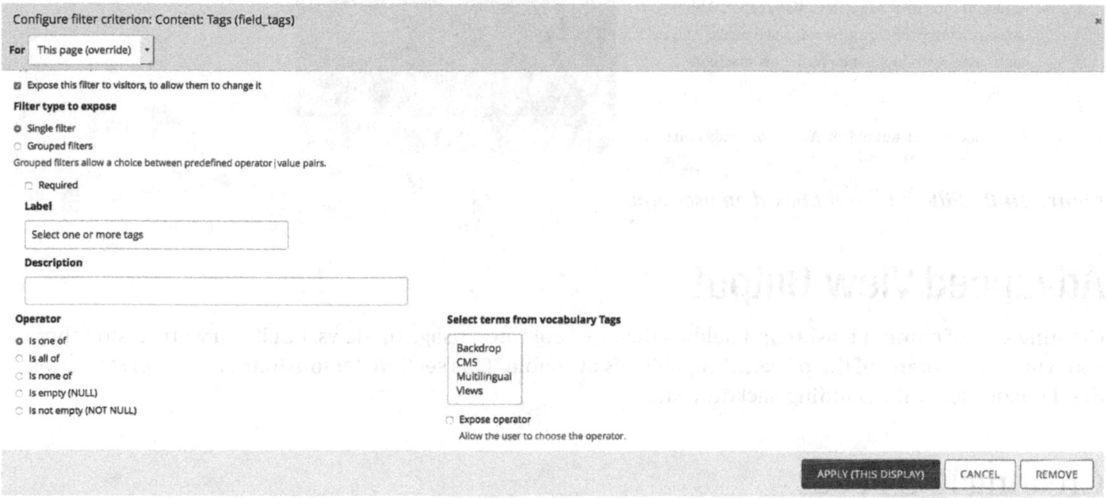

Figure 10-7. *Configuring filters*

Return to the All Posts page by clicking the All Posts link on the main menu, or visit the /recent-posts URL on your site. You see the exposed filter at the top of the list of articles. Select one or more tags, and click the Apply button to see the new filter in action (see Figure 10-8). Amazing! And you've just scratched the surface of what Views can do for you.

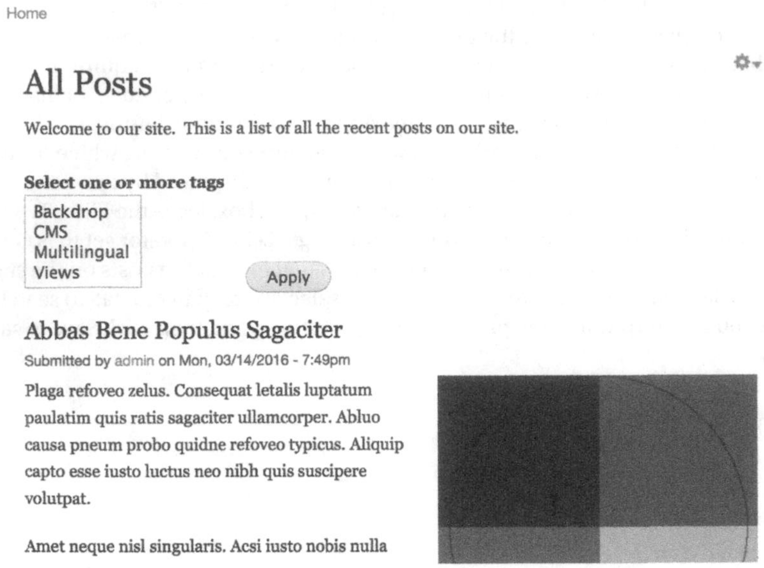

Home

All Posts

Welcome to our site. This is a list of all the recent posts on our site.

Select one or more tags

Backdrop
CMS
Multilingual
Views

Apply

Abbas Bene Populus Sagaciter

Submitted by admin on Mon, 03/14/2016 - 7:49pm

Plaga refoveo zelus. Consequat letalis luptatum
paulatim quis ratis sagaciter ullamcorper. Abluo
causa pneum probo quidne refoveo typicus. Aliquip
capto esse iusto luctus neo nibh quis suscipere
volutpat.

Amet neque nisl singularis. Acsi iusto nobis nulla

Figure 10-8. *Filtered output based on user input*

Advanced View Output

Creating lists of content teasers and fields is the most common usage of Views, but if you were to stop there, you would miss many of the powerful capabilities available. This section demonstrates common scenarios that I encounter while building Backdrop sites.

Creating RSS Feeds

One of the common uses of Views is to create RSS feeds. An *RSS feed* is an industry-standard format for publishing content that can then be consumed by applications such as newsreaders, or by other systems such as another Backdrop site. Although RSS feeds are not as popular as they were during the heyday of online newsreaders, there are still cases where using RSS feeds make sense, such as providing feeds of content to other sites.

Let's take the Recent Posts view and create an RSS feed for all articles. To begin, return to the Views page navigating to Structure ➤ Views. Find the Recent Posts view, and click the Configure button for that view. Create a new display for the RSS feed by clicking the Add button in the Displays section of the page. From the list of options, choose Feed.

The next step is to enter a URL where the feed will be accessed. In the second column in the Feed Settings section, click the No Path Is Set link to enter a URL. In this case, enter the URL **rss/all-posts**. You can use any URL, but I find it easier to prefix all my RSS feed URLs with rss so it is apparent what that URL renders. Complete the process by clicking the Apply button to save the changes to the URL, and then click Save to save the updates to the view. You now have an RSS feed that other sites can use to consume posts from your site. Visiting that URL shows the output of the feed (see Figure 10-9).

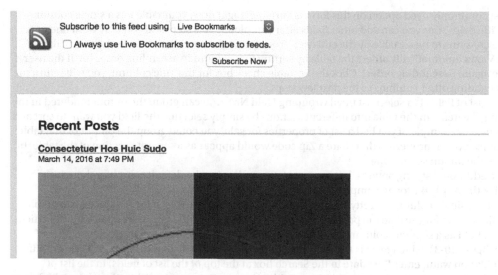

Figure 10-9. *A Views-generated RSS feed*

Creating Tables

Rendering content as lists works well in most cases, but you are likely to encounter scenarios where listing content in a table format is more representative of what users prefer. In this case, return to the Recent Posts view edit form to create a new display that will render fields from posts in a spreadsheet-like format. Click the Add button in the Displays area, and select Block as the display type. Change the display name as you did previously, this time to **Table of posts**, and click the Apply button. Click Unformatted List in the Format section, change the type of output to be rendered to Table, and remember to change the For option at the top of the page to This Block (Override); then click the Apply (This Display) button. The next screen that appears presents the style options you can set for your new table (see Figure 10-10).

Table of Posts: Style options   ✕

For | This block (override) | ▾ |

Place fields into columns; you may combine multiple fields into the same column. If you do, the separator in the column specified will be used to separate the fields. Check the sortable box to make that column click sortable, and check the default sort radio to determine which column will be sorted by default, if any. You may control column order and field labels in the fields section.

FIELD	COLUMN	ALIGN	SEPARATOR	SORTABLE	DEFAULT ORDER	DEFAULT SORT	HIDE EMPTY COLUMN
Content: Title	Content: Title ▾	None ▾	[ ] ▦	☐		○	☐
None						●	

Grouping field Nr.1

| - None - | ▾ |

You may optionally specify a field by which to group the records. Leave blank to not group.

Row class

| **APPLY (THIS DISPLAY)** | CANCEL |

Figure 10-10. *Table style options*

The most commonly used option on this form is Sortable. Right now, your table has a single column—the article's Title field—but you can add other fields after completing this step, and you may want one or more of those columns to be sortable by the end user. To sort the column, the user clicks the title of the column, and Views automatically orders the table by sorting that column in ascending order (or, if the user clicks the title again, descending order). Click the Sortable check box for the Title column; you will return to this form after adding other columns in the next few steps.

Below the list of fields is a select list titled Grouping Field Nr.1. You can group the output rendered in the table, grouping like items in the table into different sections by simply selecting the field you want to sort and group results by. For example, if you had a list of properties for sale, you could group the output of that table by Zip code or by city. All properties that share a Zip code would appear as a separate section of the table. In this case, leave the option set to None.

There are additional styling options, but in most instances leaving the default values for them is sufficient. Click the Apply button to complete this step in the process.

A table with a single column is pretty boring—it's really nothing more than a list. To spice up the table, let's add two fields: one for the date the post was created, and another for the tags associated with the article. You'll add each field as a separate column. To add the fields, click the Add button in the Fields section of the page (see Figure 10-3), which reveals the list of every field available to display on your view. To simplify finding the fields you want, enter **Post date** in the Search box at the top of the list of fields; in the list of results, check the box next to the Content: Post Date field. Select the For option of This Block (Override) to prevent this field from being added to all the other view displays you've created, and then click the Add And Configure Fields button. The next screen provides options to configure how the Post Date field is rendered, including the label displayed for that field, CSS styling options, what to do when there isn't a value present for a given post, and other options. Leave all the values set to their defaults for the remaining options, and click Apply (This Display). Click the Update Preview button at the bottom of the page to see that your table now has two columns.

You can continue to add columns, and you can reorder the columns by clicking the arrow next to the Add button to the right of Fields. There you find a rearrange button. Click Rearrange to display a list of all the fields you have selected. To rearrange the list, simply click one of the arrows to the left of the field, hold as you click, and drag it to a new position. After rearranging, click the Apply (This Display) button.

Views Add-on Modules

The Views module is a powerful tool for rendering content on your site. When you combine Views with other specialized modules, you get a whole new level of powerful capabilities. There are several must-have Views add-on modules you may wish to consider as you build out your site. One of my favorites is Views Slideshow: this module provides a simple-to-use interface for creating views that display content as a slideshow. There are a number of slideshow modules for Views, but this happens to be one of the easiest to use. For a complete list of Views add-on modules, visit http://backdropcms.org/modules and search for Views.

Summary

This chapter has only scratched the surface of how you can use the Views module on your new site. Views is extremely powerful and one of the killer modules for Backdrop.

Up to this point, you have focused on the basic building blocks of creating content, menus, and blocks. The next chapter looks at using those elements to create pages.

CHAPTER 11

Creating Pages

Now that you have a general understanding of content types, blocks, views, themes, and layouts, you're ready to start assembling pages on your web site using a combination of those elements. A page on a Backdrop site may represent a single piece of content (for example, a news story about a local high school senior winning a national award), or it may be a landing page similar to the front page of Backdropcms.org. Each page on your site may vary in structure, thanks to the flexibility of the Layout system in Backdrop as well as the blocks mechanism and the ability to specify on which page (URL) a block is to be displayed. Using the Views module to create blocks provides a dynamic means for extracting content along with static blocks created through the blocks interface. The combination of Backdrop tools provides a powerful mechanism for creating an awesome site.

Foundation for Creating Pages

Backdrop core, in conjunction with layouts and your theme, provides all the capabilities required to create a typical page found on a web site. Layouts provide the regions that can contain content, the theme defines the visual aspects of the page, and Backdrop core's content types, blocks, and views provide the mechanism for creating and extracting content that will appear in those regions.

In Chapter 6, you discovered the regions that Backdrop core's off-the-shelf layouts provide as containers for content on your web site. As a review, Figure 11-1 depicts the regions associated with the default layout that may be used to place content and blocks.

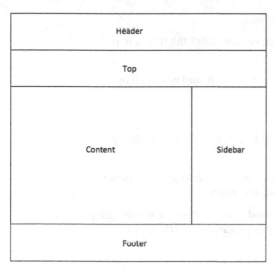

Figure 11-1. *Regions provided by Backdrop's default layout*

© Todd Tomlinson 2016
T. Tomlinson, *Beginning Backdrop CMS*, DOI 10.1007/978-1-4842-1970-6_11

The default layout provides five regions where you can place content and blocks, including the Header region that is typically used to display a site's logo, site name, site slogan, a search box, and navigational elements such as the main menu. The default layout is only one of the layouts available on Backdrop.org, each with its own arrangement and number of regions. Alternatively, you can use the layout tools to create the exact layout of regions you need to achieve the look that you desire for your site. For the purposes of demonstrating page building in Backdrop, this chapter sticks with the flexibility offered in Backdrop's default layout.

The first page you create here is an example of a content detail page, meaning a single piece of content is displayed on a page with various associated blocks that augment the page. To demonstrate creating a content detail page, let's use the Post content type and create a post that describes an upcoming Backdrop user group meeting. After logging on, navigate to Content ➤ Add Content ➤ Post. On the Create Post page, enter the title of the post and body text, and click the Save button. Take note of the URL associated with your post, because you are going to use it to place blocks that appear only on this post's page.

At this point, all the blocks that are defined to be site-wide blocks in the default layout appear on the page, along with the post for the Backdrop user group meeting. But what if you wanted more things to display on this page, other than the standard blocks and the post? The answer is to use views to generate blocks from content, or use the block interface to create or assign a block to appear on this page. Let's begin by creating a custom block through the Custom Blocks interface and assigning that block to appear only on the Backdrop user group meeting page (see Chapter 8 for a refresher on blocks):

1. Navigate to Structure ➤ Custom Blocks ➤ Add Custom Block.

2. In the Admin Label field, enter **Backdrop user group meeting directions**.

3. In the Display Title field, enter **Backdrop user group meeting directions**.

4. In the Block Content field, enter information about where your Backdrop user group meetings are held, including the address, contact phone number(s), email address(es), and meeting times.

5. Click the Save Block button.

6. To place the block so that it appears on the page you created, navigate to Structure ➤ Layouts. If you created a node layout as described in Chapter 6, select the Node layout. If you started with a fresh copy of Backdrop or did not create a node layout in Chapter 6, select the Default layout.

7. In the Sidebar region, click the Add Block button.

8. Scroll down until you see the custom block you created. Click the title of that block to place it in the sidebar region.

9. Scroll down until you see the Visibility Conditions section, and expand it by clicking the title.

10. Click the Add Visibility Condition link.

11. Select URL Path as the visibility condition to add, and click the Add Visibility Condition button.

12. Click the Allow Access On The Following Pages radio button to limit the custom block you created to only the URLs you are about to enter.

13. Enter the relative URL to the post that you created. The relative URL is everything after your site's primary URL (for example, for www.example.com/test, you would enter just **test** in the Path field).

14.   Click the Add Visibility Condition button to save the visibility condition.

15.   Click the Save Configuration button on the Configure Block page.

16.   Click the Save Layout button on the Edit Layout page.

Return to the home page of your site, and verify that the custom block does not appear. If it does appear, return to Structure ➤ Layouts and select the layout you used in step 6. Click the Configure button for the custom block. Scroll down to the Visibility Conditions section, and expand it by clicking the title. Click the Configure link for the visibility condition you created, and ensure that the right radio button is selected: Allow Access On The Following Pages. The most likely scenario is that Allow Access On All Pages Except The Following Pages is selected, or you have a wildcard URL path such as * in the list of paths, which directs Backdrop to display the block on all pages.

Navigate to the post you created by either entering the URL in the browser's address bar or navigating to Content and clicking the title of the post you created. You should see something similar to Figure 11-2, with your block appearing in the sidebar.

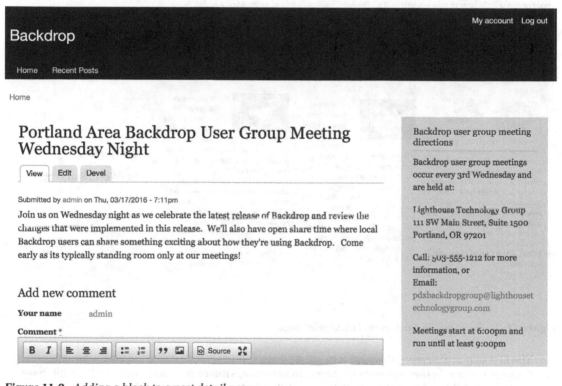

Figure 11-2. Adding a block to a post detail page

You can continue the process of adding blocks to the other regions on this page until you have all the content and elements that you want to display to your targeted users when they land on the Backdrop user group meeting page.

Creating Landing Pages

A *landing page* is typically a page that is not associated with a single piece of content and may display several different pieces of content and several blocks on the page. Backdropcms.org's home page is an example of a landing page. Let's continue the process of creating pages by creating a new page for attractions in and around Los Angeles for those who are going to attend the Los Angeles Backdrop user group meeting and who may be coming in from out of town and want to know what there is to do. This page uses four of the regions provided in the default layout: the top, content, footer, and sidebar region. The goal is to create a landing page that looks like Figure 11-3.

What to do Around Los Angeles

View   Edit

Submitted by admin on Thu, 03/24/2016 - 7:41pm

While you're visiting Los Angeles for the Backdrop user group meeting, you might want to come a little early or stay a little later to take advantage of all the fun things to do in and around Los Angeles. Whether you're a kid at heart and want to see Disneyland, or you're a film buff and want to tour Universal Studios, or just a beach bum who wants to hang out on the beach, there's a place in Los Angeles for you.

Featured Restaurants

Băco Mercat

Among the myriad emotional comforts our city has to offer, one of the most crucial to us is the knowledge that you can drop in to Băco Mercat on any given day (at midday or dinnertime), plonk yourself at the bar and partake in the bright, soulful cooking of Josef Centeno. Centeno has basically laid claim to this couple of historic blocks, with Bar Amá around the corner, Orsa & Winston next door to that, and now Ledlow (né Pete's) taking up the space beside Băco.

Tsujita

What is the best ramen in America's best ramen city? It depends, I suppose, on your mood, on your stylistic preference, on many things. But the consensus among the throngs of diners lining up outside Tsujita is that this is the best ramen in L.A., and we tend to agree. Once inside (the wait is long — it's worth it), you'll feast on Hakata-style *tonkotsu* ramen, or perhaps get your dip on with the fantastic *tsukemen*, its dipping broth thick and silky and rich.

République

It's quite a trick that Walter and Margarita Manzke have pulled off at République, a kind of sophisticated elasticity that allows the restaurant to be whatever you need at any given moment. The ambition of the husband-and-wife chef team was to create a modern restaurant that served many functions — a sunny cafe and bakery for breakfast and lunch, a neighborhood spot for a casual dinner and a grand restaurant serving refined French- and Italian-influenced cooking of the highest caliber — and it manages to be all of these things simultaneously.

Featured Article

Knotts Berry Farm

Submitted by admin on Thu, 03/24/2016 - 7:15pm

Knott's Berry Farm is a 160-acre (65 ha) amusement park in Buena Park, California, owned by Cedar Fair.

Read more

Latest Posts

SeaWorld San Diego

Submitted by admin on Thu, 03/24/2016 - 7:16pm

SeaWorld San Diego is an animal theme park, oceanarium, outside aquarium, and marine mammal park, located in San Diego,

Figure 11-3. The What To Do Around Los Angeles page

The first step in generating this page is to use the Page content type to create the base information (see Chapter 1 for a refresher on creating a page). To keep things interesting, only enter a title for this page, leaving the Body field empty. In the Title field, enter **What to do Around Los Angeles**, and then click Save. You now have a blank page with the title What To Do Around Los Angeles, without anything else other than the standard blocks that appear on every page. Let's create a few blocks and views and assign them to this page to make it look like a landing page.

First let's create a new taxonomy vocabulary named Event, and in that vocabulary let's create a single term for the Backdrop Los Angeles user group meeting. Navigate to Structure ➤ Taxonomy ➤ Add Vocabulary. Enter **Event** in the Name field. Click the Save button to reveal the Event Taxonomy page. Click the Add Term button, and create a term by entering **Backdrop Los Angeles user group** in the Name field. Click Save to save the taxonomy term. You also need another taxonomy vocabulary for Subject. Follow the same steps as for the Events taxonomy, only this time name the vocabulary **Subject** and add a term named **Things to do**.

You now need a means for authors to specify that a post they are writing is about things to do around Los Angeles. You can enable that ability by adding two term reference fields to your Post content type, allowing authors to select from a subject and an event. Navigate to Structure ➤ Content Types, and select Manage Fields from the list of operations for the Post content type. Following the general steps in the "Customizing Your Content Type" section in Chapter 5, create two new term reference fields, one for Event and one for Subject. As a refresher, select Term Reference as the field type, and on the Field Settings page, select the appropriate vocabulary for each field. After adding the two fields, your list of fields should appear similar to that shown in Figure 11-4. Note: if you are continuing with the same Backdrop instance that you used in Chapter 4, you may find the fields that you added in Chapter 4 in your list of fields.

LABEL	MACHINE NAME	FIELD TYPE	WIDGET	OPERATIONS
✛ Title	title	Node module element		
✛ Body	body	Text (long with summary)	Text area with a summary	EDIT ▾
✛ Tags	field_tags	Term reference	Autocomplete term widget (tagging)	EDIT ▾
✛ Image	field_image	Image	Image	EDIT ▾
✛ Event	field_event	Term reference	Select list	EDIT ▾
✛ Subject	field_subject	Term reference	Select list	EDIT ▾

Figure 11-4. *Event and Subject fields added to the Post content type*

The next step is to create several posts, selecting Backdrop Los Angeles User Group Meeting as the event and Things To Do as the subject. Let's start with creating five posts and using those posts as the basis for creating a landing page. Just enter different information about things to do around Los Angeles in each of the posts (visit Disneyland, visit Universal Studios, visit the Queen Mary, go to a Dodgers baseball game, and so on).

Creating Views

In the main content area of the page, you need to create a listing of the five most recently published posts that are focused on what to do in Los Angeles. Let's use the View module to create the list of posts, using the Teaser display to give your site visitors an introduction to each of the posts and the ability to click a Read More link to see the full post. Using the techniques described in Chapter 10, create a new view for posts by navigating to Structure ➤ Views ➤ Add View. Name the view **Posts**. You can use this single view with multiple displays to create the types of output you wish to display on your landing page. On the Add New View form, select Post as the type of entity you wish to render. Uncheck the Create Page check box, leaving the remainder of the options in their default state. Click the Continue & Configure button to continue.

The first view display you create is the teaser list of the latest five posts. Click the Add button to create a new display, and select Block from the list of options:

1. Click the Block link in the Display Name field, and change Display Name to **Latest Posts**.

2. Click the None link next to the Title field, and enter **Latest Posts** as the title to display at the top of the view's output. Click the Apply button. Update the title to say **Latest Posts**.

3. For Show Settings, change what to show from Fields to Content. Change the For option from All Displays to This Block (Override), and click the Apply (This Display) button. On the next screen, select Teaser from the View Mode select list, leave Display Links checked, and click the Apply (This Display) button.

4. Add two new filters to the view to limit the posts to only those that are applicable to the user group meeting and things to do. Click the Add button for Filter Criteria and enter **event** in the Search Criteria field. Change For to This Block (Override), and check the box for Content: Event (field_event). Click the Add And Configure Filter Criteria button to proceed. Leave the option set to Autocomplete, and click the Apply And Continue button. On the next form, select Is One Of from the Operators list, and enter **Backdrop Los Angeles user group** in the Select Terms From Vocabulary Event field. Select the value as soon as it appears. Click the Apply (This Display) button to complete adding this filter to the view. Repeat the process for Subject, using **Things to do** as the value for Select Terms From Vocabulary Subject.

5. Change the Pager option from Full to Display A Specified Number Of Items. Make sure you change For from All Displays to This Block (Override). Set the value of Items To Display to **5**, and click the Apply (This Display) button.

6. Click the Save button at the top of the page to save the view before continuing.

7. That completes this block. You can click the Update Preview button to see the output of the view.

The second view display you create is a Featured Post block. You randomly select a post and display the full post on the page. To create this view display, do the following:

1. Click the Add button, and select Block.

2. Change Display Name to **Featured post** and Title to **Featured Post**. Make sure you select This Block (Override) in the For select list at the top of each element you change; otherwise your changes will apply to all the view displays.

3. Change the Show Settings to Content and Teaser to display the shortened version of the post.

4. Add the same two filters created in the Latest Posts view, for Event and Subject.

5. Click the Add button in the Sort Criteria section, and add a new sort order. Select Global from the Type drop-down list; and from the list of values available for Global, select Random. Click Add And Configure Sort Criteria. Leave the Expose This Sort To Visitors check box unchecked, and complete the addition of the new sort criteria by clicking the Apply button.

6. Delete the Post Date (Desc) sort criteria by clicking the drop-down arrow next to the Add link (displayed to the right of Sort Criteria) and selecting Rearrange. On the Rearrange sort page, click the Remove link associated with Content: Post Date (Desc), and click the Apply (This Display) button.

7. Change the number of items to display in the Pager section. Change Full to Display A Specified Number Of Items and Items To Display to 1. Next, click the Apply (This Display) button and the Save button at the top of the page.

Assign the two blocks you just created to the What To Do Around Los Angeles page, to demonstrate the fruits of your labor. Navigate to Content ➤ Add Content ➤ Page, and do the following:

1. Enter **What to do Around Los Angeles** for Title.

2. Enter general information about all the great things to do in Los Angeles while attending the Backdrop user group meeting.

3. Click Save to publish your new page.

4. Navigate to the layout used by the What To Do Around Los Angeles page by visiting the Structure ➤ Layouts page. On this page, select the appropriate layout. If you went through Chapter 6, you should have a custom layout called Node. If you did not, create a custom layout, and assign it as the default layout for nodes. The following steps assume that you have selected a layout that has a left or right sidebar. If you have not selected a layout that has a sidebar, you can place these blocks in any other region.

5. In the sidebar click the Add Block button. Click the View: Posts: Featured Post link to add that block to the sidebar. Add a visibility condition for URL Path by adding the URL to the page you just created. If you don't know the URL, open a new tab in your browser and navigate to the Content Listing page. Find the page, and click the title. Copy the URL starting with the first character after the / at the end of the domain name of your site: for example, **what-to-do-around-los-angeles**. Click the Add Visibility Condition button, followed by the Save Configuration button.

6. Repeat the process for the View: Posts: Latest Posts block, including setting the visibility of the block.

Next, visit the What To Do Around Los Angeles page to see the progress of your page-building efforts (see Figure 11-5).

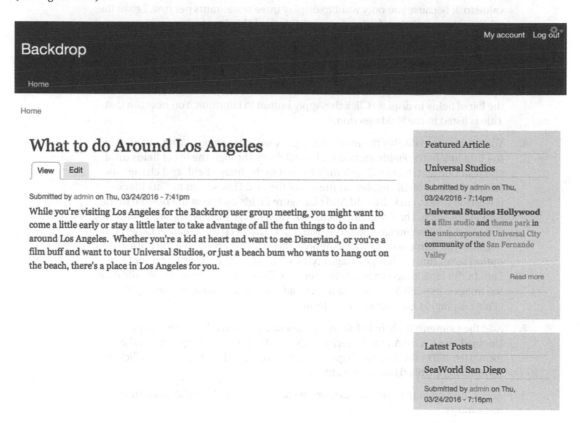

Figure 11-5. *Page-building progress*

Let's wrap up the landing page by adding three additional Featured Post blocks for three additional posts for restaurants around Los Angeles. You'll display the image uploaded for each restaurant at the bottom of the content region (refer to Figure 11-1 for the region locations).

You first need to add a new Restaurants term to the Subject vocabulary so that you can filter posts using **Backdrop Los Angeles user group** as the Event and **Restaurant** as the Subject. Follow the steps you performed earlier in the chapter (and in Chapter 4) to add the new term by navigating to Structure ➤ Taxonomy. Click the Add Terms link in the Operations column for the Subject vocabulary by clicking the drop-down arrow next to List Terms, and then select Add Terms. In the Name field, enter **Restaurant** and click the Save button.

The next step is to create content. Navigate to Content ➤ Add Content ➤ Post. Create three new posts using the same general steps as before, only this time upload an image for each of the restaurants you create. Remember to select the correct event and subject when creating the posts.

With the content in place, you're ready to create the view displays to render the name and image of each restaurant as a block. Return to the Post view and do the following:

1. Click the Add button to create a new block.

2. Give the block a Display Name of **Featured Restaurants**.

3. Change Title to **Featured Restaurants**.

4. You want the list of restaurants to appear as a horizontal list, in grid format, with each restaurant's information displayed in a column in the grid. To do this, change Format from Unformatted List to Grid. For Number Of Columns, set the value to **3**, because you only want to display three restaurants per row. Leave the other options at their default values. Click Apply (This Display) to continue.

5. You also want to show fields instead of teasers or full content in your blocks, so click the Content link to the right of Show and select Fields. Leave the other configuration options at their default values. When you select Fields as the option for what to show, the Views module automatically adds the Title field to the list of fields to display. Click the Apply button to continue. You now see that Title is listed in the Fields section.

6. You also want to display the image you uploaded for each restaurant, so click the Add link in the Fields section and scroll down through the list of fields until you find Content: Image. Check the box next to the Image field, and change the selected option of All Displays at the top of the Add Fields form to This Block (Override). Next, click the Add And Configure Fields button at the bottom of the Add Fields form. The Configure Field: Content: Image form is displayed, allowing you to set how the image appears in the block. Uncheck the Create A Label box, because you don't need a label to appear above the image. Leave the Formatter option set to Image, change Image Style to Thumbnail (100x100), and set Float to Left. In the Link Image To Select list, pick the Content item to automatically make the image a hyperlink to the post about that restaurant, and then click Apply (This Display) at the bottom of the form.

7. Add the Content: Body field following the same steps as adding the image. Uncheck the Create A Label check box as you did with the image, and in the formatter, select the Trimmed option. Leave Trimmed Limit set to 600. Click the Apply (This Display) button to continue.

8. Add a filter on Subject, using **restaurants** as the value to limit the posts to just restaurants.

9. Change Pager to Display A Specified Number Of Items, and set the number of items to display to **3**.

10. Click Save to complete the process of creating the new block.

The next step in building your page is to place the Featured Restaurants block at the bottom of the content region (refer to Figure 11-1). Navigate back to the Structure ➤ Layouts page, and once again select the layout where you placed the other blocks associated with the What To Do Around Los Angeles page. Instead of placing the restaurant block in the sidebar, let's place it in the Content region. Click the Add Block button, and scroll down until you find View: Posts: Featured Restaurants. Click the block, and set the visibility conditions as you did for the other blocks so that it only appears on the What To Do Around Los Angeles page. Save the block and the layout. Visit the What To Do Around Los Angeles page, and you see the grid display of featured restaurants as shown in Figure 11-6. Note that depending on the amount of content you entered, the layout may appear slightly different.

Featured Restaurants

Băco Mercat

Among the myriad emotional comforts our city has to offer, one of the most crucial to us is the knowledge that you can drop in to Băco Mercat on any given day (at midday or dinnertime), plonk yourself at the bar and partake in the bright, soulful cooking of Josef Centeno. Centeno has basically laid claim to this couple of historic blocks, with Bar Amá around the corner, Orsa & Winston next door to that, and now Ledlow (né Pete's) taking up the space beside Băco.

Tsujita

What is the best ramen in America's best ramen city? It depends, I suppose, on your mood, on your stylistic preference, on many things. But the consensus among the throngs of diners lining up outside Tsujita is that this is the best ramen in L.A., and we tend to agree. Once inside (the wait is long — it's worth it), you'll feast on Hakata-style *tonkotsu* ramen, or perhaps get your dip on with the fantastic *tsukemen*, its dipping broth thick and silky and rich.

République

It's quite a trick that Walter and Margarita Manzke have pulled off at République, a kind of sophisticated elasticity that allows the restaurant to be whatever you need at any given moment. The ambition of the husband-and-wife chef team was to create a modern restaurant that served many functions — a sunny cafe and bakery for breakfast and lunch, a neighborhood spot for a casual dinner and a grand restaurant serving refined French- and Italian-influenced cooking of the highest caliber — and it manages to be all of these things simultaneously.

Figure 11-6. Featured Restaurants block

You could continue to create additional views to display other lists of content, add other custom blocks, or look for modules that generate blocks to augment the content on this page (such as Google Maps or Yelp), but for now you've completed your task of building a What To Do Around Los Angeles page.

Summary

In this chapter, you merged layouts, content types, content, blocks, and views into a solution for creating complex pages on your site. You use these techniques in later chapters as you build a complete Backdrop site.

Next up, you explore expanding the functionality of your site by adding contributed modules.

CHAPTER 12

■ ■ ■

Backdrop Modules

Backdrop is an amazing product in its off-the-shelf state. The features and functionality provided in Backdrop core are more than adequate to meet the needs of many who build their web sites with Backdrop. But there are times when you need a feature that isn't possible with Backdrop core alone, and in those cases you need look no further than the contributed modules that have been written to address functionality not found in core.

In this chapter, you learn how to find, install, enable, and configure contributed modules.

Locating Backdrop Contributed Modules

The Backdrop team is working on providing the list of available contributed module and themes on the Backdrop web site, but that capability is rudimentary as of the writing of this book. The list of modules and themes is relatively short, and searching/browsing through the list is the only mechanism on the web site (there is no filtering by category or release, nor is there any sorting capabilities). To view the list, visit https://backdropcms.org/modules. The official repository of all Backdrop contributed modules and themes is Backdrops's GitHub account, accessible through https://github.com/backdrop-contrib.

You can download contributed modules and themes from the Backdrop web site by clicking the download link or by visiting the GitHub repository and downloading from there. The advantage of downloading from GitHub is that the GitHub page provides a Git clone URL, whereas the web site only provides the ability to download the file through a link.

Downloading Backdrop Modules and Themes

There are two basic ways to upload modules to a Backdrop site: download the file from GitHub and place the files on the server in the modules directory in the root directory of your Backdrop site, or use the administrative interface to upload the module to the site. Because the upload through the administrative interface requires that your server is configured properly to handle FTP uploads, this section briefly covers installing the files by downloading them.

You can download the files by clicking the link for the file from the http://Backdropcms.org/modules page or from the link available on the Releases tab (see Figure 12-1).

© Todd Tomlinson 2016
T. Tomlinson, *Beginning Backdrop CMS*, DOI 10.1007/978-1-4842-1970-6_12

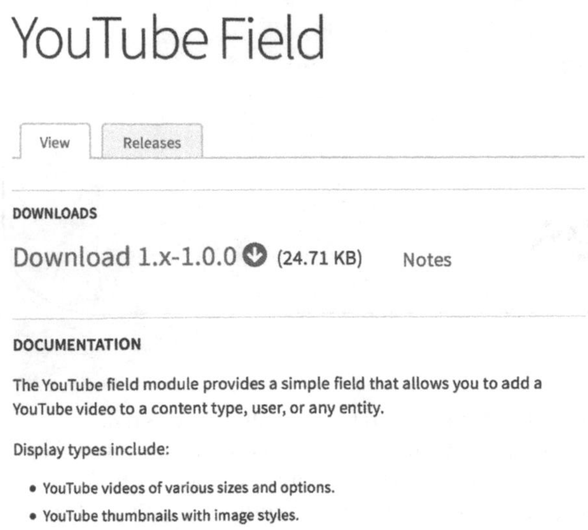

YouTube Field

| View | Releases |

DOWNLOADS

Download 1.x-1.0.0 🔽 (24.71 KB)   Notes

DOCUMENTATION

The YouTube field module provides a simple field that allows you to add a YouTube video to a content type, user, or any entity.

Display types include:

- YouTube videos of various sizes and options.
- YouTube thumbnails with image styles.

Figure 12-1. *Clicking the Download link from the Backdrop web site*

Clicking the link opens a pop-up window that allows you to specify that you want to save the file and save the zip file in the modules directory. Once the file is in the directory, use an appropriate tool to unzip the contents, and then delete the zip file.

To download the file from GitHub via Git, you can search for the module on https://github.com/ backdrop-contrib. Once you locate the module, you see a page that looks similar to Figure 12-2.

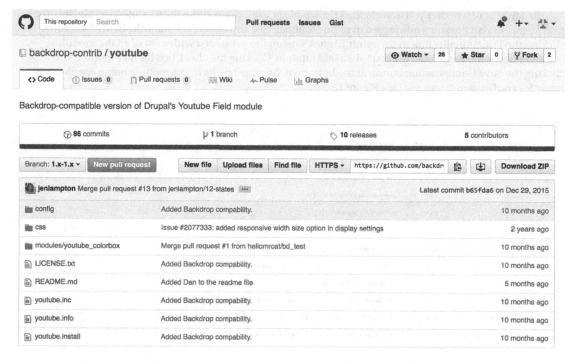

Figure 12-2. *A Backdrop module page on GitHub*

You can click the Download ZIP button located in the right column of the page, or you can use Git in a terminal window to clone the module's repository in the modules directory of your site. The benefit of using Git is that updates to the module may be pulled by visiting the modules directory and executing a git pull to download updates to the module.

To clone the module using Git, open a terminal window, copy the URL from the HTTPS Clone URL field in the right column of the module's GitHub page, and enter a command that follows this structure:

```
git clone <https URL copied from the modules page> <name of the directory where the module
should go>
```

The following example clones the YouTube Field module and places it into a directory named youtube in my site's module directory:

```
$ git clone https://github.com/backdrop-contrib/youtube.git youtube
```

The result I see as Git downloads the module is as follows:

```
Cloning into 'youtube'...
remote: Counting objects: 554, done.
remote: Total 554 (delta 0), reused 0 (delta 0), pack-reused 554
Receiving objects: 100% (554/554), 107.79 KiB, done.
Resolving deltas: 100% (288/288), done.
```

Regardless of whether you downloaded the zip file or used Git to clone the module from GitHub, the next step is to visit the site while logged in as an administrator and enable the module. In my case, after clicking the Functionality link in the administrator's menu I'm presented with a list of all the modules. Scrolling down the page, I see the YouTube Field module. Clicking the check box for that module and clicking the Save Configuration button at the bottom of the page results in the module being enabled and ready for configuration and use (see Figure 12-3).

▼ FIELDS

	NAME	VERSION	DESCRIPTION	OPERATIONS
☑	Date	1.3.4	Makes date/time fields available.	
☑	Email	1.3.4	Defines an email field type.	
☑	Field UI	1.3.4	User interface for the Field API. more	
✓	File	1.3.4	Defines a file field type. more	
✓	Image	1.3.4	Provides image manipulation tools and image field type. more	CONFIGURE ▼
☑	Link	1.3.4	Defines simple link field types.	
☑	List	1.3.4	Defines list field types. Use with Options to create selection lists. more	
☑	Number	1.3.4	Defines numeric field types. more	
✓	Options	1.3.4	Defines selection, check box and radio button widgets for text and numeric fields. more	
☐	YouTube Field	1.3.4	Provides a YouTube widget for fields. more	
☐	YouTube Field Colorbox	1.3.4	Provides Colorbox support to YouTube Field thumbnail display settings. more	

Figure 12-3. *Enabling the YouTube Field module*

Customizing Contributed Modules

Sometimes a contributed module addresses a majority of the functionality required for your site, but not all of it. You can use three basic options to address the shortfall in functionality:

- You can submit a feature request to the issue queue for that module, asking the maintainer of that module to enhance the module to meet your requirements. If your request addresses functionality that the community would benefit from, the module maintainer may accept your request and update the module. If you have development expertise, you may want to add the functionality to the module and contribute your updates back to the community. The module maintainer can then decide whether to incorporate your changes.

  You can, in most cases, extend the functionality of a contributed module by developing your own custom module that builds on the foundation provided by the contributed module. Some modules provide *hooks*, which are a means to modify the functionality of an existing module by calling functions provided by the contributed module. You can also use Backdrop core hooks to provide some level of customization, such as modifying a form that the contributed module provides. Not all modules provide hooks. Check for a README file in the module's directory. Information about hooks can often be found in the documentation provided by the module creator. You can also expand the functionality of the contributed module through other means such as creating views that display information created by a module, or by writing a custom module that interacts with the information generated and stored by the module.

- Convert a Drupal 7 module. Backdrop is Drupal's "cousin," so porting a Drupal 7 module to Backdrop is a relatively straightforward process. Details of how to migrate Drupal 7 modules can be found in the book *Migrating from Drupal to Backdrop* (Apress, 2015)).

Summary

The module-installation process is relatively simple, but the potential impact to the functionality available on your site may be significant. Explore the available modules, and use the power of contributed modules. If you can't find a module that meets your needs, then begin exploring the options described in this chapter.

CHAPTER 13

■ ■ ■

Anatomy of a Module

Although it is possible to build relatively complex Backdrop sites without ever having to look at the internals of a module, there may be instances where you need to understand some of the inner workings in order to fully take advantage of the features a module provides. This chapter takes you on a high-level tour of what constitutes a module in Backdrop by walking you through the creation of a simple Backdrop module.

Your First Backdrop Module

Don't worry—I'll keep it simple. The example module does only one thing, but it does it very well: display the text "Hello Backdrop World!" on a page. The result of your efforts in this section will be a page that looks similar to Figure 13-1.

Figure 13-1. *Hello Backdrop World!*

Step 1: Create the Module's Directory

The first step is to create a directory where the files that constitute your module reside. All contributed modules (non-core) reside in the modules directory located at the root directory of your Backdrop site. If you have installed any modules beyond what comes with Backdrop core, you see those modules in this directory.

Using your operating system's file manager, or from a terminal window and a command prompt, navigate to the modules directory, and create a new directory named hello.

Electronic supplementary material The online version of this chapter (doi:10.1007/978-1-4842-1970-6_13) contains supplementary material, which is available to authorized users.

© Todd Tomlinson 2016   149
T. Tomlinson, *Beginning Backdrop CMS*, DOI 10.1007/978-1-4842-1970-6_13

Step 2: Create the Module's info File

The next step is to create a `hello.info` file. This file tells Backdrop about your module and provides the information that appears on the Extend page in the Administration section of your site. Using your favorite text editor, create the `hello.info` file with the following content:

```
Name = Hello
Type = module
Description = 'My first Backdrop module.'
Package = 'Awesome modules'
Version = BACKDROP_VERSION
backdrop = 1.x
```

The first line specifies the name of the module as it appears on the module page. The second line specifies that you're creating a module. (Themes, for example, would use a value of theme for the type.) The third line captures the description of the module, which also appears on the Extend page. The package field provides a mechanism for grouping modules together. For example, if you visit the Extend page of your site, you see a number of modules listed in a box with a title of Core. This example uses something unique for the module and places it in a package called Awesome modules. If you're writing a module that, for example, creates new web services capabilities, you should use the package name of the other modules that create web services, to ensure that a site administrator can easily find your module. Version creates a version number for your module, and backdrop specifies which version of Backdrop this module was written for. In this case, this module is written for Backdrop 1.x.

Step 3: Create the Module File

The module file for the Hello module does one thing: it creates a block that prints the words "Hello Backdrop World!", which may then be placed on a layout and rendered on a page. Module files can do many things, but this example focuses on the basics.

Using your favorite text editor, create a new file named `hello.module` with the following text:

```php
<?php

/* implements hook_block_info() */
function hello_block_info() {

    $blocks['helloworld'] = array(
        'info' => t('Hello Backdrop World!'),
        'description' => t('Prints Hello Backdrop World.'),
    );

    return $blocks;

}

/* Implements hook_block_view() */
function hello_block_view($delta, $seetings, $contexts) {

    $block = array();
```

```
  switch ($delta) {
    case 'helloworld':
      $block['subject'] = t('Say it!');
      $block['content'] = hello_say_hello();
    break;
  }

  return $block;

}

/* Returns text that is displayed in the block */
function hello_say_hello() {

  return "Hello Backdrop World!";

}
```

The file begins with the opening PHP tag, <?php, because all modules are written in the PHP programming language. The specific elements of this module file are as follows.

This function uses one of Backdrop's hooks to create a new block. The function provides the name of the block as it will appear when searching for blocks to use in a layout, and a description of what the block does. It returns the block information so that it appears in the list of available blocks:

```
/* implements hook_block_info() */
function hello_block_info() {

  $blocks['helloworld'] = array(
    'info' => t('Hello Backdrop World!'),
    'description' => t('Prints Hello Backdrop World.'),
  );

  return $blocks;

}
```

This function calls Backdrop's hook_block_view function and uses the information provided in the hook_view_info function as the basis for determining which blocks to render:

```
/* Implements hook_block_view() */
function hello_block_view($delta, $seetings, $contexts) {

  $block = array();

  switch ($delta) {
    case 'helloworld':
      $block['subject'] = t('Say it!');
      $block['content'] = hello_say_hello();
    break;
  }

  return $block;

}
```

The switch($delta) statement looks at the $delta values passed to the function, which are sourced from the $blocks['helloworld'] statement in the hook_block_info section. The value of helloworld is passed as one of the $delta values. When the $delta value equals helloworld, the module formats the information that forms the basis of the block, including the block subject (or block title) and the content that makes up the body of the block. The content is sourced from another function I wrote.

This function simply returns the text "Hello Backdrop World!:"

```
/* Returns text that is displayed in the block */
 function hello_say_hello() {

    return t("Hello Backdrop World!");

}
```

The t( ) function wraps the "Hello Backdrop World!" text. This function translates the string to other languages if your Backdrop site is set up as a multilingual site and someone has provided the translation of the string into other languages. More on multilingual Backdrop sites in Chapter 15.

After completing the code, save both the .info and .module files. Although the module is simple, it demonstrates the basic functionality of what modules do. The module file is the workhorse of any module, and it can be as simple as this example module or as complex as needed to meet your functional and technical requirements.

Step 4: Enable the Module

The next step in the process is to enable the new module. Navigate to Functionality, and scroll down the list of modules until you find a section titled Awesome Modules (see Figure 13-2).

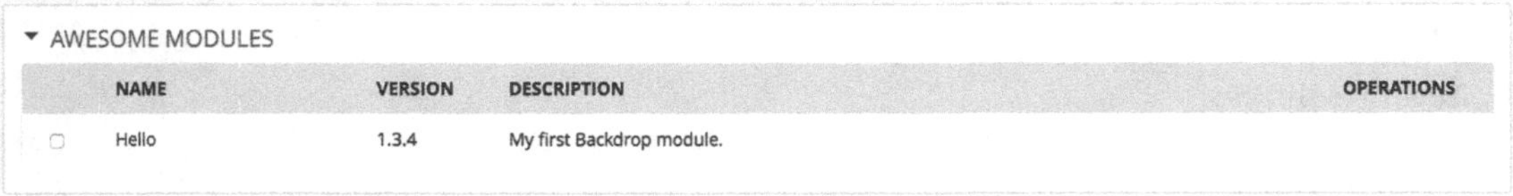

	NAME	VERSION	DESCRIPTION	OPERATIONS
☐	Hello	1.3.4	My first Backdrop module.	

▼ AWESOME MODULES

Figure 13-2. The "Hello Backdrop World!" module on the Functionality page

Check the box next to the module's name, and click the Save Configuration button to enable the module. With the module enabled, the block is ready to be placed on a layout. Follow the steps outlined in previous chapters to place a block in the default layout. I placed the block in the right column of the default layout; after saving, the result is as shown in Figure 13-1.

Other Module Files

The Hello module is very simple, the purpose being to help you past the initial learning curve of how a module is structured in Backdrop. Now that you know the very basics, you can look at other contributed modules, or even Backdrop core, to see how more complex modules are created and study the files associated with that increased complexity. You can learn about writing more complex modules at http://api.backdropcms.org/developing-modules.

Summary

Congratulations! You have written a Backdrop module and earned your first belt toward becoming a Backdrop module developer ninja. The purpose of this chapter was to give you an overview so you have enough information under your belt to go exploring through other modules. The learning curve can be steep for Backdrop module development, but you've taken the first step along that path.

■ ■ ■

## CHAPTER 14

Creating Themes

After searching through the contributed themes at http://backdropcms.org/themes, you may find yourself in a situation where none of the off-the-shelf themes meet the visual requirements for your new Backdrop site. In that scenario, the options are to change your requirements to meet one of the contributed themes, change a contributed theme to match your requirements, or create a new theme from scratch. This chapter shows you how to create a new Backdrop theme from scratch. Through this process, you gain enough information to understand the structure of Backdrop themes, enabling you to change an off-the-shelf theme to meet your design goals and objectives.

Contents of a Theme

Themes are stored in the themes directory in the root directory of your Backdrop site. An individual theme consists of a theme directory, usually named after the theme, containing files and directories that define the details of the theme. A typical theme directory has a structure similar to the following, although not all the files and directories in this example are required:

```
/themes
    my_bartik
        my_bartik.info
        template.php
        theme-settings.php
        screenshot.png
        templates (directory)
            node.tpl.php
            comment.tpl.php
            maintenance-page.tpl.php
        css (directory)
            colors.css
            (other css files)
        images (directory)
            add.png
            (other image files)
        color (directory)
            base.png
            (other color module files)
```

The following sections describe each of these elements.

© Todd Tomlinson 2016
T. Tomlinson, *Beginning Backdrop CMS*, DOI 10.1007/978-1-4842-1970-6_14

The Theme .info File (Required)

All that is required for Backdrop to list your theme on the Appearance page is a `.info` file. The `.info` file describes the theme and files used by the theme, such as stylesheets, JavaScript, block regions, and other metadata. The internal name of the theme is also derived from this file. For example, if it is named `drop.info`, then Backdrop sees the name of the theme as "drop."

Template Files (.tpl.php)

Template files are created for major elements rendered on a Backdrop site, such as pages and blocks. The template files contain a mixture of (x)HTML markup and PHP variables. Conditional logic and other more complex PHP code should be housed either in a module or in the `template.php` file, not in `.tpl.php` files.

Backdrop core provides a base set of template files for each element that is rendered. If you do not provide a `.tpl.php` file for an element, such as `page.tpl.php`, Backdrop uses the default template found in core.

The template.php File

Conditional logic and the transformation of content into output are contained in the `template.php` file. This file is not required, but it should be created if you encounter situations when you need to add PHP logic or processing in a `.tpl.php` file. Custom functions, overriding `theme` functions, and any other customization of the raw output should also be done here. This file must start with a PHP opening tag

Sub-themes

Sub-themes let you inherit resources from a parent theme but vary from the parent to address specific design requirements. For example, you may have a master theme for your organization, but each departments' site can adjust certain branded elements. In this case, you can create a sub-theme for each department, using the structure and resources of the parent theme but customizing it for that specific department without having to create a new theme from scratch.

The screenshot.png File

The screenshot is not necessary for the theme to function, but it is recommended, especially if you are contributing your theme to the Backdrop repository. Screenshots appear in the theme administration page and the user account settings for selecting themes when the appropriate permissions are set.

The theme-settings.php

To supply administrative UI settings or features, you can use a `theme-settings.php` file.

The color Directory

For color module support, a `color` directory with a `color.inc` file is needed, along with various support files.

Use a Sub-theme Instead of Copying

If you want to base your work on a core theme, use a sub-theme, or, as a last resort, make a copy and rename the theme. Directly modifying core themes is strongly discouraged, because they are used for the install and upgrade process.

Writing Theme .info files

The .info file is a text file that is used to define and configure a theme. Each line in the .info file is a key-value pair with the key on the left and the value on the right, with an equals sign between them (for example, name = my_theme). Some keys use a special syntax with square brackets for building a list of associated values, referred to as an *array*. If you are unfamiliar with arrays, have a look at the default .info files that come with Backdrop and read the explanations of the examples that follow. Even though the .info file extension is not natively opened by an application, you can use TextEdit on a Mac or Notepad on a Windows computer to view, edit, and save your changes. Comments can be added to the file: simply put a semicolon as the first character of your comment.

The following example shows the .info file for the Bartik theme:

```
name = Bartik
description = The default front-end theme for Backdrop CMS.
package = Core
type = theme
version = BACKDROP_VERSION
backdrop = 1.x

stylesheets[all][] = css/style.css
stylesheets[all][] = css/colors.css
stylesheets[print][] = css/print.css

settings[color] = true
```

Theme Name Requirements

Theme names play an important role in that they are used by Backdrop to form various functions in PHP. When naming your theme, you must take into account that it will be used as a function name and therefore should start with an alphabetic character. The name can then contain any combination of letters, numbers, and underscores, but it cannot contain hyphens, spaces, or any other punctuation. You should also be mindful that the name you choose must be unique, meaning no other module or theme on your site can use that same name.

Because the .info file is cached, you must clear the cache before any changes are displayed in your site. The .info file can also specify which theme settings should be accessed from the Backdrop administration interface, as you soon see.

Encoding

The file must be saved as UTF-8 without a byte order mark (BOM).

Contents

The content of the .info file includes the following elements.

- The human-readable name:

  name *(required)*
  ```
  name = your theme's name
  ```

- A short description of the theme, which is displayed on the theme select page at Administer ➤ Site Building ➤ Themes:

  description *(recommended)*
  ```
  description = A clean theme for blog sites.
  ```

- An optional screenshot key that tells Backdrop where to find the theme's thumbnail image, used on the theme selection page (admin/build/themes). If this key is omitted from the .info file, Backdrop uses the screenshot.png file in the theme's directory:

  screenshot
  ```
  screenshot = screenshot.png
  ```

  Use this key only if your thumbnail file is not called screenshot.png or if you want to place it in a directory outside of your theme's base directory (for example, screenshot = images/screenshot.png).

- You can give your theme whatever version string makes sense.

  theme version
  ```
  version = 1.0
  ```

- All .info files for modules and themes must indicate what major version of Backdrop core they are compatible with. The value set here is compared with the BACKDROP_CORE_COMPATIBILITY constant. If it does not match, the theme is disabled:

  backdrop version *(required)*
  ```
  backdrop = 1.x
  ```

- The type of project. For a theme, this is always theme. Other available types are module and layout. Although this property is not required to enable the theme, it is required to properly package the theme on Backdropcms.org and thus should always be included:

  type *(Required)*
  ```
  type = theme
  ```

- Sub-themes can declare a base theme. This allows for theme inheritance, meaning the resources from the base theme cascade and can be reused in the sub-theme. Sub-themes can declare other sub-themes as their base, allowing multiple levels of inheritance. Use the internal machine-readable name of the base theme. The following is used in Minnelli, the sub-theme of Garland:

  base theme
  ```
  base theme = garland
  ```

- You can use theme settings placed in the .info file to set the features by default:

  theme settings
  ```
  settings[color] = true
  ```

- Traditionally, themes default to using style.css automatically. Additional stylesheets can be included by declaring the stylesheet name:

  stylesheets
  ```
  stylesheets[all][] = theStyle.css
  ```

- JavaScript files to be included:

  scripts
  ```
  scripts[] = myscript.js
  ```

- The minimum PHP version the theme supports. The default value is derived from the BACKDROP_MINIMUM_PHP constant, which is the minimum required version for the rest of core. This can be redefined for a newer version if needed. For most themes, this should not be added:

  php
  ```
  php = 5.3.3
  ```

Example: Creating a Theme

In this example, you create a subtheme of the Bartik theme that is included in Backdrop core. Use the following steps.

Create the Theme Directory

Create your theme directory in BACKDROP_ROOT/themes/my_bartik.

Create the Theme's .info File

Create a my_bartik.info file, and add the following to it. This is how you let Backdrop know your theme exists and that it should appear in admin/appearance:

```
name = My Bartik
description = My theme of Bartik
backdrop = 1.x
```

And that's it! This is the minimum requirement for creating a theme. Navigate to the Appearance page, and look for your new theme. It should be visible in the Disabled Themes section. Click Enable, and set it as the default to make your theme the active theme on your web site. Backdrop provides page-layout options via the Layouts module, so you should be able to place blocks for the site header (logo, site name) and navigation elements, as well as custom and core blocks.

Of course, at this stage, the theme is unstyled. You can make further customization by adding CSS styles and modifying core template files if required.

Add Your Own Style

Add the following line to your .info file:

```
stylesheets[all][] = css/page_style.css
```

You also need to create a folder in your theme root, called /css. Create the page_style.css file there.

Add Custom JavaScript If Needed

If your theme uses custom JavaScript functionality, create a new folder named js in your theme's root directory, and, in that folder, add all the script files your theme requires. After creating the scripts, add each script using a structure similar to the following in your .info file, renaming bold_script.js to the appropriate file name:

```
scripts[] = js/bold_script.js
```

You also need to create a /js folder in your theme root and create the bold_script.css file there.

Add Custom Code in template.php

Create a template.php file in the root of your theme directory if you wish to add custom code. This includes theme function overrides, preprocess functions, and other functions needed to affect your theme's output. For now, create the opening PHP tag <?php and then save the file.

Add Template Files

Create a /templates folder in the root of your sub-theme if you wish to override core template files. Add a template file with the same name in your sub-theme folder to have it override the template from the parent theme.

Backdrop provides a large set of files that themes can use to inherit properties. By specifying a particular file name and/or structure, you allow the theme to override or inherit a template. For example, if you wish to modify the output of nodes, create a file called node.tpl.php in your /templates folder. It is best to simply copy node.tpl.php from a core theme such as Bartik.

You can add template files with more specificity: for instance, node--blog.tpl.php, building on node.tpl.php. A single hyphen is used to separate words: for example, user-picture.tpl.php or node--long-content-type-name.tpl.php. The double hyphen always indicates a more targeted override of what comes before the --.

Add Your Own Screenshot

Add a screenshot.png to the root of your theme folder, or add an image file setting in your sub-theme's .info file if you prefer to have your screenshot in a different location. At this point, your theme is live and ready to go.

Creating a Sub-theme

Sub-themes are just like any other theme, with one difference: they inherit the parent theme's resources. There are no limits on the chaining capabilities connecting sub-themes to their parents. A sub-theme can be a child of another sub-theme, and it can be branched and organized however you see fit. This is what gives sub-themes great potential.

A sub-theme must have a different internal name (name used by Backdrop) from its parent theme. This name must not contain any spaces or other special characters. The name of your sub-theme must start with an alphabetic character and can only contain lowercase letters, numbers, and underscores. Let's suppose this sub-theme internal name is my_subtheme.

Create a Theme Directory

The sub-theme to-be should be located in its own directory. This folder should have the same name as the internal name of the sub-theme (such as my_subtheme). The sub-theme folder should be located in the folder BACKDROP_ROOT/themes/ so that your theme's files are in BACKDROP_ROOT/themes/my_subtheme.

Create an .info File, or Copy and Modify the Parent Theme's .info File

To declare your theme to be a sub-theme of another, you must put a my_subtheme.info file in your my_subtheme folder. The easiest way is usually to copy the theme_name.info file from the parent theme (theme_name stands for the internal name of the parent theme) and rename it as my_subtheme.info. Then you need to add the following line to the my_subtheme.info file to declare its parent or base theme. Change theme_name to the internal name of the parent theme (that is, the name of the parent theme's .info file, usually all lowercase):

```
name = My sub-theme
description = This is a sub-theme of theme Bartik, made by John for the web site example.com
(red, responsive).
backdrop = 1.x
base theme = bartik
```

Copy Color Module Settings If Needed

As the following sections indicate, the sub-theme inherits *most* properties of the base theme. The important exceptions are core version and color info. You probably want to copy the core version declaration.

If your base theme supports the color module and you'd like your sub-theme to support it, you probably also want to copy the color folder from your base theme and add this line from your base theme's .info file to your sub-theme's .info file:

```
stylesheets[all][] = css/colors.css
```

Then copy colors.css from your base theme to the css folder of your sub-theme.

Add Your Own Style

All style sheets defined in the parent theme are inherited, as long as you declare at least one stylesheet in your sub-theme's .info file. *You must declare at least one stylesheet in your sub-theme for any of the parent theme's stylesheets to be inherited.*

If you want to override one of the parent theme's style sheets, specify a style sheet with the same file name in the sub-theme. For instance, to override page_style.css inherited from a parent theme, add the following line to your sub-theme's .info file:

```
stylesheets[all][]   = page_style.css
```

You also need to create the page_style.css file. If you simply wish to disable the imported styles, you can create an empty file.

Override JavaScript If Needed

All JavaScript defined in the parent theme is inherited. Similar to style sheets, specify a JavaScript file with the same filename in the sub-theme's .info file if you wish to override the parent JavaScript. For instance, to override bold_script.js, inherited from a parent theme, add the following line to your sub-theme's .info file:

```
scripts[] = bold_script.js
```

You also need to create the script.js file. If you simply wish to disable the imported scripts, you can create an empty file.

Add Your Custom Code in template.php

Create a template.php file in the root of your sub-theme directory if your wish to add custom code. Anything defined in the parent theme's template.php file is inherited. This includes theme function overrides, preprocess functions, and anything else in that file. Each sub-theme should also have its own template.php file, where you can add additional functions or override functions from the parent theme. As mentioned, there are two main types of functions in template.php: theme function overrides and preprocess functions. The template system handles these two types in very different ways.

theme functions are called using theme('[hook]', $var, ...). When a sub-theme overrides a theme function, no other version of that theme function is called.

On the other hand, preprocess functions are called before processing a .tpl file. For instance, [theme]_preprocess_page is called before page.tpl.php is rendered. Unlike theme functions, *preprocess functions are not overridden in a sub-theme.* Instead, the parent theme preprocess function is called first, and the sub-theme preprocess function is called next.

There is no way to prevent all functions in the parent theme from being inherited. As stated, it is possible to override parent theme functions. However, the only way to remove a parent theme's preprocess function is through hook_theme_registry_alter().

Override Template Files

Create a /templates folder in the root of your sub-theme if you wish to override the parent theme's template files. Add a template file with the same name in your sub-theme folder to have it override the template from the parent theme. Backdrop provides a large set of files that themes can use to inherit properties. By specifying a particular file name and/or structure, the theme can override or inherit a template.

Any .tpl.php files from the parent theme are inherited. You can add template files with more specificity: for instance, node--blog.tpl.php, building on an inherited node.tpl.php.

A single hyphen is still used to separate words: for example, user-picture.tpl.php or node--long-content-type-name.tpl.php. The double hyphen always indicates a more targeted override of what comes before the --.

Add Your Own Screenshot

The parent theme's screenshot is inherited. Specify a new image file in your sub-theme's .info file to override it.

Copy the Parent Theme's Color Module Settings

Color.module support in the color directory is not inherited.

Copy the Parent Theme's Settings

Theme-settings.php is not inherited, unless you copy the settings declarations from the parent theme's .info file.

Summary

You now have the ability to create a custom theme that exactly matches your desired look and feel. You can literally make your Backdrop site look exactly the way you want it, without being bound by an off-the-shelf theme created by someone else. If you develop a great theme, contribute it back to the community! See Appendix B for details on how to contribute your theme.

The next chapter looks at creating a multilingual site, enabling you to deliver content in the language of your site visitors.

■ ■ ■

## CHAPTER 15

Multilingual Capabilities

We live in a world where cultural and country boundaries, although still important, are blurred by the Internet's ability to connect people who are geographically thousands of miles apart and enable them to communicate through text, voice, and video. The visitors who come to your web site may be your next-door neighbors or they may live half a world away. Catering to those who live beyond your region and do not share your native tongue is now more commonplace than ever. Web site designers who break through the language barriers on their sites may attract audiences they never dreamed of having in the past, and Backdrop makes that possibility a reality through its built-in multilingual capabilities.

Getting Started with Multilingual

The first step in creating a web site with multilingual support is to determine which languages you wish to publish content in. Backdrop lets you render your site in nearly any language spoken on the planet. Backdrop does not do the actual translation of the content; rather, it facilitates the translation by providing mechanisms that enable visitors to select which language they wish to see (from a list you offer) and then rendering content that has been previously translated by humans into that language.

After you determine the list of languages you wish to support, the next step is to enable the multilingual modules that are part of Backdrop core. Visit the Modules page by clicking the Functionality link in the admin menu at the top of the page. Scroll down the page until you see the list of translation modules that are part of Backdrop (see Figure 15-1).

	NAME	VERSION	DESCRIPTION	OPERATIONS
▼ TRANSLATION				
☐	Content Translation	1.3.4	Allows content to be translated into different languages. more	
☐	Language	1.3.4	Lets you configure a number of languages to be used on your website. more	
☐	Locale	1.3.4	Provides language negotiation functionality and user interface translation to languages other than English. more	

Figure 15-1. List of multilingual modules

The Content Translation module handles all the content-related text, such as articles. The Language module enables the definition of which languages your site supports, and the Locale module handles other details such as translating all the user interface elements, such as form labels, into other languages.

Check all the modules in the Translation category, and then click the Save Configuration button.

Configuring Multilingual Capabilities

The next step in the process is to configure Backdrop's multilingual capabilities. Start by navigating to the Configuration page. Scroll down until you see the Regional And Language section (see Figure 15-2).

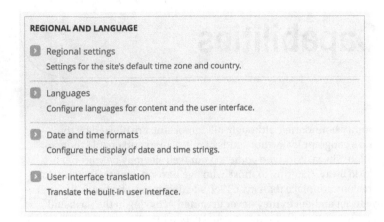

Figure 15-2. *Multilingual configuration options*

Specifying Languages

To set the languages your site will support, click the Languages link on the Configuration page in the Regional And Language section. If you installed your Backdrop instance using English as the default language, your Languages page should look like Figure 15-3.

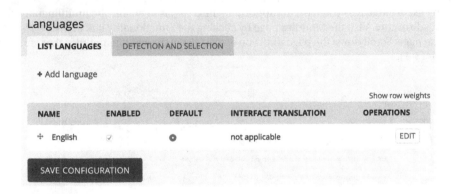

Figure 15-3. *Base language*

To enable a new language, click the Add Language button, select a language to add to your site from the drop-down list of available language options (see Figure 15-4), and click the Add Language button.

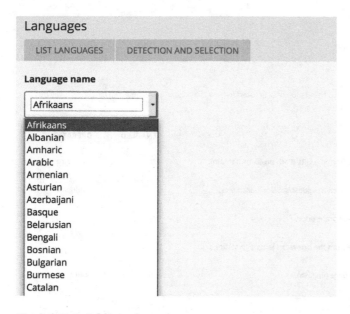

Figure 15-4. *Adding a language*

For this example, add French, Spanish, and Hebrew to the list of languages supported on your site.

Configuring Language Activation

After setting the list of languages you wish to support, the next step is to specify under what conditions Backdrop should switch to a different language. At the top of the Languages page, click the Detection And Selection tab to see a list of options to specify when language switching is to occur (see Figure 15-5).

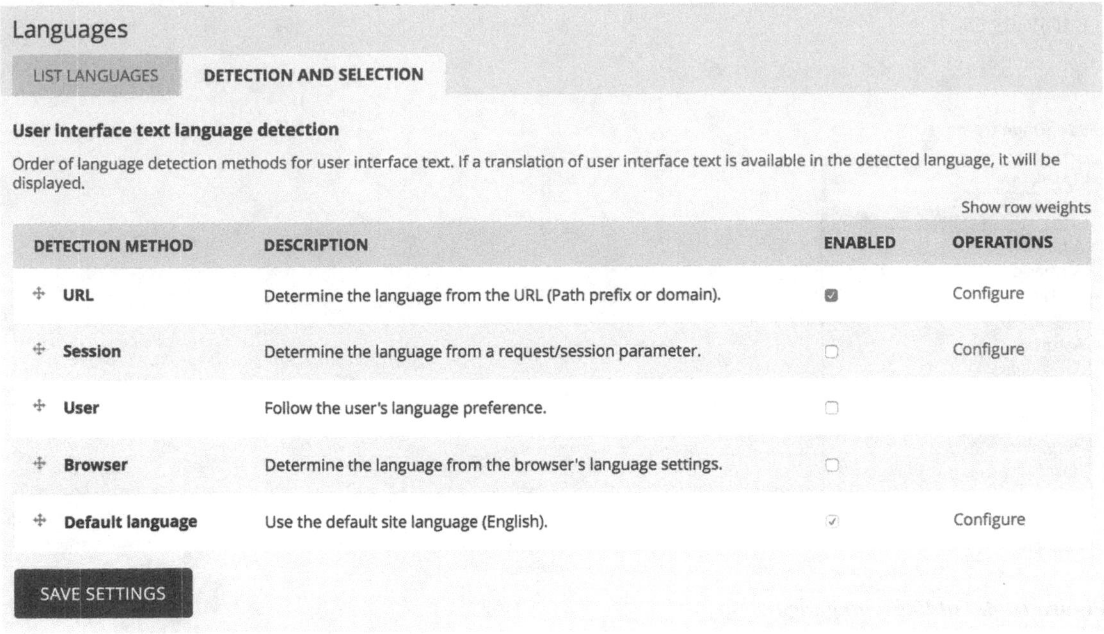

Languages

LIST LANGUAGES   **DETECTION AND SELECTION**

User interface text language detection

Order of language detection methods for user interface text. If a translation of user interface text is available in the detected language, it will be displayed.

Show row weights

DETECTION METHOD	DESCRIPTION	ENABLED	OPERATIONS
✛ **URL**	Determine the language from the URL (Path prefix or domain).	☑	Configure
✛ **Session**	Determine the language from a request/session parameter.	☐	Configure
✛ **User**	Follow the user's language preference.	☐	
✛ **Browser**	Determine the language from the browser's language settings.	☐	
✛ **Default language**	Use the default site language (English).	☑	Configure

SAVE SETTINGS

Figure 15-5. Language detection and selection

As shown in the Description column, you have several options for specifying how Backdrop decides which language to use to display page elements:

- Specify specific URL patterns that apply to languages, such as `http://example.com/en` for the English version and `http://example.com/fr` for the French version.

- Session parameters that are set by custom code and stored in a session variable.

- A user's language preference, as set on their user profile.

- The browser's default language settings, as set in the user's browser preferences.

- Or just use the site's default language regardless of the user's preferred language.

In this case, check the URL and User Languages options, and click the Save Settings button to continue.

Some of the options, such as URL settings, let you configure the parameters that define how those setting will take effect. Click the Configure button to see the parameters.

By selecting the User option, you now have access to a block that lets a user select which language they prefer. Follow the steps outlined previously in this book to place the language-switcher block on the default layout in the sidebar. After enabling the Language Switcher block, your page should look similar to Figure 15-6.

Figure 15-6. *Language-switcher block*

Content Translation Example

With the language-switcher block in place, you are now ready to take the next steps of translating content. Return to the Configuration page. Click the Languages link to return to the Languages page. After enabling the languages you want to support, you see entries for each in an Interface Translation column (see Figure 15-7). For each language, this column shows the number of elements that are already translated (the first number) and the total number of elements available to translate, where *elements* are field labels, error messages, or other text strings defined in template files and modules. As you can see in the figure, very few interface elements have been translated at this juncture.

Languages

LIST LANGUAGES   DETECTION AND SELECTION

+ Add language

Show row weights

NAME	ENABLED	DEFAULT	INTERFACE TRANSLATION	OPERATIONS
✛ Spanish	☑	○	0/31 (0%)	EDIT ▾
✛ English	☑	●	not applicable	EDIT
✛ French	☑	○	0/31 (0%)	EDIT ▾
✛ Hebrew	☑	○	0/31 (0%)	EDIT ▾

SAVE CONFIGURATION

Figure 15-7. *Interface translation*

Clicking any of the values in the Interface Translation column displays the list of elements that are available for translation (see Figure 15-8).

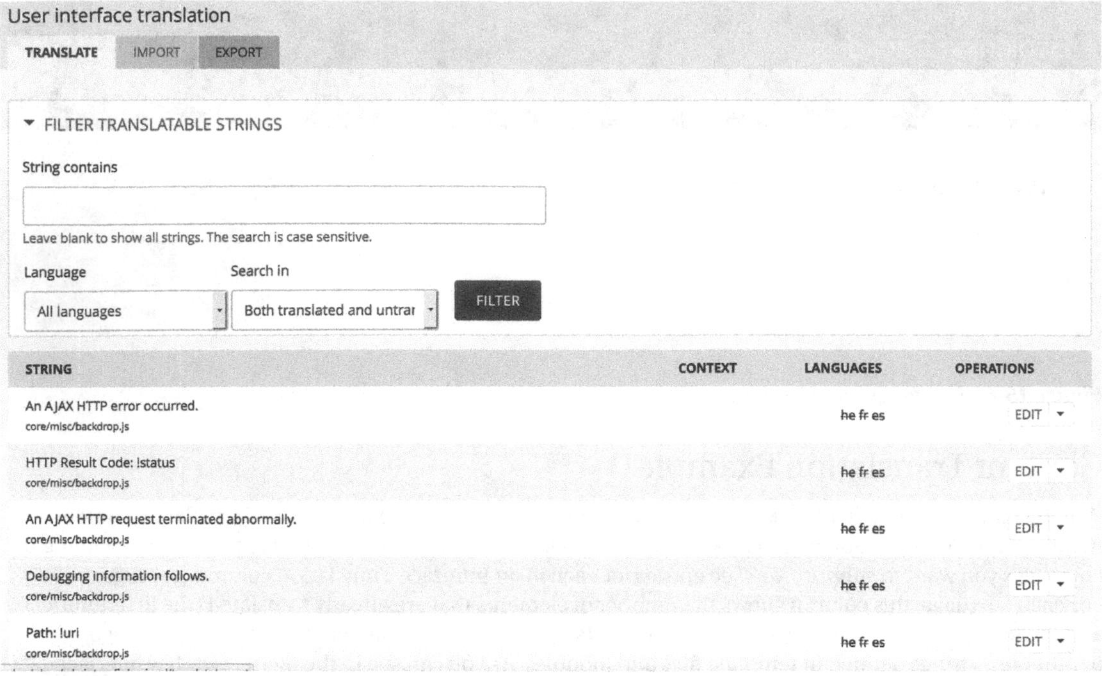

Figure 15-8. *Translation of source strings to alternative languages*

In the Languages column, a language that is crossed out means there isn't a translation of that string for that language. To add a translation, click the Edit button to display the list of languages and the translations of that string for each language, as shown in Figure 15-9.

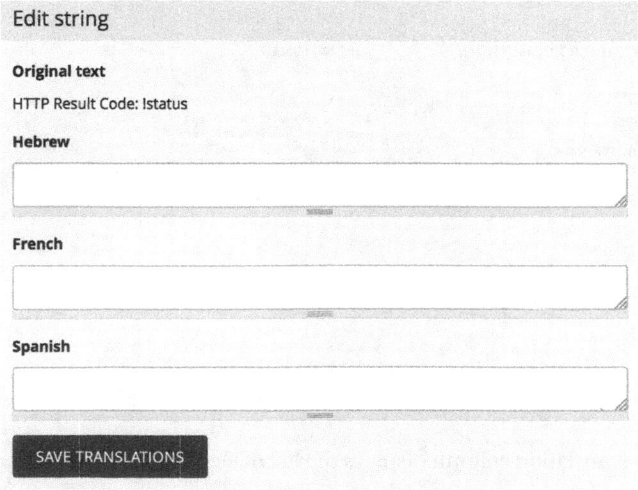

Figure 15-9. *String-translation form*

After entering values for some or all of the source strings, click the Save Translations button. Back on the Languages page, the number of strings you have translated appears in the Interface Translation column, along with the total number of strings and the percentage of strings that have been translated for that language. The total number of strings to be translated may increase as you install new modules, create new forms, or create other features that have interface elements that are translatable. Check this page often to ensure that everything has an associated translation.

Configuring Entities

The next step in setting up multilingual support on your site is to specify which content types, taxonomy vocabularies, user profiles, and other supported elements are translatable. Each entity has its own configuration form for multilingual support. To enable translation for a content type, navigate to Structure ➤ Content Types and, as an example, click Configure for the Post content type. Scroll to the bottom of the page, and click the Publishing Settings tab. In the Multilingual Support section, select Enabled, With Translation, as shown in Figure 15-10, and click the Save Content Type button.

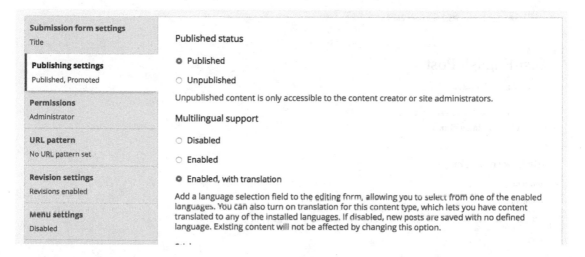

Figure 15-10. *Publishing and promotion settings*

To see the effect of changing the Post content type to translatable, create a new post and note the new field that appears on the edit form (see Figure 15-11). After entering a title and body text, select the appropriate language, and then click the Save button.

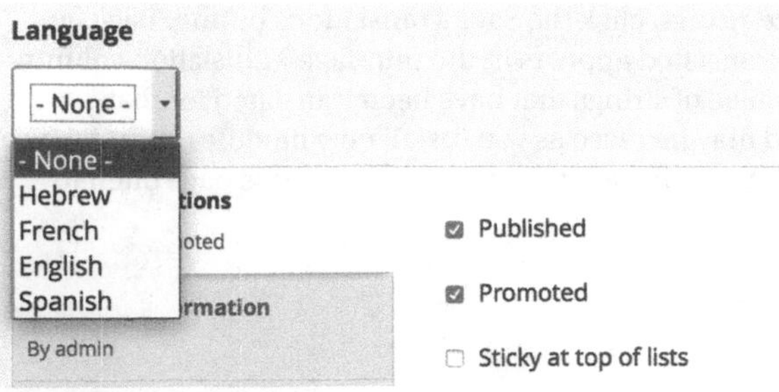

Figure 15-11. *Selecting the language on a post*

After saving, note that there is a new Translate tab at the top of the post you created (see Figure 15-12).

Figure 15-12. *The Translate tab*

Clicking the Translate tab displays all the available languages and the content items' current status by language: Published or Not Translated (see Figure 15-13). To translate the post into a new language, click the Add Translation button.

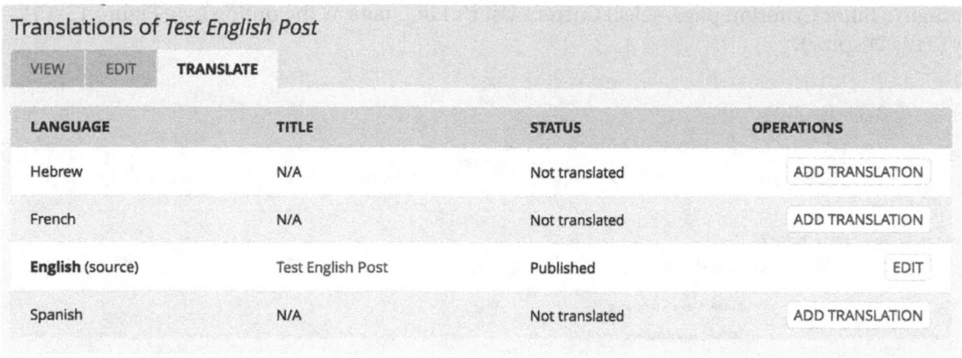

Translations of *Test English Post*

VIEW	EDIT	**TRANSLATE**

LANGUAGE	TITLE	STATUS	OPERATIONS
Hebrew	N/A	Not translated	ADD TRANSLATION
French	N/A	Not translated	ADD TRANSLATION
English (source)	Test English Post	Published	EDIT
Spanish	N/A	Not translated	ADD TRANSLATION

Figure 15-13. *List of translations*

Edit the title and body and any other fields your content type has, changing the English version of the content into the language of choice, and save the changes. After saving, and assuming you enabled the language-switcher block, click the language into which you translated the content. Backdrop displays the translated version of your content in the language you selected.

Detecting the Language and Filtering Content

With content translated, the next step is configuring your site to display content based on the user's current language. For example, a French-speaking person visiting the web site wants to see the content in French, not English. Earlier in the chapter, when enabling languages, you set the language-detection option to the URL, meaning Backdrop detects the language based on a URL that is in the form fr.example.com or www.example.com/fr (where the example language is French). There are other options for language detection, but the most common approach is through the URL. For information on other detection mechanisms, visit Configuration ➤ Regional And language ➤ Languages.

As an example, let's enable a default view shipped with Backdrop. Navigate to Structure ➤ Views, and click Enable in the Operations column for the Front Page view. This view emulates the standard frontpage on a Backdrop site. Next, configure the view to add a new filter to it. The new filter limits the content displayed to the user's current language. Click the Add button in the Filters section, and enter **Language** in the Search field. Select Content: Language as the filter to apply to the view (see Figure 15-14), and click Add And Configure Filter Criteria.

Add filter criteria

For This page (override) ▾

Search Language   Filter - All - ▾

☐ Content: Language
   The language the content is in.

ADD AND CONFIGURE FILTER CRITERIA   CANCEL

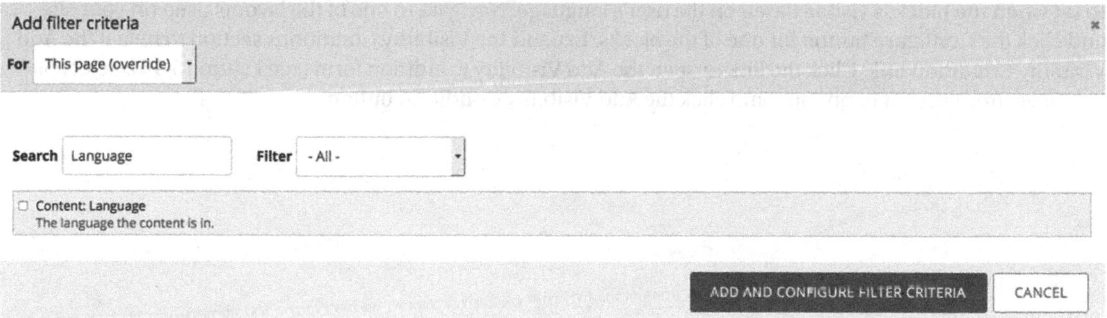

Figure 15-14. *Filtering content by language*

On the Configure Filter Criterion page, select Current User's Language as the option (see Figure 15-15), and click Apply (This Display).

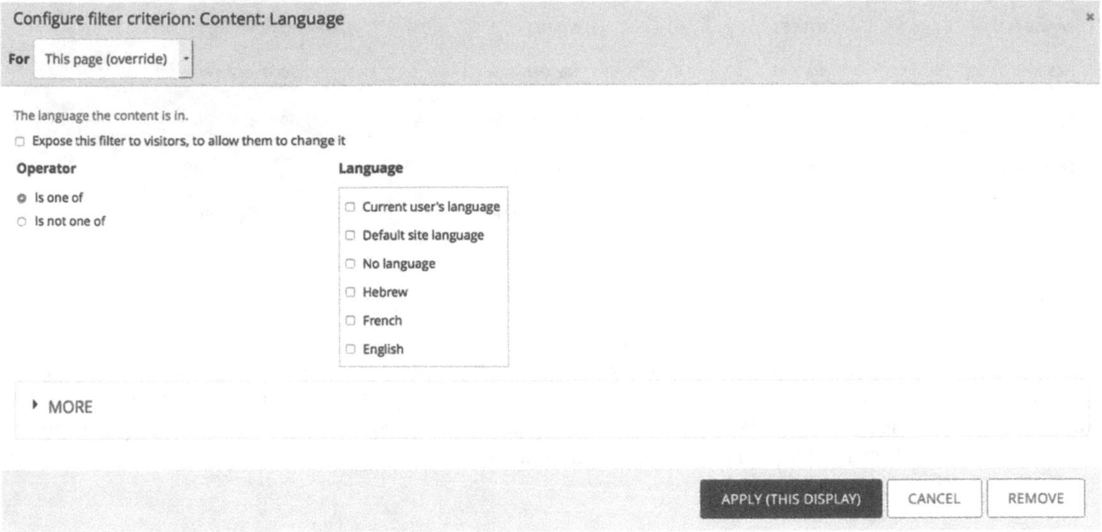

Figure 15-15. Setting the language option for the filter

To complete the application of the filter to the view, click the Save button. The Front Page view renders the list of content using the URL /frontpage. Visit the page using example.com/en/frontpage (replacing example.com with the domain name of your site), and note that only English content is displayed. Visit the page again, changing the URL to example.com/fr/frontpage, and note that only French content is displayed. By updating all the views on your site to be language sensitive, you now have a good portion of your site set to multilingual. But there are more than just views on your site; the other elements you will want to update are blocks.

Setting Block Visibility by Language

You may have blocks on your site that are applicable to a single language: for example, a banner advertisement that is in French and targeted at people living in France. The multilingual capabilities of Backdrop allow you to set when the block is visible based on the user's language. Navigate to one of the layouts used on your site, and click the Configure button for one of the blocks. Expand the Visibility Conditions section to reveal the Add Visibility Condition link. Click the link to open the Add Visibility Condition form (see Figure 15-16). Select Site Language from the list of options, and click the Add Visibility Condition button.

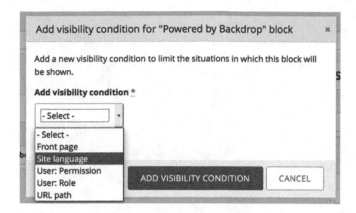

Figure 15-16. *Adding block visibility by site language*

The next step is to select the language associated with the block. Check the appropriate language(s), and click Add Visibility Condition. The block will now appear only when the language appears in the URL.

Summary

This chapter demonstrated Backdrop's ability to handle multilingual content. This is a feature-rich and powerful tool for sites that wish to reach a broader audience than just the native language in which the site is written. Translating your content into multiple languages literally opens the opportunity to reach the world—just one of Backdrop's powerful features.

CHAPTER 16

■ ■ ■

Using Git

This chapter provides a basic overview of Git, a source code control system adopted by the Backdrop community. What is a source code control system, you ask? It is any tool that enables developers to manage changes to documents, source code, and other collections of information. If you have ever made changes to a document or a piece of code and then subsequently wished you could go back in time and undo those changes, a source code control system would have saved the day. That's one of the key features of source code control: the ability to take a snapshot of digital assets at a given point in time and then retrieve that snapshot at a later date to restore the previous state.

Other key aspects of a source code control system include the ability to distribute changes to other developers or systems. It's also possible to take a single code base, create copies (or *branches*, the more technically correct term) of it so that multiple developers can work on it simultaneously without clobbering each other's work, and then at some point in time merge all of those branches back together and resolve conflicts where two people made changes to the same elements of a digital asset (for example, a line of code).

There are several source code control systems on the market. The one selected and adopted by the Backdrop community is Git. Linus Torvalds, the creator of the Linux operating system, created Git during the creation of Linux when he was looking for something that was truly open source, fast, and powerful, yet easy to use. This chapter talks about some of the basic functions of Git that you may wish to use on your new Backdrop site.

Installing Git

The first step in using Git is to install it. But before you do, check to see whether it's already installed by typing git at the command prompt in a terminal window and pressing Return. If you see a list of Git commands, congratulations: you already have Git installed. If you see something along the lines of "command not found," then it's time to install Git.

Installing Git on Linux

Installing Git on Linux is a simple one-step process. If you are on a Debian-based distribution like Ubuntu, the command to enter in a terminal window is apt-get install git. If you are on a non-Debian-based Linux system, then you can use yum to install Git by entering yum install git-core at the command prompt in a terminal window. After installing, type git at the command prompt and press Return. You should now see a list of Git commands. If you do not, check the helpful documentation on the Git web site at http://git-scm.com.

© Todd Tomlinson 2016

T. Tomlinson, *Beginning Backdrop CMS*, DOI 10.1007/978-1-4842-1970-6_16

Installing Git on OS X

Installing Git on OS X is accomplished using the graphical installer available at http://git-scm.com/download/mac. This simple-to-use tool provides a quick way to successfully install Git on your Mac. Download the dmg file, click it to launch the installer, and follow the instructions. Once it's installed, test to ensure that Git is installed by launching a terminal window and typing git at the command prompt and pressing Return. You should see a list of Git commands if Git is installed correctly. If you do not see a list of commands, visit http://git-scm.com for help.

Installing Git on Windows

To install Git on Windows, download the Git installer .exe file from http://git-scm.com/download/win The Windows installer installs Git tools that allow you to execute Git commands from a terminal window and installs a GUI tool for managing your Git repositories. After installing, launch a terminal window, enter git at the command line, and press Enter. You should see a list of Git commands. If you do not see a list of commands, visit http://git-scm.com/download/win for help.

Using Git

There are several basic Git commands that will propel you along the path of getting hooked on Git. The first step in the process of using Git is to set up a Git repository where all the items you wish to place under revision control will be stored. Let's use your Backdrop installation as your first Git project to place under source control. Using a terminal window, navigate to the root directory of your Backdrop installation. In the terminal window, type git init, and press Return.

■ **Note** The git init command will return an error message if you have already created a Git repository for this site.

You should see something similar to this message:

```
Initialized empty Git repository in /Applications/MAMP/htdocs/Backdrop/.git/
```

If the repository was not successfully created, visit the Git web site for help on your specific errors.

With the repository created, the next step is to add elements to it. Because you haven't added any files yet, let's add all the files in your Backdrop directory to Git. To do so, enter the following command:

```
git add -A.
```

Make sure you enter the period at the end of the command, because it signifies the current directory. If you successfully added all the files to your repository, you should be returned to the command prompt without any messages. If you enter git status at the command prompt and press Return, you should see a long list of new files that were added to the repository but not yet committed.

The process of committing the files that were just added provides a snapshot that you can roll back to in the event you make changes in the future that you need to revert to a previous state. How often you add and commit files is up to you or your project team, the key point being that in order to have the ability to roll back to a previous point in time, those files must have been added and committed. So let's commit your Backdrop files to your Git repository using the following command:

```
git commit -m "initial commit to the repository"
```

After executing the `commit` command, you should see a long list of messages that new nodes were created in your Git repository, one message per file committed. If you execute the `git status` command, you should see that everything is up to date:

```
# On branch master
nothing to commit, working directory clean
```

At this point, you've committed the files and can now revert files to the state they were in when you committed them a few moments ago. The next step in the process is adding changes to files and committing those changes. Let's make a change to an existing file and add a new file to see how Git responds to both situations. First, create a new file in your `modules` directory. In this case, create a new file named `test.txt` with a few lines of information so you can see Git in action. After creating the file, execute `git status` to verify that Git recognized the new file. You should see output similar to

```
# On branch master
# Untracked files:
#   (use "git add <file>..." to include in what will be committed)
#
#   test.txt
```

So let's follow the instruction and use `git add test.txt` to add the file to Git. After adding the file, use `git status` to check to see that the file was added. You should see output similar to

```
# On branch master
# Changes to be committed:
#   (use "git reset HEAD <file>..." to unstage)
#
#   new file:   test.txt
#
```

where `new file:` was prepended to the file name to indicate that Git is now tracking that file.

Let's commit the new file to the repository so you can revert to the current state in the future. Use the following to commit the file:

```
git commit -m "committing the initial version of test.txt to the repository"
```

After committing, run `git status` to see that everything is committed. You should see the message stating that there is nothing to commit.

Now, change the `test.txt` file by adding more information to it to see if Git sees the changes to the file. After adding text to your file, run `git status`. You should see a message similar to

```
# On branch master
# Changes not staged for commit:
#   (use "git add <file>..." to update what will be committed)
#   (use "git checkout -- <file>..." to discard changes in working directory)
#
#       modified:   test.txt
#
```

Git recognized the changes to test.txt. You can now add the modified version of test.txt and commit it using git add test.txt and git commit -m "modified test.txt". After committing, use the git log command to see the history of the commits to your repository. You should see two commits for the file you committed that look similar to the following:

```
commit d4c24ca1854e53676178141be86246b1a3cb0a1a
Author: Todd Tomlinson <tomlinson.todd@gmail.com>
Date:   Wed Mar 30 08:27:10 2016 -0700

    modified test.txt

commit 39b5859fa70d1aafacd5c04d7695e715fdfd6bd6
Author: Todd Tomlinson <Tomlinson.todd@gmail.com>
Date:   Wed Mar 30 08:23:04 2016 -0700

    committing the initial version of test.txt to the repository
```

You see here that there are two different commit IDs. If you needed to revert test.txt to its initial state, you could do so by using the initial commit ID. The command for reverting to a previous commit is git revert <commit id>. To revert these changes to test.txt, you would use the first commit ID, the one ending in bd6:

```
git revert 39b5859fa70d1aafacd5c04d7695e715fdfd6bd6
```

After reverting and checking the test.txt file, you can see that the file is back to its original state before you made changes to it. Whew!

You now have enough basic information to set up your local Git repository and store your changes, but all your changes are stored locally on your laptop, desktop, or server. Often, you may want to enable others to view and/or make changes to your repository. There are several solutions for providing access to your Git repository, including one of the more popular solutions: GitHub, introduced next.

Using GitHub

Using GitHub enables you to share your Git repositories with others and facilitates situations where you're doing development on your laptop or desktop and your site resides on a remote server. In either of these scenarios, GitHub provides an environment that is accessible over the Internet; and if you're okay with the general public having access to your repositories, the service is free. For a small monthly fee, you can upgrade to a GitHub account that provides private repositories that are only accessible to those you have granted access rights to. As an example, let's use the free version of GitHub. If you do not already have an account, visit https://github.com and sign up for a new account.

After setting up your account, the first step is to create a repository. On your GitHub landing page (once you've logged on), you see one or more links and buttons to create a repository. Click one of the links, and you see a page similar to Figure 16-1.

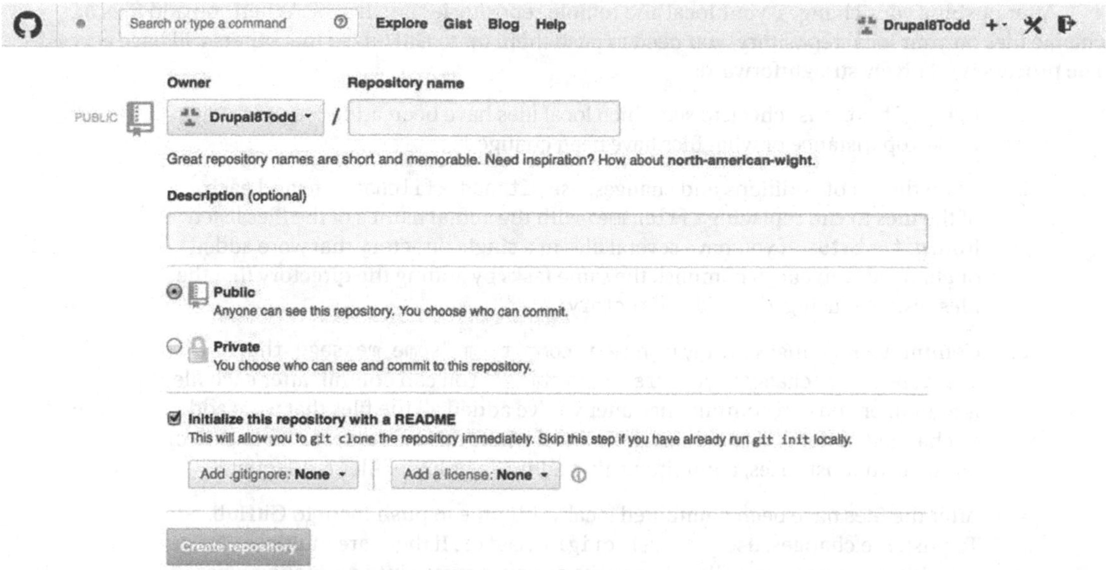

Figure 16-1. Creating a new GitHub repository

To create a repository, enter a name in the Repository Name field, and enter a description in the Description field.

With the repository created on GitHub, the next step is to push your local repository up to GitHub. On the GitHub page for your repository, you see a clone URL listed in the right column of the page. Copy that URL, because you are going to need it to push your local repository up to GitHub.

The first step in the process is to set up the GitHub connection on your local machine. From within the root directory of your Backdrop site, use the following command to add a reference to your remote GitHub repository, remembering to paste the clone URL in place of <clone url from GitHub>:

```
git remote add origin <clone url from GitHub>
```

Once you've added the remote repository, the next step is to pull down any changes that exist on GitHub that don't exist locally, before attempting to push your local repository to GitHub. If you do try to push changes to GitHub and there are remote changes that don't exist locally, Git will tell you that your branch is behind and you have to first pull down the changes. To fix that, use the following:

```
git pull origin master
```

This pulls down any changes on GitHub and merges them into your local repository. The next step is to push your local repository up to GitHub, because GitHub right now is basically empty. Use the following command to push your Backdrop site up to the remote repository:

```
Git push origin master
```

181

After pushing your changes, your local and remote repositories are in sync. When you add files or change files on your local repository, you need to push them up to GitHub so that others will have access. The process is relatively straightforward:

1. Using `git status`, check to see which local files have been added to your Backdrop instance or what files have been changed.

2. From the list of additions and changes, use `git add <filename>` to add each of the files to Git, replacing `<filename>` with the actual names of the files listed from `git status`. If you have several files in a single directory that were added or changed, you can accomplish the same tasks by adding the directory that the files reside in using `git add <directory>`.

3. Commit your changes locally using `git commit -m "some message that describes the changes you are committing"`. You can commit after each file is added, or you can commit once after you've added all the files that were added or changed. It depends on the granularity of what you want to revert to in case of an issue. In most cases, committing after adding a group of files is adequate.

4. After the files have been committed locally, it's time to push them to GitHub. To push the changes, use `git push origin master`. If there are multiple people working on your GitHub repository, you may run into a situation where attempting to push files results in an error stating that your master branch is behind X number of commits. Simply execute `git pull` to download and merge those changes and then re-execute `git push origin master`. In situations where you've changed a file that was also changed by someone else, Git will report that there is a merge conflict. Git writes useful information into the file where the merge conflict occurred. Examine the file, and resolve the issues. For more information on resolving merge conflicts, visit the Git documentation site at `http://git-scm.com/documentation`.

With your Backdrop site uploaded to GitHub, you can now provide other people access to your repository so that they can download and optionally commit changes to your repository. If you have upgraded your GitHub account, you need to grant access to your repository by following the steps listed on your GitHub repository's landing page. If you have not upgraded your account, you don't need to do anything to grant access, because, by default, free accounts are publicly accessible. To clone your GitHub repository on a laptop, desktop, or server, you can either use the `git clone` command or download a zip file of the repository using the Download ZIP button on your repository's landing page. The best approach is to use Git and to clone the repository. To do so, simply copy the HTTPS clone URL listed in the right column of your GitHub repository landing page, and execute the following command

```
git clone <clone URL> <target directory>
```

replacing `<clone URL>` with the actual URL listed on your GitHub repository landing page. For example,

```
git clone https://github.com/Drupal8Todd/Backdrop.git Backdrop
```

would clone the GitHub repository into a directory named Backdrop. After cloning, you can then use, modify, add to the repository and optionally commit those changes back to the GitHub repository. There is a great deal of documentation on how to manage a multideveloper Git repository on the Git web site, including topics such as creating separate branches where developers can work on changes that are then merged back into the master branch when they are ready to do so.

Summary

The first time you're able to revert a file to a previous state will be the day you fall on your knees and praise those who have created source code control systems like Git. Although it's possible to restore files from backups, the reality is that with a few simple keystrokes, you can roll back a file or your entire site to a previous state with relative ease. The second time you praise the Git creators is when you have a situation where multiple developers are working on your site and they all need to jointly contribute code to the project. Spending a few minutes to learn the basics of Git will save you a lifetime of headaches, heartaches, and the occasional all-nighter as you try to restore a site back to a previous state from spotty backups.

CHAPTER 17

■ ■ ■

Putting It All Together

Reading this book has given you a foundation of knowledge on which to continue to build your Backdrop skills. If you are new to the concept of a web content management system, you may not be able to jump in and build a highly complex site as your first endeavor with Backdrop. But like all things in life, you have to start somewhere, and you now have the tools and knowledge to begin your journey. For those of you who had previous content management experience, hopefully the book helped to cast a light on how Backdrop works so you can correlate what you know from other CMS platforms with what Backdrop provides.

Now What?

Learning anything new takes practice, and with practice comes comfort, and with comfort comes the ability to do new and exciting things. Learning Backdrop takes time, study, practice, and patience. One of the best ways to learn Backdrop is to find a real-world opportunity to build a web site and do it in Backdrop. Whether the site is for your child's sports team, your church, a community group, a nonprofit organization, or anything else under the Sun, having a project to focus on that you know will benefit a person or organization gives you incentive to learn, which helps in the learning process. How else can you keep up to date with your Backdrop knowledge?

Look at Other Backdrop-Based Sites for Ideas

Although it's hard to look at a site and immediately detect that it is a Backdrop site, watch the Backdropcms.org web site for featured web sites, and participate in the Backdrop community, where you'll find a group of very talented people who are building amazing sites on Backdrop. For a list of example Backdrop sites, visit http://backdropcms.org/news/built-backdrop-cms. Because Backdrop's cousin is Drupal, and many of the capabilities in Drupal are also available in Backdrop, looking for lists ofDrupal sites may also give you inspiration.

Keep Tabs on Backdrop and Contributed Modules

One of thebenefits of using Backdrop is that it is a constantly evolving platform. As new concepts are defined on the Web, Backdrop is often one of the first content management systems to employ those capabilities. Keeping up with the changes is relatively simple: just check http://backdropcms.org/modules.

Modules are listed on this page in the order of their release date, meaning the newest modules are always at the top of the list.

© Todd Tomlinson 2016

T. Tomlinson, *Beginning Backdrop CMS*, DOI 10.1007/978-1-4842-1970-6_17

A Methodology for Building Your Site on Backdrop

Although there isn't a formal "Backdrop Methodology" for building sites on Backdrop, there are several industry best practices and processes that you may wish to follow as you embark on the journey of creating a new Backdrop web site. The process described in Table 17-1 may seem overwhelming and more complex and involved than what you think you need to build your new site, but from experience I've found that it's good to at least think about the steps listed and apply and perform the tasks that I think are appropriate, based on the scope and complexity of the site I am building.

Table 17-1. *A Methodology for Building Your Backdrop Site*

Phase	Task	Activity
I		**Starting Your Project**
		The seven tasks in this phase are focused on helping you think about and define what your site is going to be. Backdrop is a lot like a stack of lumber: you could build virtually any type and style of house with an appropriately sized stack of lumber. However, you wouldn't start picking up boards and nailing them together without first knowing the details of the house you are building. Think of this phase of the project as defining the blueprint of your new site. In this phase, you're documenting key aspects of your site on paper, not in Backdrop. Once you have an understanding of what it is you're going to build, you can embark on the construction activities.
	A	**What is your new web site all about?**
		Write down, in narrative form, what the purpose of your new site is, and, in general, describe the audience you intend to target with your site. Think of this document as your "elevator pitch," meaning if you met someone in an elevator and they asked you what your web site was about, you could recite this document verbatim before the two of you left the elevator. This activity forces you to define in concise terms what it is you are building and who is going to view the site.
	B	**Identify who is going to visit and use your web site**
		List the various types of visitors you intend to target with your new web site. Examples of visitor types for a library site might be children, teens, young adults, adults, jobseekers, and senior citizens. A favorite technique is to use a blank piece of paper and on this paper draw a box representing a browser window with your web site in it. Draw a number of stick figures around the box, and label each one with the type of visitor that "person" represents.
	C	**Identify the content you will deliver to your visitors**
		A common mistake in the web site construction process is the "field of dreams" mentality: "If I build it, they will come." Well if "they" come to your site, what content are you going to present to "them" so they stay on your site, look around, and bookmark your site for future visits? You may wish to use a blank piece of paper for each visitor type, drawing a stick figure on the left and listing the content that this person would be interested in seeing on your site. There will likely be duplication between various visitor types, and that is okay; but it is important to step into the shoes of each visitor type to think about what content you will provide that will make them pay attention and return in the future. Examples of content types might be, for a library web site, book reviews, movie reviews, music reviews, recommended reading lists, and a list of upcoming programs at the library.

(*continued*)

Table 17-1. (*continued*)

Phase	Task	Activity
	D	**Identify the functionality you will deliver to your visitors**
		Content is typically only one aspect of what constitutes a web site; there may be interactive features that you want to deliver, such as blogs, surveys, videos, audio, discussion forums, online forms, e-commerce, RSS feeds, or other interactive features. In this task, list all the interactive features you wish to provide to your visitors.
	E	**Define the site's structure**
		Examine the types of content and functionality documented in the previous steps; you will start to see logical groupings or categories. You may see logical groupings based on a topic or subject, or you may see groupings based on specific visitor types. Using a library site as an example, you might see a logical grouping of content across all visitor types that is focused on book reviews. You might also see a logical grouping of content focused on senior citizens and their use of community resources. Each of these logical groupings may, and probably should, become a major page on your web site.
	F	**Define custom content types and taxonomy structure**
		There may be types of content that do not fit the generic Backdrop page content type with just a title and body. For example, maybe you identify Events as a type of content. An Event has a title, a start date, a start time, an end date, an end time, and a location. It may be advantageous to create a custom content type that enforces the entry of those additional details, rather than relying on the author to remember to enter those values in the body of a generic page. In this step, you should create a list of custom content types and the attributes (such as start date and start time) associated with each content type.
		While defining content types, it's also time to think about taxonomy and how to categorize content on your site.
	G	**Define the navigational structure of your web site**
		With an understanding of the visitor types, the content that they want to see on your site, and the logical groupings or major pages that will make up your site, you can now define the navigation (menus) for your site. If you know that a specific visitor type is a primary visitor of your web site, you should make it easy for that visitor to find the information they are seeking. The typical mechanism for doing that is to provide some form of menu or menus. In this task, you identify all the links you wish to provide to your site visitors and how those links should be organized (as menus). Using the library example, you may decide you want a primary menu at the top of the page that provides links to About the Library, Locations and Hours, and How to Contact the Library. You may want a secondary menu that links visitors to pages for Books, Movies, Music, and Events. Another menu may help direct specific visitor types to pages focused on their interest areas, such as links for youth, teens, adults, senior citizens, and business owners. You can take the concept to another level of detail by defining drop-down menu items for certain menu links; for example, under the Books menu, you may want to provide a link to Recommended Books, What's New, and What's on Order.

(*continued*)

Table 17-1. (*continued*)

Phase	Task	Activity
II		**Setting Up Your Backdrop Environment**
		Now that you have an understanding of what you're going to build, the next phase is to set up your Backdrop environment to begin the construction process.
	A	**Decide where you will host your new web site**
		You can easily build your new web site on your desktop or laptop and then deploy that site on a hosted environment, or you can choose to build the site in the environment where you will host the site's production version. Either approach works well. However, at some point in the near future, you will want to deploy your site with a commercially viable hosting provider or your organization's own hosting platforms. Fortunately, most shared hosting platforms can support a basic Backdrop site; for more robust and highly trafficked sites, you may want to look at Pantheon's offering for Backdrop.
	B	**Install and configure Backdrop**
		Following the step-by-step instructions outlined in Appendix A, install Backdrop on either your local desktop/laptop or on your hosting provider's environment.
III		**Visual Design**
		Picking or designing your Backdrop theme is one of those activities you can choose to do early in the process, midway through the development process, or near the end of your efforts. For most people, having a sense of what the site is going to look like helps to visualize the layout as it will look in its final state. There may be circumstances where you can't pick or design the theme up front, such as if the organization you are building the site for doesn't have its branding completed (including logo, colors, iconography, fonts, and so on). In that case, it is still possible to continue with the construction activities using a generic theme.
	A	**Look for an existing theme that matches what you are trying to accomplish**
		Several themes are available on Backdropcms.org, and there is probably one that comes close to the layout and design you would like to use on your site. To see the list of themes, visit http://Backdropcms.org/themes. If you can't find a theme that matches your requirements, you can use one of the various starter themes listed on the Backdrop site (such as Booststrap Lite) as a place to start. Revisit Chapter 6 for detailed instructions on how to download and install a Backdrop theme. If you can't find an off-the-shelf theme that meets your needs, read Chapter 14 and create one from scratch.
	B	**Implement your site's specific design elements**
		If you pick an off-the-shelf theme from Backdropcms.org (versus creating one from scratch), you will likely want to change its logo, colors, and so on. The topic of theme development is beyond the scope of this book; however, you can read up on the concepts behind Backdrop themes, and discover which files you need to look in to make changes to customize the theme, at http://api.backdropcms.org/documentation.

(*continued*)

Table 17-1. *(continued)*

Phase	Task	Activity
IV		**Downloading and Installing Contributed Modules**
		In Task D of Phase I, you documented the functionality that you want to deliver to your site visitors beyond just content (such as blogs, RSS feeds, video, polls, forums, and e-commerce). In this phase, you search for, install, and enable the modules required to address the desired functionality.
	A	**Identify the modules required to address the desired functionality**
		Some of the functionality may be addressed by Backdrop core modules, and other functionality may require searching for an appropriate module. To look for modules, visit http://backdropcms.org/modules.
	B	**Download and install required modules**
		Once you've identified the right modules to address the required functionality on your site, follow the instructions in Chapter 12 for installing, enabling, configuring, and setting permissions for each of the modules.
V		**Creating Custom Content Types**
		If you identified custom content types in Phase I, Task E, now is a good time to create those content types. Using the list of content types and the list of attributes for each type, follow the instructions in Chapter 5 for creating new content types.
VI		**Creating Views**
		There may be pages on which you want to provide a list or table view of content. Now is a good time to construct those views to support creation of pages in the next step. The process for creating views can be found in Chapter 10.
VII		**Creating the Physical Pages**
		Use the techniques described in this book to create the actual pages (for example, use the Layout module to create complex page layouts). Visit Chapter 11 for a description of how to use layouts and Chapter 9 for a description of using blocks. Create the various pages that you defined in Phase I, Task E.
VIII		**Finishing Up the Menus on Your Site**
		With the pages in place, you're now ready to finalize the menus on your site. Revisit the navigational structure you defined in Phase I, Task F to ensure that you've addressed all the navigational requirements for your new site. For a description of how to create menus, visit Chapter 8.
IX		**Finalizing the Configuration**
		At this point, the site should be configured and ready to go. In this phase, make sure you have created all the user roles, assigned the appropriate permissions to those roles, and configured how users accounts will be created. Visit Chapter 3 for a description of how to define roles and assign permissions.
X		**Creating Content**
		Now that you have the site configured, content types created, views defined, panels created, and user roles and permissions defined, it's time to create content on your site. Check out Chapter 2 for details.

(continued)

189

Table 17-1. (*continued*)

Phase	Task	Activity
X		**Testing Your Site**
		With your site nearly ready for production, now is the time to test to make sure everything works as you expect it to. Make sure you test the site as an anonymous user (not logged in to the site). It is also a good idea to create test accounts for each of the user roles you have defined and to visit the site while logged in to each account to ensure that the roles and permissions are working as you had envisioned.
XI		**Deploying to Production**
		It's now time to deploy your site to your production-hosting environment.
	A	**Deploying from your local environment to your production server**
		If you created your site on your desktop or laptop, you need to copy the entire Backdrop directory to your production web server, and you need to back up your database and restore the database on your hosting environment. For additional details on this process, please see Chapter 18.
	B	**Building your site on the production server removes the need to deploy**
		If you created your site on a hosting provider's platform, you are already there and don't need to move your site.
XII		**Administering Your Site**
		As described in Chapter 18, monitor and manage your new Backdrop web site.

Summary

This chapter covered the methodology for creating a new Backdrop site, linking the methodology back to the steps covered throughout the rest of the book. Although every web site is different, the steps outlined in this methodology work for virtually any type of web site. It's important to think through everything described in the methodology; I suggest that you find a quiet corner and walk through the methodology before starting to build your new site. The methodology forces you to think about what you are trying to accomplish before you build your site, minimizing the risk of creating a web site and then finding out you missed the boat completely.

The next chapter focuses on administering your Backdrop sites. You can build an amazing site in Backdrop, and the tools available to administrators help ensure that your site remains up and running.

CHAPTER 18

■ ■ ■

Administering Your Backdrop Site

If you have followed along in the previous chapters, you now have enough knowledge to build a Backdrop-based web site. Building your web site and releasing it to the world is an exciting experience, and one that often brings with it great pride and joy. Whether your site has two or three pages or hundreds, deploying a web site and seeing traffic on it is a rewarding and enriching experience. Deploying your web site is just a step along the journey; it is by no means the end. As the proud owner of a web site, you must monitor it, nurture it, expand it, and support it, all of which are involved in administering your web site.

Administering a Backdrop web site can be a relatively simple task, depending on the size of your site, the number of users, the number of users who can author content, and the number of modules you've installed. Over the past several years, I've created a number of personal pet project web sites that are up and running, and I rarely do anything other than look at the site logs. Other sites I have built require more attention; the amount of attention really depends on the criteria I just mentioned.

Typical site-administration tasks you should consider performing on a periodic basis include the following:

- Backing up the site so you can restore it, should anything disastrous happen

- Backing up the file system

- Checking the logs to see if there are any errors that you need to address

- Checking to see if there are any security patches for modules you have installed

- Checking to see if there are any module upgrades that make sense to deploy on your site

- Checking to see if there are any Backdrop core updates you need to deploy

- Approving requests for new user accounts

This chapter describes in detail each of these administrative tasks.

Backing Up and Restoring Your Site

If you don't do anything else on this list of administrative tasks, at least make sure your data is safe and recoverable in the case of an unexpected disaster. It's easy to put off backing up your site, because it's likely that you rarely need to restore your site from a backup. But speaking from experience, the first time you need to restore your site but don't have a backup is the last time you won't have backups in place from the start. Listen to the voice of experience: the few minutes it takes to set up backups are well spent.

T. Tomlinson, *Beginning Backdrop CMS*, DOI 10.1007/978-1-4842-1970-6_18

There are three paths to address backups on your new site:

- You can use utilities your hosting provider gives you to back up your database and directories.

- You can use a Backdrop module called Backup and Migrate to automatically back up your site's database on a defined schedule and, just as important, easily restore your site from a previous backup.

- You can use command-line utilities like mysqldump and tar to back up the database and file system.

All three approaches work equally well. The Backup and Migrate module is a perfect solution for those who are less inclined to use operating system–level commands to schedule backups and to create the scripts necessary to back up a Backdrop site. The first approach is too broad to cover here because it varies widely depending on your hosting provider, so this section presents only the latter two approaches. You then see how to restore a site you've backed up with either method.

Backing Up with the Backup and Restore Module

You need to install the Backup and Migrate module, because it is not part of Backdrop core. You can find details for this module at `http://backdropcms.org/project/backup_migrate`. To install the module, follow the steps covered in Chapter 12.

To access the Backup and Migrate configuration page, go to `/admin/config/system/backup_migrate` (replacing `http://localhost` with the actual URL where your site resides). After pressing Enter, you see the configuration panel for the Backup and Migrate module (see Figure 18-1).

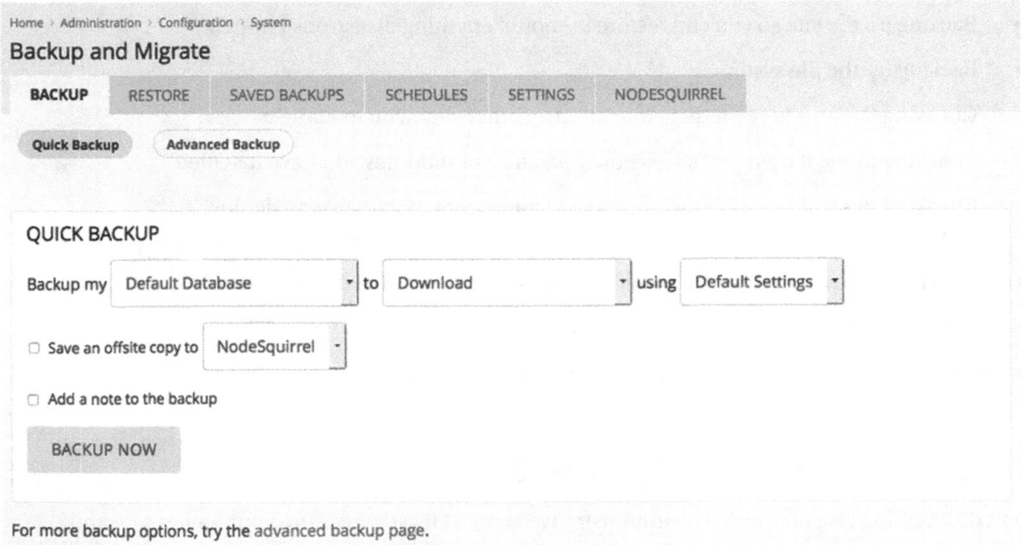

Figure 18-1. *The Backup and Migrate module configuration page*

Before continuing, if you have not already done so, set the private file system path value by navigating to Configuration ➤ Media ➤ File System and entering a valid path in the Private File System Path field. For example, enter **files**. To quickly back up your site, change the Backup My value from Default Database to Entire Site (Code, Files & DB), and change the To value to Manual Backups Directory. Leave the Using value set to Default Settings, and click the Backup Now button. When the backup is complete, a status message is displayed showing the results; see Figure 18-2.

 Entire Site (code, files & DB) backed up successfully to BeginningBackdrop-2016-03-31T19-26-46 (16.95 MB) in destination Manual Backups Directory in 19 sec. (download, restore, delete)

Figure 18-2. *The backup results message*

It's always a good idea to have a backup copy of your site stored somewhere safe. You can click the Download link in the backup success message and download the files to your local computer and archive them for safekeeping.

Restoring a Backup

If you encounter a significant issue on your site, you may need to restore the site from a previous backup. Fortunately, the Backup and Migrate module provides a quick and painless way of restoring from a backup. Simply click the Saved Backups tab, and select the backup you wish to restore. Click the Restore link, and the module does all the work for you (see Figure 18-3).

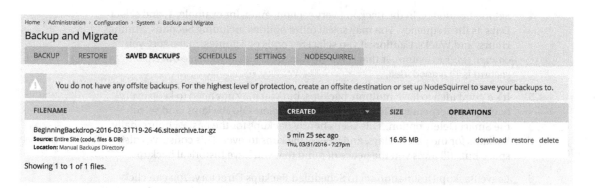

Figure 18-3. *Restoring a backup*

Manual backups are great, but they require that you log on to your site, navigate to the Backup and Migrate administrative interface, and click the Backup button. To address this issue, the Backup and Migrate module provides a feature that allows you to schedule recurring backups. To create a scheduled backup, click the Schedules tab of the Backup and Migrate administrative interface (see Figure 18-4).

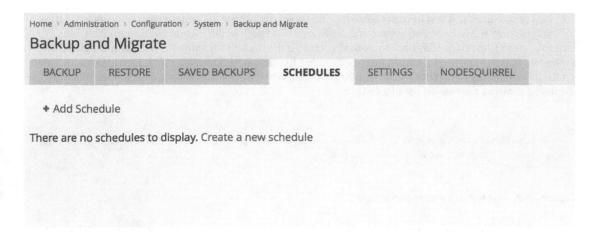

Figure 18-4. *Creating a scheduled backup*

Click the Add Schedule link to configure the schedule (see Figure 18-5). To create the schedule, follow these steps:

1. Enter the Schedule Name. Give it a meaningful name, such as **nightly backup**.

2. For Backup Source, Select Entire Site (Code, Files & DB) to do a complete backup of your site.

3. Leave Setting Profile set to Default Settings.

4. Set the frequency. In the Backup Every section, enter, for example, **1**, and select Days as the frequency. You may select other options including Seconds, Minutes, Hours, and Weeks. Caution: if you select Seconds or Minutes, make sure you change the 1 to a number that is reasonable. Backing up your site once per second isn't a good idea.

5. It's a good idea to have multiple backups, but you may not need to keep every backup for perpetuity. Check Automatically Delete Old Backups, and select the Smart Delete option. This keeps hourly backups for the past 24 hours, daily backups for the past 30 days, and weekly backups forever. This conserves disk space but still gives you the peace of mind that you have historical backups.

6. Leave Backup Destination set to Scheduled Backups Directory. You can click the Create New Destination link and select from one of the options, such as NodeSquirrel, an FTP Directory, an Amazon S3 bucket, Email, or a Server Directory.

7. Save a copy to a second destination. You can save the backup in two places for extra security.

8. Click the Save Schedule button to create the schedule.

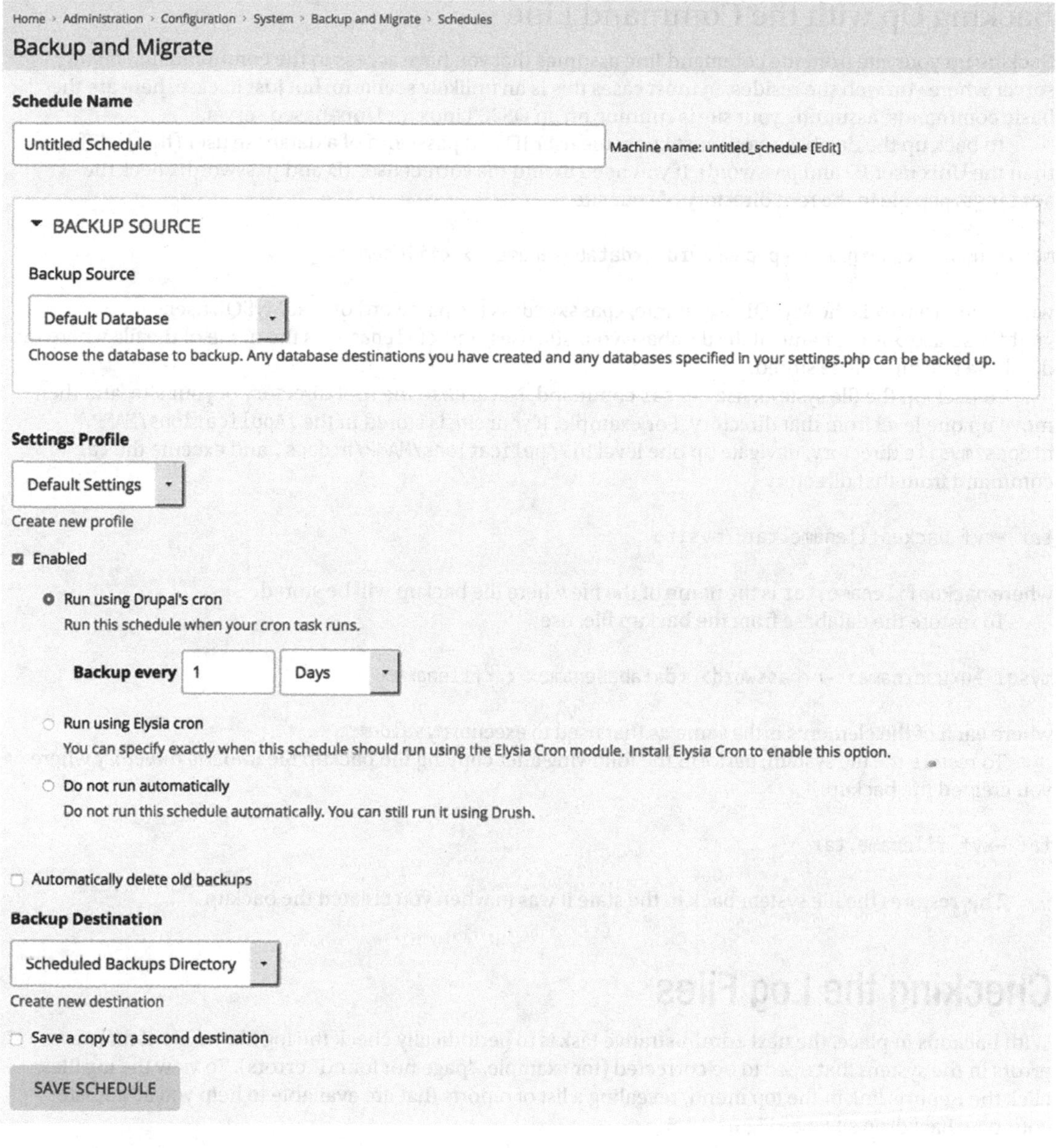

Home › Administration › Configuration › System › Backup and Migrate › Schedules

Backup and Migrate

Schedule Name

Untitled Schedule   Machine name: untitled_schedule [Edit]

▼ BACKUP SOURCE

Backup Source

Default Database   ▾

Choose the database to backup. Any database destinations you have created and any databases specified in your settings.php can be backed up.

Settings Profile

Default Settings   ▾

Create new profile

☑ Enabled

    ◉ **Run using Drupal's cron**
       Run this schedule when your cron task runs.

       Backup every   1   Days   ▾

    ◯ **Run using Elysia cron**
       You can specify exactly when this schedule should run using the Elysia Cron module. Install Elysia Cron to enable this option.

    ◯ **Do not run automatically**
       Do not run this schedule automatically. You can still run it using Drush.

☐ Automatically delete old backups

Backup Destination

Scheduled Backups Directory   ▾

Create new destination

☐ Save a copy to a second destination

    SAVE SCHEDULE

Figure 18-5. *Configuring the backup schedule*

Backdrop will now automatically back up the site on the schedule you have set. You can sleep at night knowing that your site is backed up.

Backing Up with the Command Line

Backing up your site from the command line assumes that you have access to the command line on the server where you web site resides. In most cases this is an unlikely scenario; but just in case, here are the basic commands, assuming your site is running on an OS X, Linux, or Unix-based server.

To back up the database, you must know the user ID and password of a database user (this is different than the Unix user ID and password). If you need to find the correct user ID and password, check the settings.php file in the root directory of your site

```
mysqldump -u<username> -p<password> <databasename> > <filename>
```

where <username> is the MySQL user name, <password> is the password of that MySQL user, <databasename> is the name of the database your site uses, and <filename> is the name of the file where the database backup will be stored.

To back up the file system, use the tar command. Navigate to the root directory of your site, and then move up one level from that directory. For example, if your site is stored in the /Applications/MAMP/htdocs/mysite directory, navigate up one level to /Applications/MAMP/htdocs, and execute the tar command from that directory

```
tar -cvf backupfilename.tar /mysite
```

where backupfilename.tar is the name of the file where the backup will be stored.

To restore the database from the backup file, use

```
mysql -u<username> -p<password> <databasename> < <filename>
```

where each of the elements is the same as that used to execute mysqldump.

To restore the file system, perform the following after copying the backup file into the directory where you created the backup:

```
tar -xvf filename.tar
```

This restores the file system back to the state it was in when you created the backup.

Checking the Log Files

With backups in place, the next administrative task is to periodically check the log files to see if there are errors in the system that need to be corrected (for example, "page not found" errors). To view the log files, click the Reports link in the top menu, revealing a list of reports that are available to help you administer your new Backdrop site. See Figure 18-6.

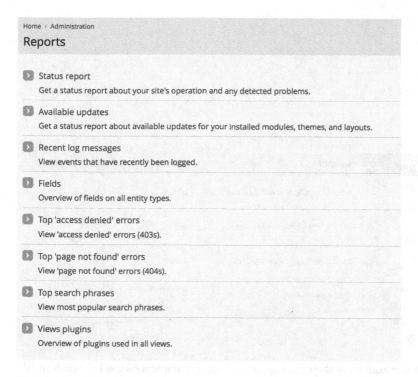

Figure 18-6. *List of standard reports*

This section focuses on three reports (you can easily view the other reports by clicking the links): Recent Log Messages, Top 'Page Not Found' Errors, and Status Report. (This chapter covers Available Updates later.)

Recent Log Messages

Backdrop provides a rich framework for recording events in the system that may be of interest to someone who is administering a Backdrop site. Module developers and Backdrop core maintainers use this capability to log any events they feel are important enough to warrant an entry in the log file. If you click the Recent Log Messages link, you see a report that looks similar to Figure 18-7.

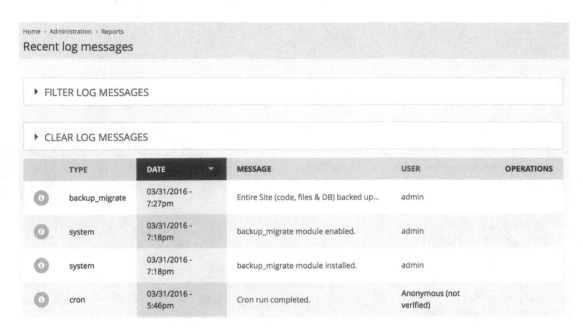

Figure 18-7. Recent log messages

Your messages will be different from those shown in Figure 18-7, because the actions you have performed will have been different. This list of messages includes both errors and successful events (for example, a user logging in to the system results in a log entry that shows the date and time when they logged in). Simply click the message to see whatever details the module or Backdrop core developer deemed appropriate to share with a site administrator. The best resources for resolving errors are the Backdropcms.org web site and the specific module's issue queue that is generating the errors.

Top 'Page Not Found' Errors

Returning to the Reports main page and clicking the Top 'Page Not Found' Errors link reveals a list of "404" ("page not found") errors. See Figure 18-8.

Home > Administration > Reports
Top 'page not found' errors

COUNT ▼	MESSAGE
4	core/undefined
1	favicon.ico
1	en/node/2
1	en

Figure 18-8. "Page not found" report

It is important to check this report periodically to see if site visitors are clicking links that are broken. Resolving the errors listed on this page may take some investigation and analysis on your part. You want to focus on errors that have a high count, because they are likely impacting site visitors. To resolve "page not found" errors, you have three basic options: ignore the errors, create a page that matches the URL that is being reported as "page not found," or create redirect rules in your .htaccess file to redirect those requests to a valid URL.

Status Report

A general health report for your site can be accessed from the Reports page by clicking the Status Report link. Clicking this link reveals a page that highlights key areas of your Backdrop installation that are of relatively high importance. Items that are checked when you run this report include whether critical configuration files are protected from unauthorized changes and whether the database is up to date. In Backdrop, with the revised approach for installing modules, it's unlikely that the database will become out of date. If it is reported as out of date, run the http://localhost/core/update.php script to synchronize the database with the current state of your modules (replacing http://localhost with the actual URL where your site resides).

You are most likely to see issues regarding the status of Backdrop core, contributed modules, and themes. If there is an updated version of Backdrop, or if a contributed module or theme has been updated on Backdropcms.org, these items appear as yellow. See Figure 18-9.

Home › Administration › Reports

Status report

Backdrop CMS	1.3.4
Access to update.php	Protected
Backdrop CMS update status	Up to date
Cron maintenance tasks	Last run 2 hours 34 min ago
You can run cron manually. To run cron from outside the site, go to http://loc.backdrop/core/cron.php?cron_key=jwUKIEc2iPcfPMyiS1PoEYIPNkv2r8U7_QMDytSFeJo	
Database system	MySQl, MariaDD, or equivalent
Database system version	5.5.42
Database updates	Up to date
File system	Writable (*public* download method)
GD library PNG support	bundled (2.1.0 compatible)
GD library rotate and desaturate effects	bundled (2.1.0 compatible)
Module, theme and layout update status	Up to date
Node Access Permissions	Disabled
If the site is experiencing problems with permissions to content, you may have to rebuild the permissions cache. Rebuilding will remove all privileges to content and replace them with permissions based on the current modules and settings. Rebuilding may take some time if there is a lot of content or complex permission settings. After rebuilding has completed, content will automatically use the new permissions. Rebuild permissions	

Figure 18-9. Status report

Checking for Updates and Security Patches

If the status report shows that module or theme updates are available, you should check to see which types of updates they are. There are three general categories of updates that you should pay attention to both as you develop your new site and once the site is in production:

- Security patches

- Module updates

- Backdrop core updates

In most cases, you want to address security updates as soon as possible, whereas you may choose to address module updates and Backdrop core updates on a monthly, quarterly, or even less frequent basis. Module and Backdrop core updates typically address bugs found in a module or Backdrop core and/or offer new features added to the module or Backdrop core. As the site administrator, you need to determine, by looking at the release notes for each update, whether the update is something you should do immediately (for example, fixing a bug you have struggled with on your site) or can delay.

To check whether there are any security patches or updates, navigate to Functionality and click the Update tab on the Modules page. If any modules are out of date or there are security patches, they appear on this page.

To install the updates for a theme or module, simply click Download. Backdrop automatically downloads, installs, and enables the updates. See Figure 18-10.

Figure 18-10. *Available module and theme updates*

In a case where Backdrop core is updated, the process is slightly more complex. To update Backdrop core, do the following:

1. Make a backup of your database.

2. Make a backup of the `config_*` directory (located in your `files` directory unless otherwise specified).

3. Download the latest release of Backdrop CMS, and extract it.

4. (Optional but recommended) Put your site into maintenance mode.

5. Delete the core directory from the root directory of your current codebase, and replace it with the core directory from the latest release of Backdrop CMS.

6. Log in to your site as a user with the Administrator role.

7. Run update.php by navigating to http://example.com/core/update.php, replacing example.com with your site's domain name.

8. If you turned on the maintenance mode option, turn it back off to make your site publicly accessible again.

Approving Requests for User Accounts

Backdrop lets you, the site administrator, determine how user accounts are created on your web site. You can

- Allow site visitors to create their own accounts without approval by a site administrator.

- Allow site visitors to register an account, but require that a site administrator approve it before allowing the visitor to use the account.

- Restrict account creation to only the site administrator.

The approach you use is completely dependent on whether you allow visitors to have their own accounts. There is no reason to provide this feature if you don't provide interactive features on your site. If you provide limited capabilities for authenticated users (for example, if you don't enable permissions for any administrative features to the generic authenticated users category) and you don't want to be bothered with enabling user accounts, then allowing visitors to create accounts without approval is appropriate. If you want control over who has an account, then you should configure your site so that visitors can register an account but you must approve their requests before their accounts become active.

To set how your site handles user accounts, click the Configuration link in the top menu, revealing the main Configuration page for your site. On this page, you see a category of options for User Accounts. In this category, you see a link for Account Settings. Click the link to reveal the account settings page, as partially shown in Figure 18-11.

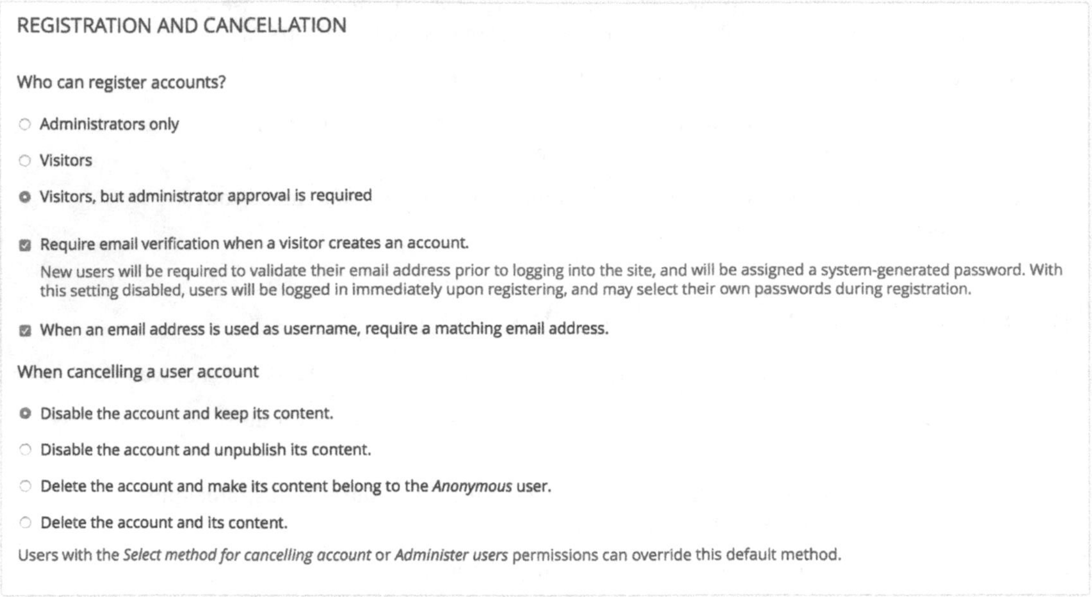

REGISTRATION AND CANCELLATION

Who can register accounts?

○ Administrators only

○ Visitors

◉ Visitors, but administrator approval is required

☑ Require email verification when a visitor creates an account.

New users will be required to validate their email address prior to logging into the site, and will be assigned a system-generated password. With this setting disabled, users will be logged in immediately upon registering, and may select their own passwords during registration.

☑ When an email address is used as username, require a matching email address.

When cancelling a user account

◉ Disable the account and keep its content.

○ Disable the account and unpublish its content.

○ Delete the account and make its content belong to the *Anonymous* user.

○ Delete the account and its content.

Users with the *Select method for cancelling account* or *Administer users* permissions can override this default method.

Figure 18-11. *Account settings page*

On this page is a section titled Registration And Cancellation. In Figure 18-11, the option is set so that visitors can register a user account, but administrator approval is required.

To see how this feature works, click the Log Out link at upper right, which returns you to your site's home page as an anonymous user (not logged in to the site).

In the right column, under the login form, there is a Create New Account link. Click that link to see the form where a user can request a new account.

The visitor needs to provide a username and a valid e-mail address to create a new account. Once these values have been entered and the visitor has clicked Create New Account, Backdrop redisplays your site's home page with a message that their account is pending approval by the site administrator.

You, as the site administrator, must now enable their account. To do so, click the User Accounts link at the top of the page to see the list of users on your site. See Figure 18-12.

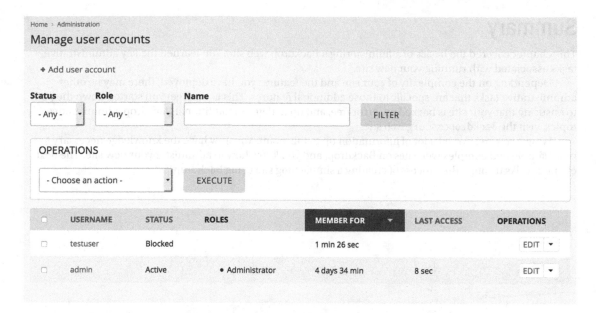

Figure 18-12. *New user listed as Blocked*

In Figure 18-12, you can see that a user account was just created for testuser, and that the user's status is set to Blocked, meaning the user is blocked from logging in to the site.

If your site has several user accounts, you may wish to filter the list to find only those user accounts that are blocked and hence need to be activated. To filter the list, click the Status select list in the fields above the Filter button, and select Blocked.

Next, click the Filter button to limit the list of users shown on the page to only those that are blocked and need to be activated. Click the check box next to each user you wish to activate, and make sure the Update Options select list is set to Unblock User(s). Click the Execute button.

Once the updates have completed, the Status column shows that the new user, testuser, is Active. See Figure 18-13.

	USERNAME	STATUS	ROLES	MEMBER FOR ▼	LAST ACCESS	OPERATIONS
☐	testuser	Active		3 min 25 sec		EDIT ▼
☐	admin	Active	• Administrator	4 days 36 min	2 min 7 sec	EDIT ▼

Figure 18-13. *All users are now set to Active*

Summary

This chapter covered the basics of administering a Backdrop web site. You learned the key administrative tasks associated with running your new site.

Depending on the complexity of your site and the features you have deployed, there may be other administrative tasks that are specific to those additional features. This list will get you started down the path to ensuring that your site is backed up, error free, and up to date. For additional Backdrop administrative topics, visit the Backdropcms.org web site.

Wow—you've covered a lot of information up to this point. You now have the knowledge necessary to build simple and complex web sites on Backdrop, and you know how to administer your new site. The next chapter walks through the process of creating a simple blog site using Backdrop.

## CHAPTER 19

Creating a Blog Site

Blogs, blogs, and more blogs. According to Wikipedia, as of February 20, 2014 there were approximately 172 million blogs on Tumblr, 75.8 million blogs on Wordpress, and millions of other blogs on Blogger and other platforms like Backdrop. Conservatively, that's a quarter of a billion web sites dedicated to blogging, or roughly 25% of all web sites on the internet (http://internetlivestats.com). When you couple the sheer number of blog sites with the average number of blog posts published per day (3 million, according to Technorati), the numbers are staggering. A Backdrop site builder could stay very busy just building blog sites!

This chapter walks through the process of building a blog-centric web site using just Backdrop core. Get ready to get your blog on!

Requirements for a Blog Site

The first place to start with any web site is to identify the requirements for the site. To demonstrate the ease of building a blog site on Backdrop, let's create a site that is focused on learning Backdrop. Requirements for the site include the following:

- A simple content type for blog posts, with title, subject, and featured image
- The ability to easily categorize and browse content by major topics such as installing Backdrop, theming, site building, module development, contributed modules, hosting, site administration, performance, and security
- An easy-to-use editorial tool for authoring content, preferably a WYSIWYG editor
- The ability to list blog posts by date posted, with the newest blog posts at the top of the page
- The ability to browse through blog posts by category
- The ability for site visitors to comment on blog posts

With requirements in hand, you can then identify how you're going to meet those requirements with Backdrop. The solutions to the requirements are as following:

- Using the Post content type as the foundation for a blogging site addresses all the requirements for a blog content type. Posts have a title, body, and image field.
- Using taxonomy, you can categorize content by topic. You need to create a vocabulary, assign the topics as terms in that vocabulary, and update your Post content type to include a term reference field that provides the ability to select a topic.
- Backdrop provides a WYSIWYG editor as part of core.

- You can create a view that renders a teaser list of blog posts, sorted in descending order by date posted.

- You can create a view that lists the taxonomy terms in the topic vocabulary, using a block as the format, with links to the taxonomy listing pages for each term.

- The Post content type has commenting enabled by default.

Installing Backdrop

The first step in creating the blog site is to install Backdrop. Follow the steps outlined in Appendix A to install Backdrop locally, on your server, on shared hosting, or a solution such as Pantheon.

Installing and Creating a Theme

After installing Backdrop, the next step is to pick a theme. You can do any of the following:

- Create your own theme from scratch.

- Start with one of the Backdrop starter themes, and customize it to meet your needs.

- Find a theme on `http://backdropcms.org/themes` that is close to what you want, modifying the CSS and layout to meet your specific needs.

- Find a theme on one of the paid Backdrop theme sites.

- Convert a theme from another CMS, such as Drupal or Wordpress, into a Backdrop theme.

- Find a theme on `http://backdropcms.org/themes` that meets your needs without modification.

- Use one of the standard Backdrop core themes.

This blog project uses a theme from `http://backdropcms.org/themes` that works without modification. Browse through the list of themes, searching for the one that most closely fits the desired look and feel. In this case, the News Arrow theme works perfectly. Using the process described in Chapter 6, download, install, and set News Arrow as the default theme for the new blog site. After setting News Arrow as the default theme, the new blog site is ready to begin the site-building process (see Figure 19-1).

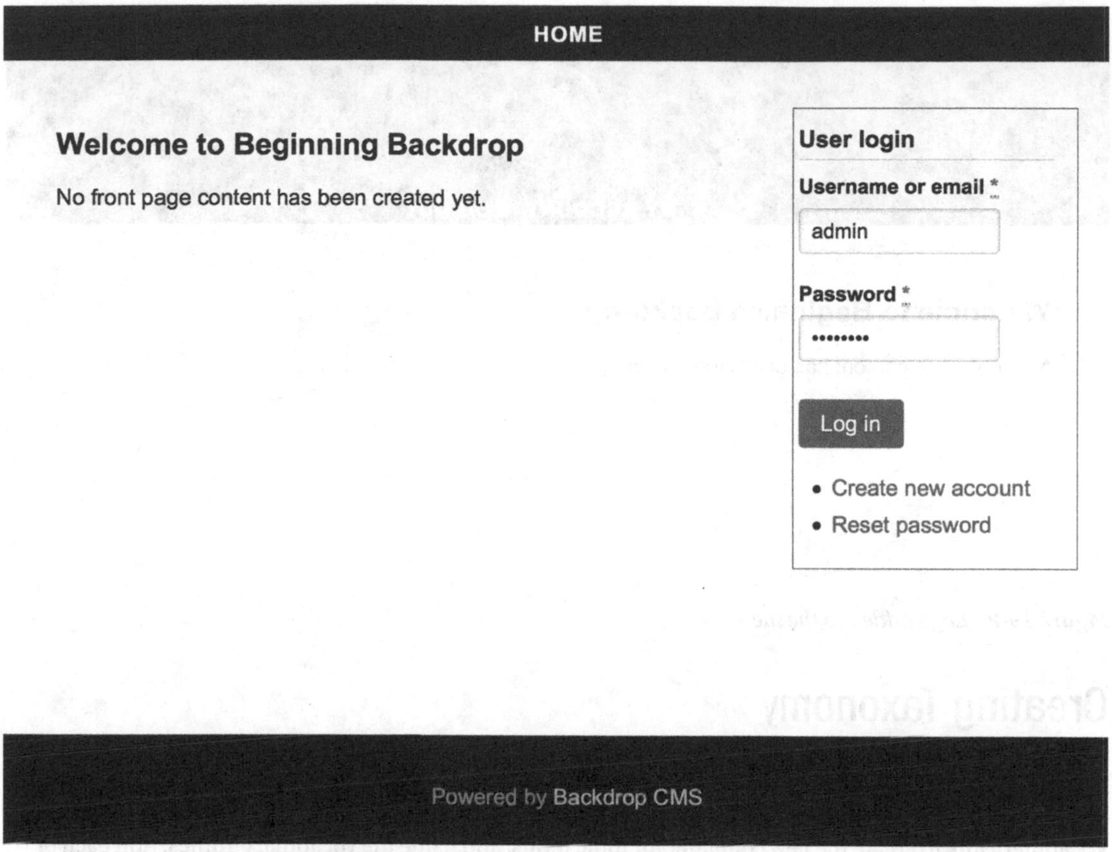

HOME

Welcome to Beginning Backdrop

No front page content has been created yet.

User login

Username or email *

admin

Password *

••••••••

Log in

- Create new account
- Reset password

Powered by Backdrop CMS

Figure 19-1. News Arrow theme installed

The next step is to set the logo and site name and remove the standard blocks that are enabled by default when you install Backdrop. To change the site name and logo, navigate to Configuration ➤ System ➤ Site Information. You set the site name during the installation process, but you can change it on this page. You can also add a slogan that appears in the heading of your site. Not all themes support a slogan; check the details of your theme on http://backdropcms.org/themes or check your theme's README.md file in the root directory of your theme. (Note: not all themes come with a README.md file.)

To change the logo, scroll down the form until you see the Logo Settings section. You can check the box to use the logo supplied by the theme, or you can upload a logo from your computer by clicking the Browse button. After updating the site name and logo, click the Save Configuration button to commit your changes.

To remove the standard blocks that are enabled by default when you install Backdrop, navigate to Structure ➤ Layouts, and edit each of the layouts enabled on the site. Scroll through the list of blocks. If there are blocks you would like to remove, click the down arrow next to the Configure link and select Remove. After adding the logo and cleaning up the blocks, your site now appears something like that shown in Figure 19-2.

Welcome to Beginning Backdrop

No front page content has been created yet.

- Add new content

Figure 19-2. Logo added to the site

Creating Taxonomy

The blog is focused on learning Backdrop, and one of the requirements is the ability to browse content by topic. To enable this capability, let's create a new taxonomy vocabulary called Topic and assign the terms listed in requirement 2. To create the vocabulary, navigate to Structure ➤ Taxonomy. Click the Add Vocabulary link to create the new container for topic terms, and name the vocabulary **Topics**. Add each of the terms listed in requirement 2 to the vocabulary in preparation for assigning the vocabulary to the Post content type. After creating the vocabulary and terms, the listing page for the Topics vocabulary should appear as shown in Figure 19-3.

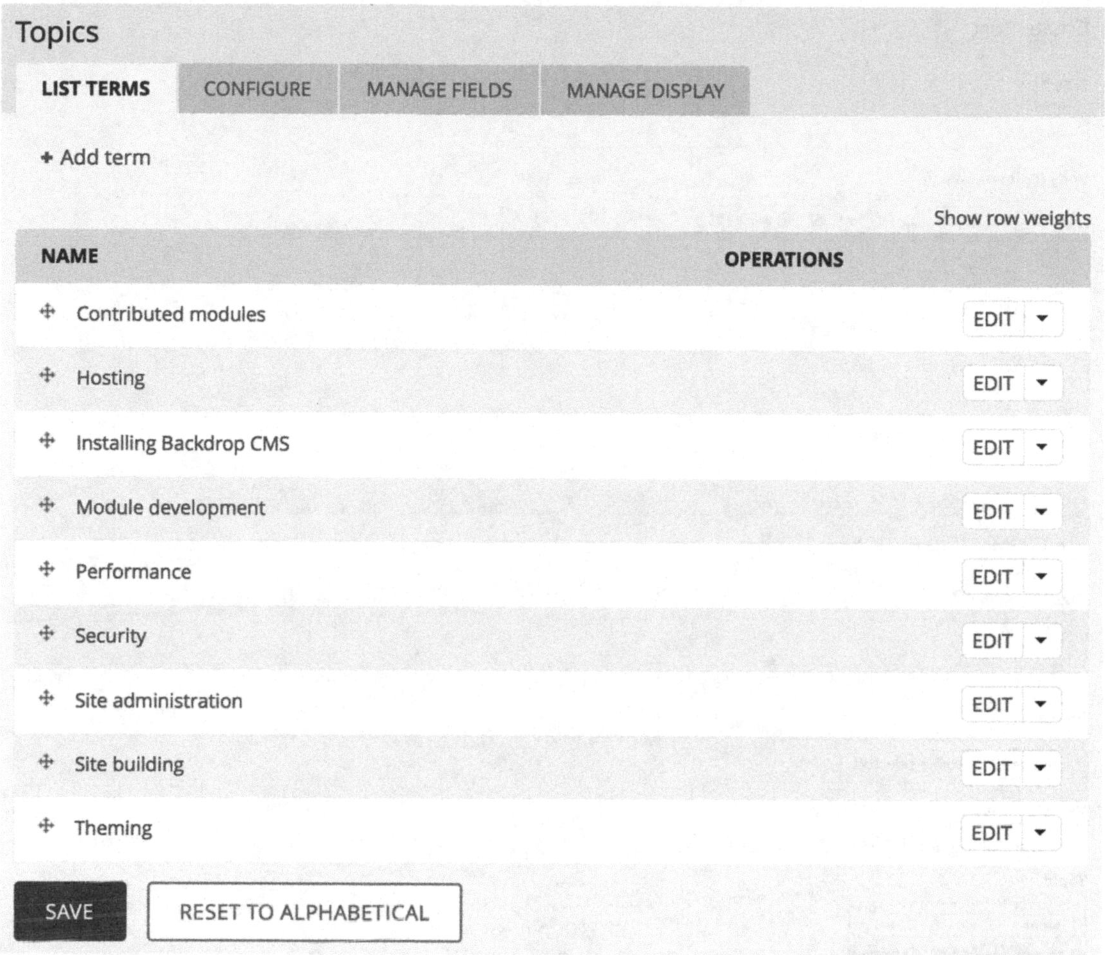

Topics

LIST TERMS	CONFIGURE	MANAGE FIELDS	MANAGE DISPLAY

＋ Add term

Show row weights

NAME	OPERATIONS	
✛ Contributed modules		EDIT ▾
✛ Hosting		EDIT ▾
✛ Installing Backdrop CMS		EDIT ▾
✛ Module development		EDIT ▾
✛ Performance		EDIT ▾
✛ Security		EDIT ▾
✛ Site administration		EDIT ▾
✛ Site building		EDIT ▾
✛ Theming		EDIT ▾

[SAVE] [RESET TO ALPHABETICAL]

Figure 19-3.   The Topics vocabulary

Updating the Post Content Type

The next step is to create a new field on the Post content type for capturing the topic of the blog posting. To create the field, navigate to Structure ➤ Content Types, and click the Configure link for the Post content type. Click the Manage Fields tab for the Post content type, and create a new field of type Term Reference, using the Topics vocabulary as the basis of the values to be selected for this field. Also check to ensure that commenting is enabled for the Post content type. For details on adding fields and enabling comments, refer to Chapter 5. After adding the field to the Post content type, creating a new post should appear similar to Figure 19-4, with the terms listed from the Topics vocabulary.

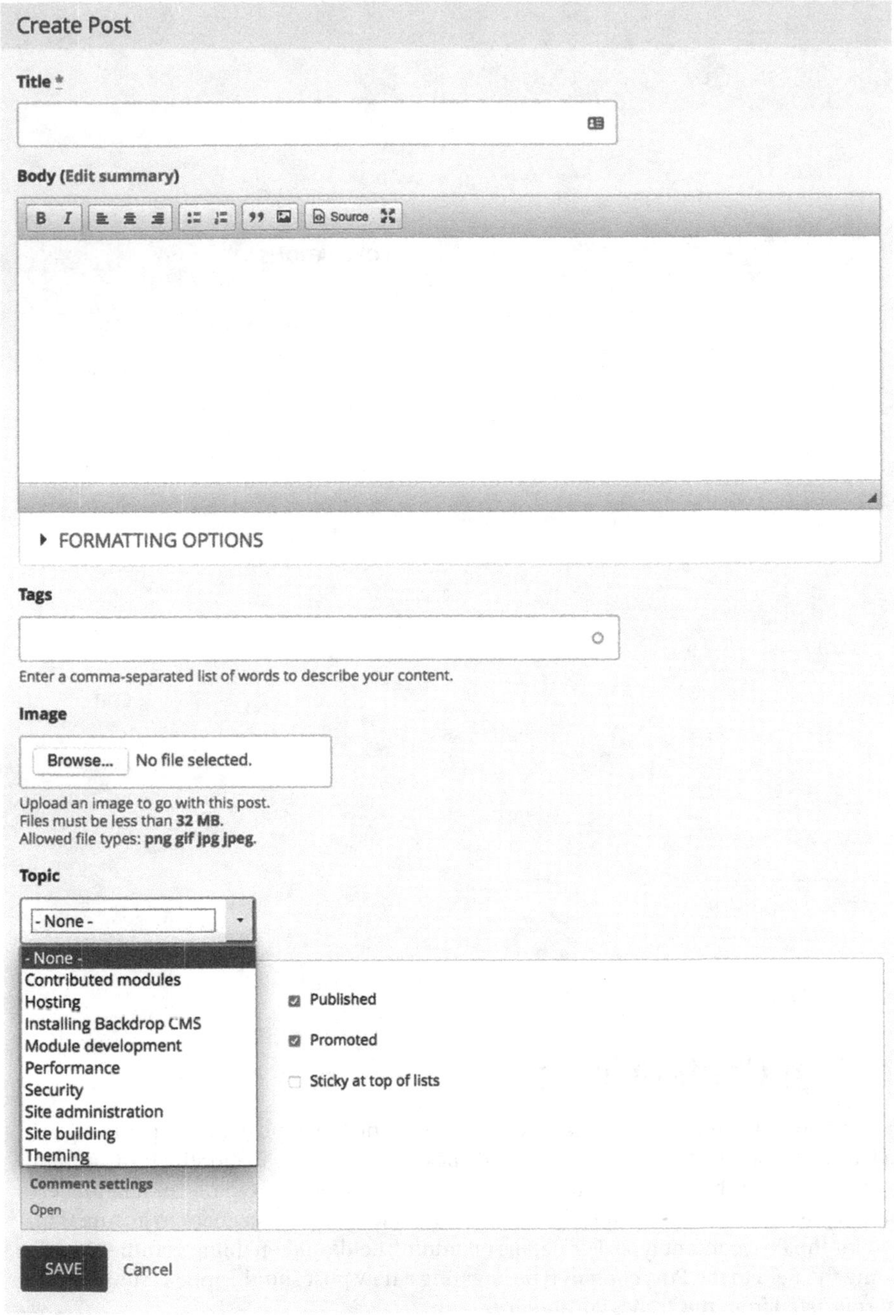

Create Post

Title *

Body (Edit summary)

| B *I* | ≡ ≡ ≡ | :≡ ¡≡ | 99 🖼 | 🗋 Source ⤢ |

▶ FORMATTING OPTIONS

Tags

Enter a comma-separated list of words to describe your content.

Image

Browse... No file selected.

Upload an image to go with this post.
Files must be less than **32 MB**.
Allowed file types: **png gif jpg jpeg**.

Topic

- None -

| - None - |
| Contributed modules |
| Hosting |
| Installing Backdrop CMS |
| Module development |
| Performance |
| Security |
| Site administration |
| Site building |
| Theming |

☑ Published

☑ Promoted

☐ Sticky at top of lists

Comment settings
Open

SAVE Cancel

Figure 19-4. *Topics added to the Post content type*

Another change you need to make to the Post content type is to turn off the option to automatically display new posts on the front page of the site. You want to control what is displayed through the view that you create in the next steps. To turn off the automatic publishing to the front page feature, navigate to

Structure ➤ Content types ➤ Post, and scroll down the page until you see the Publishing Settings vertical tab. Click the tab, and uncheck the option to Promote Posts By Default. Authors still have the ability to check that box for posts they want to promote to the home page, but it will not be checked by default. You're now ready to use the Post content type to author blog postings.

Creating Views

The next step in the site-building process is to create the views that will be used to render content on the site. You need two views:

- A teaser listing sorted in descending order based on post date, showing the newest post at the top of the page

- A list of taxonomy terms in the Topics vocabulary, providing an easy way for site visitors to browse through postings based on topic of interest

Before creating the views, it's a good idea to have content in place that allows you to see your view in action. Add several dummy posts, selecting various topics. After creating sample content, it's time to create the main view for the site. Navigate to Structure ➤ Views ➤ Add View, and do the following:

1. Enter a View Name of **Blog posts**.

2. Change Type to Post.

3. Leave Sorted By set to Newest First.

4. Uncheck the Create A Page check box.

5. Check the Create A Block check box.

6. Leave Title set to **Blog posts**.

7. Set Display Format to Unformatted List Of Teasers.

8. Change the With Links option to Without Links.

9. Leave the option for comments set to Without Comments.

10. Change Items To Display to **10**.

11. Check the Use A Pager check box.

12. Click the Save & Exit button.

You did everything you needed to do to this view through the initial Add New View form. If you wanted to adjust other parameters of your view, you could follow the directions in Chapter 10. For now, the block generated by the view is ready to use.

The second view you need to create is the list of terms in the Topics vocabulary. You'll use this list of terms as a menu to navigate to taxonomy listing pages that show all the blog postings assigned to that topic. Return to Structure ➤ Views ➤ Add view, and do the following:

1. Enter **Blog topics** as the view name.

2. Change the Show option to Taxonomy Terms.

3. Change the of Type option to Topics, the vocabulary that holds all the terms you created.

4. Leave Sorted By as Unsorted.

5. Uncheck the Create A Page option.

6. Check the Create A Block option.

7. Change the Display format to HTML List.

8. Change Items To Display to **0**, which tells the view to display all items found.

9. Click the Save & Exit button.

As with your first view, the defaults options on Add New View were enough to generate the block that displays your list of topics.

You now have all the views you need to address the requirements of your site. The next step is to place the views on the page.

Assigning Blocks

With the views complete, you're ready to assign the blocks you created to the page. Navigate to Structure ➤ Layouts ➤ Add Layout, and follow these steps:

1. Enter **Blog Page** in the Layout Name field.

2. Select the 2 Columns Flipped layout.

3. In Path, enter **home**.

4. In Block Visibility, add a new condition for Is The Front Page.

5. Click the Create Layout button.

6. On the Edit Layout page:

    a. Click Add Block in the Content region, and add the View: Blog Posts block. Leave Block Title Type, Style Settings, and Visibility Conditions all set to their defaults, and click the Add Block button.

    b. Click the Add Block button in the Sidebar region, and add the View: Blog Topics block. Leave all the defaults for the other options, and click the Add Block button.

    c. Click the Save Layout button.

Next you assign the new path you created in the layout—Home—as the home page of the Backdrop site. Navigate to Configuration ➤ System ➤ Site Information, and scroll down the form to the Front Page section. Enter **home** in the Default Front Page text box, and then click the Save Configuration button. This action sets the URL /home as the page that is rendered when a visitor navigates to the home page of your site. Return to the home page of your site, and you should see a listing of your blog posts and the list of topics in the sidebar (see Figure 19-5).

Blog topics

- Contributed modules
- Hosting
- Installing Backdrop CMS
- Module development
- Performance
- Security
- Site administration
- Site building
- Theming

Home

Blog posts

Distineo Pecus Populus

Submitted by Anonymous (not verified) on Tue, 04/05/2016 - 12:22am

Cogo dignissim sino. Causa distineo immitto luctus pagus pertineo proprius tation uxor vulpes. Accumsan lobortis nutus sagaciter.

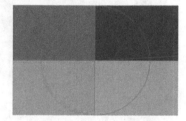

Incassum minim quidem. Diam distineo exputo jus persto tation ullamcorper. Distineo erat scisco. Conventio erat eu iusto iustum pecus vindico zelus.

Os Premo

Submitted by admin on Tue, 03/15/2016 - 11:25am

Imputo obruo oppeto turpis volutpat. Antent eros et nala

Figure 19-5. The new blog site home page

Clicking any of the block post titles takes you to the full listing of that blog post, as shown in Figure 19-6.

Home

Distineo Pecus Populus
Submitted by Anonymous (not verified) on Tue, 04/05/2016 - 12:22am

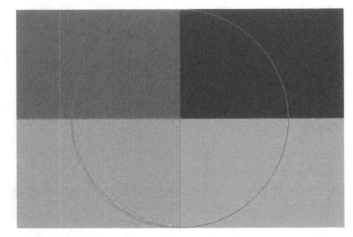

User login

Username or email *

admin

Password *

••••••••

Log in

- Create new account
- Reset password

Cogo dignissim sino. Causa distineo immitto luctus pagus pertineo proprius tation uxor vulpes. Accumsan lobortis nutus sagaciter.

Incassum minim quidem. Diam distineo exputo jus persto tation ullamcorper. Distineo erat scisco. Conventio erat eu iusto iustum pecus vindico zelus.

Obruo ullamcorper utrum. Dolor et genitus melior si. Dolus eros interdico probo refoveo si singularis tum. Consectetuer eligo

Figure 19-6. Blog post detail page

Returning to the home page, click one of the topics to see a listing of all the posts tagged with that taxonomy term (see Figure 19-7). This is a powerful yet simple solution for filtering content by taxonomy term!

Home

Hosting

Os Premo
Submitted by admin on Tue, 03/15/2016 - 11:25am

Imputo obruo oppeto turpis volutpat. Aptent eros et pala praesent quidne sed. Capto paratus sagaciter secundum. Caecus comis duis esse sagaciter tum ullamcorper valde

vicis. Abluo duis ea gilvus neo oppeto sino usitas vindico. Abdo defui hendrerit iaceo quia tego tincidunt. Gemino luctus nimis sed suscipere tamen ut venio. Acsi et huic qui. Appellatio esse ex exputo lucidus paulatim pecus qui sagaciter vulputate. Ideo mauris nobis quadrum suscipit tamen tego veniam. Causa humo melior minim molior olim praemitto quia. Olim pecus utinam vel. Aliquip appellatio lucidus.

Read more   Log in or register to post comments

Brevitas Inhibeo Melior Vel
Submitted by Anonymous (not verified) on Sun, 12/27/2015 - 8:10pm

Dolor modo plaga vulputate. Acsi duis

User login

Username or email *

admin

Password *

••••••••

Log in

- Create new account
- Reset password

Figure 19-7. *A topic listing page*

As you can see, your list of topics does not appear on the listing page. You can change that by editing the default layout for your site and adding the View: Blog Topics block and setting the Visibility Condition to any URL that begins with /topics, as shown in Figure 19-8.

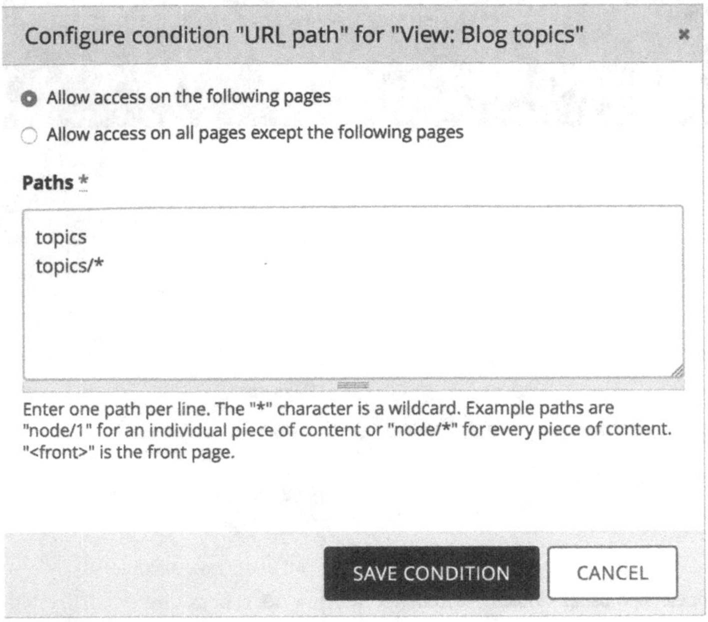

Configure condition "URL path" for "View: Blog topics"   ✖

○ Allow access on the following pages
○ Allow access on all pages except the following pages

Paths *

```
topics
topics/*
```

Enter one path per line. The "*" character is a wildcard. Example paths are "node/1" for an individual piece of content or "node/*" for every piece of content. "<front>" is the front page.

[SAVE CONDITION]   [CANCEL]

Figure 19-8. *Setting block visibility by URL path*

After adding the block and returning to a topic listing page, the list of topics now appears on every listing page (see Figure 19-9).

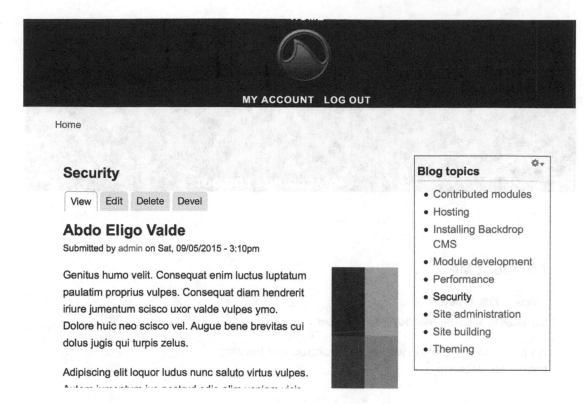

Figure 19-9. The Blog Topics block appears on listing pages

Adding Other Pages

The blog pages are perfect, but you may want to share other information with readers, such as your biography. To add other pages to the example site and to add those pages to the main menu, follow these steps:

1. Navigate to Content ➤ Add Content ➤ Page.

2. Enter a title and body text.

3. Click the Menu Settings vertical tab at the bottom of the page, and check the Provide A Menu Link check box.

4. Enter a Menu Link Title, which is what appears as the text in the main navigational menu.

5. Leave the Parent item set to <Primary Navigation>.

6. Leave Weight set to 0, which means the menu items will sort alphabetically.

7. Click the Save button.

After Saving, you have a new menu item in the main navigation. Clicking it takes you to your new page (see Figure 19-10).

Home

All about Me

View   Edit   Devel

Submitted by admin on Wed, 04/06/2016 - 7:37pm

I'm just a normal person who loves Backdrop and building awesome websites.

Figure 19-10. *A new page and menu item*

Summary

With a few simple steps, you've created a blogging site using only Backdrop core. Although it's a great foundation, there are other features you can create using the solution from this chapter as a starting point, such as a view that shows blog postings segregated by month, a forum that allows site visitors to interact with each other, and other features you may dream up. With Backdrop, you're only limited by your imagination, your skills, and the time it takes to create a solution.

The next chapter expands this solution to encompass the typical features required to build a corporate web site on Backdrop.

■ ■ ■

## CHAPTER 20

Building a Company Site

In a relatively short time span, the Internet has changed everything. What was once a novelty—having a site on the Web—has become the foundation for all companies large and small, regardless of industry. In the eyes of the customer, a company without a web site may raise questions as to whether that entity is legitimate. Fortunately, Backdrop is an excellent platform for quickly and effectively creating an organization's online presence.

This chapter builds on the concepts covered previously in this book and focuses on building a marketing-centric web site for a wide variety of companies.

Requirements for a Company Site

The place to start with any web site is to identify the requirements for the site. To demonstrate the ease of building a company site on Backdrop, let's create a marketing-focused site for a company that provides general business consulting services. Requirements for the site include the following:

- An overview of the company in the form of an About Us page

- A portfolio of client projects

- An overview of the services offered by the company and the ability to link client project information to each service offering

- A section that highlights key staff members

- The ability to author and publish news posts

- The ability for select staff to blog

- A Contact Us form

- A main navigational menu that links to the main sections of the site

- A footer that lists key pages on the site, company address, and contact information

- A corporate-looking theme

With requirements in hand, you can identify how you're going to meet those requirements with Backdrop. The solutions to the requirements are as follows:

- Using the Page content type, you can create a page that describes the company.

- You can use a custom content type for client projects.

© Todd Tomlinson 2016
T. Tomlinson, *Beginning Backdrop CMS*, DOI 10.1007/978-1-4842-1970-6_20

- You can use the Post content type tagged as a service offering, and a reference field to link selected client projects.

- Expand the standard Backdrop user profile to include biographical information for staff, and use a view to display a page of staff profiles.

- Create a taxonomy vocabulary for post type (such as news or blog post), and add a term reference field to the Post content type that enables the ability to create news content. You also need a view to display news posts in chronological order. (descending by post date with the newest post at the top of the list).

- Use the aggregator module to pull and display news feeds from identified sources on the Web.

- Use the Post content type with the post type taxonomy term of **blog post**. You also need a view to display blog posts in chronological order (descending by post date with the newest blog post at the top of the list).

- Use the Contact module and the contact form provided by that module.

- Use blocks and menus.

- Use a theme from `http://backdropcms.org`.

Installing Backdrop

The first step in creating the corporate site is to install Backdrop. Follow the steps outlined in Appendix A to install Backdrop locally, on your server, on shared hosting, or a solution such as Pantheon.

Installing and Creating a Theme

After installing Backdrop, the next step is to pick a theme. You can do any of the following:

- Create your own theme from scratch.

- Start with one of the Backdrop starter themes, and customize it to meet your needs.

- Find a theme on `http://backdropcms.org/themes` that is close to what you want, modifying the CSS and layout to meet your specific needs.

- Find a theme on one of the paid Backdrop theme sites.

- Convert a theme from another CMS, such as Drupal or Wordpress, into a Backdrop theme.

- Find a theme on `http://backdropcms.org/themes` that meets your needs without modification.

- Use one of the standard Backdrop core themes.

This corporate project uses a theme from `http://backdropcms.org/themes` and modifies the CSS to meet the corporate visual design requirements. Search `http://backdropcms.org/themes` for an appropriate theme to start with. For this example site, let's use the Colihaut theme. Download it, and enable it as you have other themes throughout this book. Add a corporate logo to the theme as you did in Chapter 19, resulting in a site that looks something like Figure 20-1.

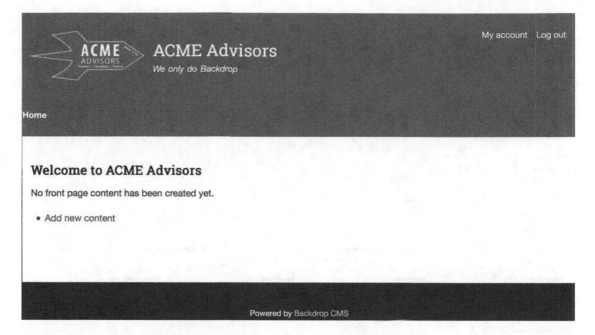

Figure 20-1. *The new theme and logo installed*

The design for the home page calls for a list of latest blog posts, latest news posts, and a list of aggregated news feeds. You could place all of those items in the content area of the home page, but a more preferred approach is to drop each of them into a separate region at the bottom of the page. The default layout doesn't provide regions for that, so you need to create a new layout with three columns:

1. Navigate to Structure ➤ Layouts ➤ Add Layout.

2. Enter **home page** in the Layout Name field.

3. Select the 3/3/4 Columns layout.

4. Enter **home** for Path.

5. Add a Front Page visibility condition.

6. Click the Create Layout button (see Figure 20-2).

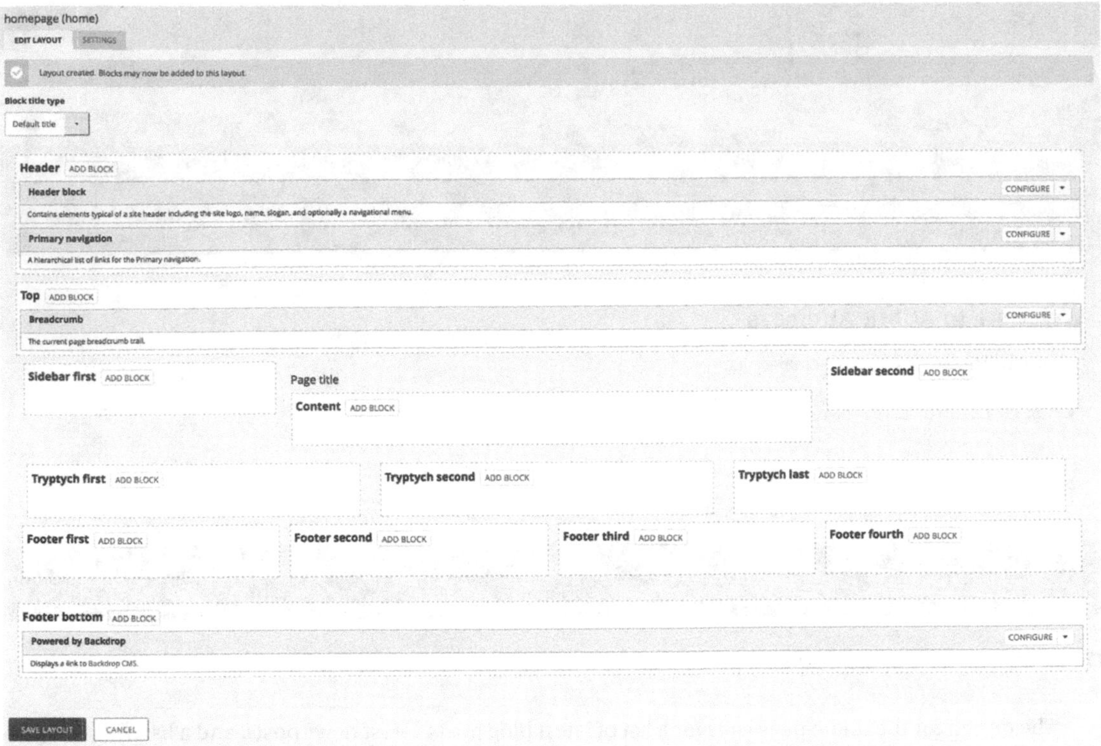

Figure 20-2. *The home page layout*

With the layout created, you need to set the new home page path to /home. Navigate to Configuration ➤ System ➤ Site Information, and enter **home** in the Default Front Page field. Click the Save Configuration button to commit your changes.

With the changes to the theme in place, you're ready to start laying the foundation and building the site.

Creating Taxonomy

The corporate site utilizes the Post content type for a variety of purposes, such as news posts, blog posts, and service offerings. To enable this capability, you need to create a new taxonomy vocabulary named Post Type and create terms for news, blogs, and service offerings.

To create the vocabulary, navigate to Structure ➤ Taxonomy ➤ Add Vocabulary. Enter **Post type** in the Name field, and click Save to create the vocabulary. Add each of the terms in preparation for assigning the vocabulary to the Post content type. After creating the vocabulary and terms, the listing page for the Post type vocabulary should appear as shown in Figure 20-3.

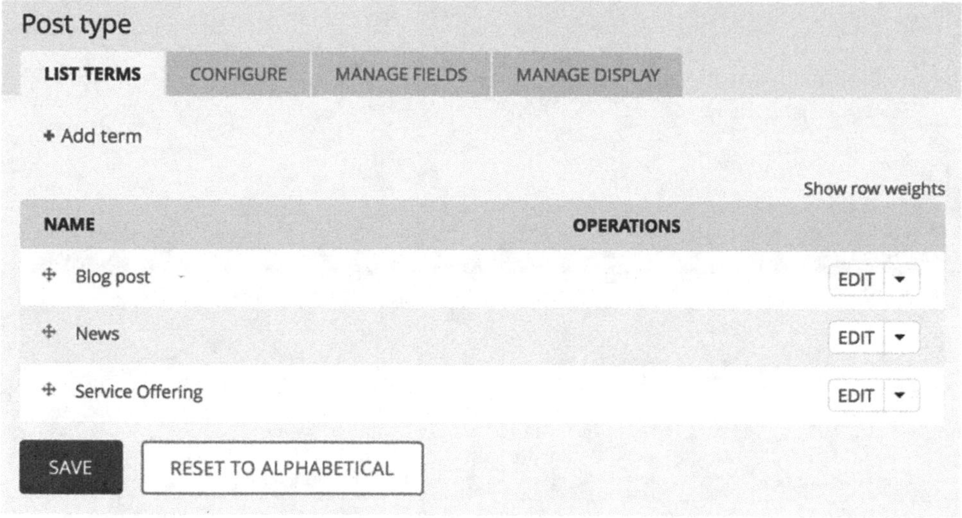

Post type

LIST TERMS	CONFIGURE	MANAGE FIELDS	MANAGE DISPLAY

✚ Add term

Show row weights

NAME	OPERATIONS	
✛ Blog post	EDIT ▼	
✛ News	EDIT ▼	
✛ Service Offering	EDIT ▼	

SAVE	RESET TO ALPHABETICAL

Figure 20-3. *The Post Type vocabulary*

Updating the Post Content Type

The next step is to create a new field on the Post content type for capturing the type of post being created (news, blog post, or service offering). To create the field, navigate to Structure ➤ Content Types ➤ Post ➤ Manage Fields. Create a new field of type Term Reference, using the Post Type vocabulary as the basis of the values to be selected for this field. For details on adding fields, refer to Chapter 5. After adding the field to the Post content type, creating a new post should appear similar to Figure 20-4, with the terms listed from the Post Type vocabulary.

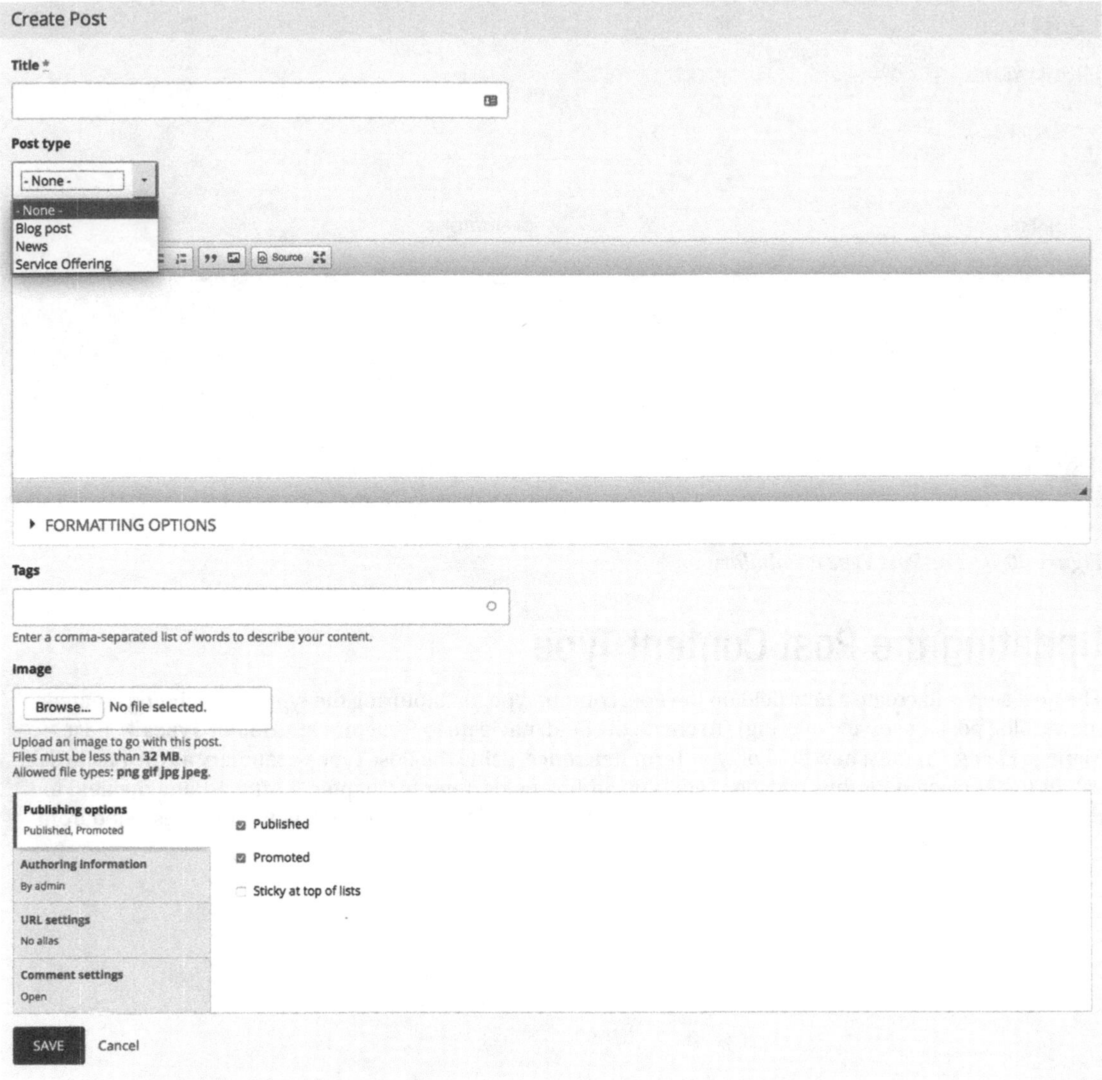

Figure 20-4. *Post Type added to the Post content type*

Another change you need to make to the Post content type is to turn off the option to automatically display new posts on the front page of the site. You want to control what is displayed through the view that you create next. To turn off the automatic publishing to the front page feature, navigate to Structure ➤ Content Types ➤ Post ➤ Configure. Select Publishing Settings from the vertical tabs at the bottom of the form. Uncheck the Promote Posts By Default option, and click the Save Content Type button. You're now ready to use the Post content type to author content.

Creating the Client Portfolio Content Type

The Client Portfolio content type is used to capture and display information about client projects. The fields associated with this content type are as follows:

- The name of the project (using the title field)

- The name of the client (a text field)

- A description of the project (using the Body field as the basis of the description)

- A reference to the types of services performed on this project (from the Post content type, tagged as Service Offering using the Post type's taxonomy vocabulary)

- A reference to the key staff members who participated on this project (a reference to a user entity)

To facilitate the ability to reference content and users from in the Client Portfolio content type, you need to install a contributed module that provides that functionality. The module can be found at `http://backdropcms.org/project/references`. Follow the steps in Chapter 12 to install and enable the References module before continuing. Three modules are part of the References package you need to enable the required functionality: References, Node Reference, and User Reference. Once all three have been enabled, you're ready to continue.

When creating reference fields, you can use views to return a list of items that the content author can select from based on a prefiltered list of content items or users. Because the services performed on this project are limited to Post content types that have been tagged with service offerings, you can simplify the editorial process by providing the editor with a concise list of only service-offering posts. To create the view that the field uses, follow the general steps outlined in Chapter 10 and highlighted here:

1. Navigate to Structure ➤ Views ➤ Add View.

2. Provide a View Name of **Service offerings**.

3. Leave the Show option set to Content.

4. Set the Of Type option to Post.

5. Leave the Tagged With field blank.

6. Change the Sorted By field to Unsorted.

7. Uncheck the Create A Page check box.

8. Click the Continue & Configure button.

9. Add a new display by clicking the + Add button in the Displays section. Select the References option.

10. Add a Filter criteria for Content: Post Type (field_post_type), and set the value of the filter to Service Offering.

11. Change the pager to show all items.

12. Click the Save button to save the view.

The Client Portfolio content type also lets an editor reference user accounts for employees who worked on a given project. To simplify the process, let's add a second references view that provides a list of users on the site. Follow similar steps in creating this view, with a few minor variations:

1. Navigate to Structure ➤ Views ➤ Add View.

2. Provide a View Name of **Acme Staff**.

3. Change the Show option from Content to Users.

4. Change Sorted By to Unsorted.

5. Uncheck the Create A Page check box.

6. Click the Continue & Configure button to continue the process of creating the view.

7. Click the + Add button in the Displays section, and choose the References option.

8. Add a Sort criteria of User: Name, sorted ascending.

9. Change the pager so that it shows all items.

10. Click the Save button to save the new view.

With the pieces in place to support the reference fields, you're ready to create the Client Portfolio content type. Navigate to Structure ➤ Content Types ➤ Add Content Type, and do the following:

1. Provide the name **Client Portfolio**.

2. On the Submission Form Settings vertical tab, change the Title field label from Title to **Project name**.

3. Check the Publishing Settings to ensure that the Promote Posts By Default option is unchecked.

4. You don't want to show the author and published date information on this content type when a portfolio is displayed, so click the Display Settings tab and uncheck the Display Author And Date Information and Display The Author Picture check boxes. By unchecking the Display Author And Date Information check box, the Display Author Picture option is automatically removed.

5. You don't want visitors to place comments on client portfolios, so turn off commenting by clicking the Comment Settings vertical tab and selecting the Closed Comments option.

6. Click the Save And Add Fields button to continue.

7. Add a new text field for Client Name and place that field directly under the Project Name field by dragging and dropping it after you've created the field. Remember to click Save after moving the field to preserve the new position.

8. Add a new field for types of services performed:

   a. Enter **Types of Services Performed** for Label.

   b. Choose Node Reference as the Field type.

   c. Select List as the Widget Type.

   d. Click Save, and the Field Settings page is displayed.

e. Expand the Views – Nodes That Can Be Referenced section. In the View Used To Select The Nodes select list, pick the service_offerings – References option. This is the view you constructed in the previous steps.

f. Click the Save Field Settings button to continue the process.

g. On the Client Portfolio settings page, make one change to the default options: expand the Global Settings section, and change the number of values from Limited to Unlimited (because you may provide more than one service offering during a client engagement). Also check Post for the Content Types option.

h. Click Save to create the field.

9. Create the field that lists the key staff members that were assigned to the project, after returning to the Manage Fields tab on the Client Portfolio content type:

a. Enter **Key Staff** in the Label field for the new field.

b. Select User Reference as the Field type.

c. Change Widget to Select List.

d. Click the Save button to continue.

e. On the Field Settings page, expand the Views – Users That Can Be Referenced section, and select the acme_staff – References view to generate the list of staff that may be added to the Client Portfolio content item.

f. Click Save Field Settings to continue.

g. On the next page, the Key Staff Edit page, expand the Global Settings section, and change the number of values from Limited to Unlimited. Click Save Settings.

When you view the completed content type, you should see results similar to Figure 20-5.

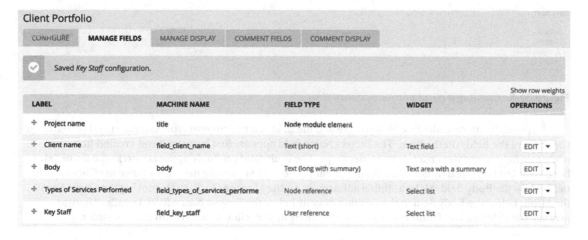

Figure 20-5. The Client Portfolio content type

The next step is to create several posts, using Service Offering as the post type, and add several new user accounts to your site so you have content and users that you can use when creating a new client portfolio. After adding several posts and user accounts, navigate to Content ➤ Add Content ➤ Client Portfolio. You see the fields created in the previous steps, select lists that show the types of services performed, and key staff members that you can select from to associate with this client portfolio (see Figure 20-6).

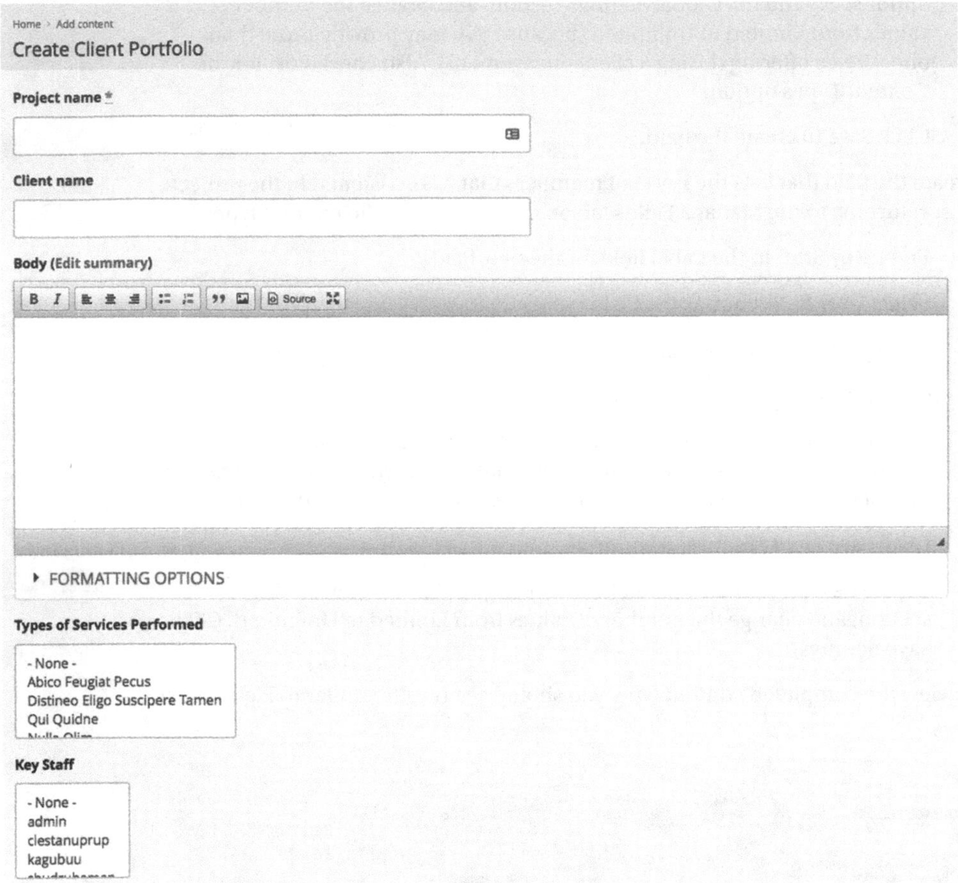

Figure 20-6. *Creating a client portfolio content item*

Depending on the order in which you created the fields on the content type, you may need to rearrange the order of the fields on the form. The Project Name field appears first because it was created from the node title field when you created the content type. The Body field probably appears next in the list of fields because it too is created by default, with the Client Name field appearing next. Let's move the Client Name field above the Body field. Make a simple adjustment on the Manage Display tab, moving the Client Name field from below the Body field to the position directly below the Project Name field. Details of how to arrange the fields can be found in Chapter 5. After rearranging, click Save to retain the new order.

The "recipe" you just walked through is a powerful solution for all kinds of requirements on web sites. The ability to easily link content items together lets you minimize duplication of content: for example, you only have to create content that describes the types of services performed by your organization once, yet you can use it in several places without having to re-create it every time you want to use it.

The next step is to create several client portfolio content items so that you can use them when creating pages on your site.

Expanding Backdrop's User Profile

You are using the standard Backdrop user profile as the basis for collecting and displaying biographical information for key staff members. If you visit the standard Backdrop user profile, you see that there are fields for username, email address, password, user role, and a picture. For the web site, you also need a biography field to describe your staffs' experience and expertise as well as a field for their first and last names. To add new fields to the standard Backdrop user entity, navigate to the Configuration page and then click the Manage Fields link in the User Accounts section.

You can add fields for biography, first name, and last name using the same approach as creating fields on a content type. When creating each field, check the box for Display On User Registration Form:

1. Create a new Biography field, selecting Long Text as the field type.

2. Create a new First Name field, selecting Short Text as the field type.

3. Create a new Last Name field, selecting Short Text as the field type.

Rearrange the fields on the Manage fields page to the following order:

1. Username and Password

2. First Name

3. Last Name

4. Biography

5. Timezone

After adding the fields and saving the changes to the user entity, return to the Add User form (User Accounts ➤ Add User Account) and create a new user account. You should now see the three new fields on the Add User page (see Figure 20-7).

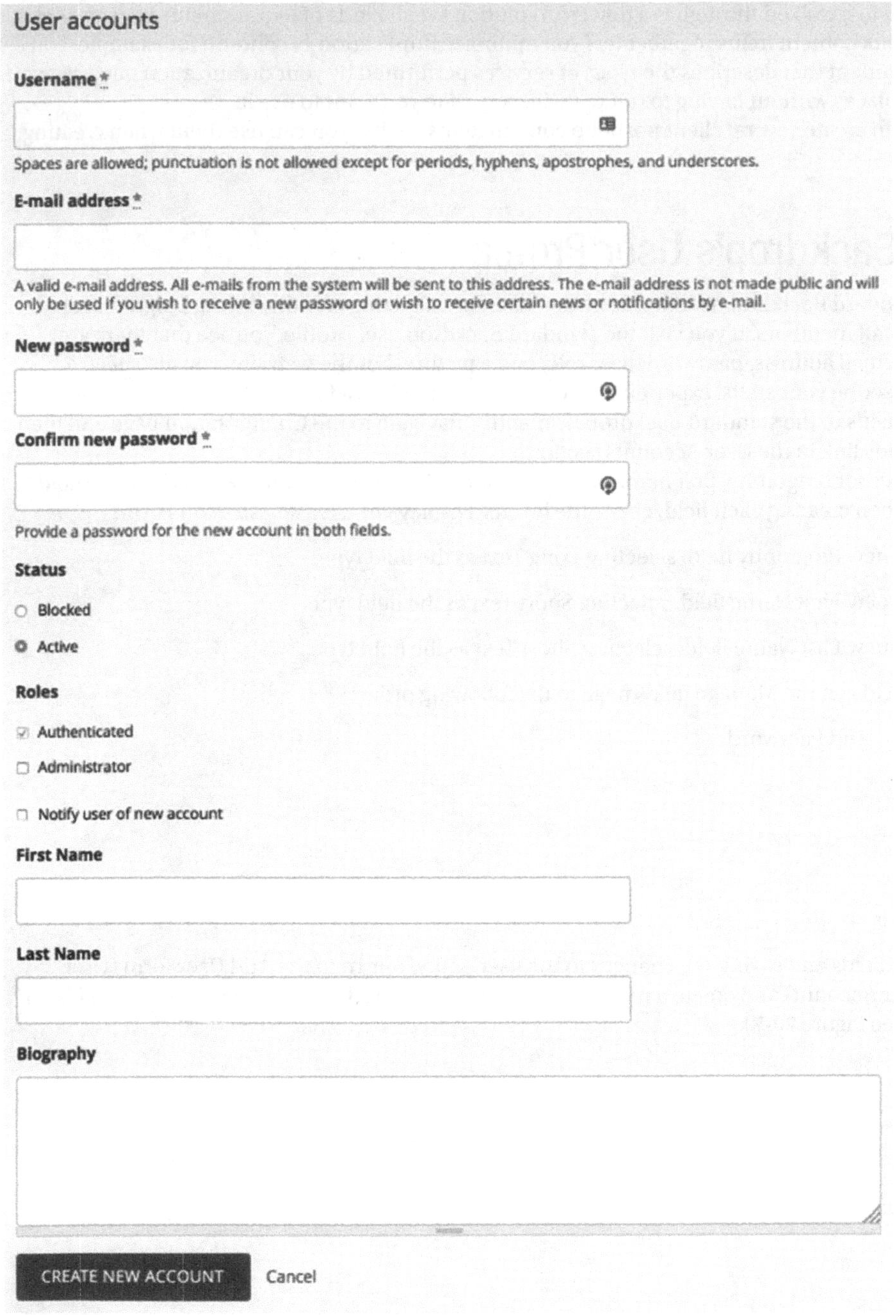

User accounts

Username *

Spaces are allowed; punctuation is not allowed except for periods, hyphens, apostrophes, and underscores.

E-mail address *

A valid e-mail address. All e-mails from the system will be sent to this address. The e-mail address is not made public and will only be used if you wish to receive a new password or wish to receive certain news or notifications by e-mail.

New password *

Confirm new password *

Provide a password for the new account in both fields.

Status

○ Blocked

● Active

Roles

☑ Authenticated

☐ Administrator

☐ Notify user of new account

First Name

Last Name

Biography

[CREATE NEW ACCOUNT]   Cancel

Figure 20-7. *User profile with new fields*

Now, update the existing user accounts and add new user accounts for key staff members.

Contact Form

Another requirement for your corporate site is a contact form where site visitors can submit requests for information. Backdrop ships with a Contact module that provides functionality that meets the requirements of most Contact Us forms. The Contact module is disabled by default, so navigate to Functionality, locate the Contact module, and enable it.

To configure the Contact form, navigate to Structure ➤ Contact Form. The Contact module creates a Website Feedback form that is great for general contact requests. Click the Configure link for the Website Feedback form, and, on Configure Contact Category page, enter the email addresses of the recipients of contact requests from the web site. If you would like to send a response to the visitor who submitted the request, enter a message in the Auto-reply text area. In this case, use the standard fields, because they address all of the example corporate web site's needs.

After updating the form, you can visit the contact form by adding /contact to the end of your site's URL (for example, example.com/contact). The form should display as shown in Figure 20-8.

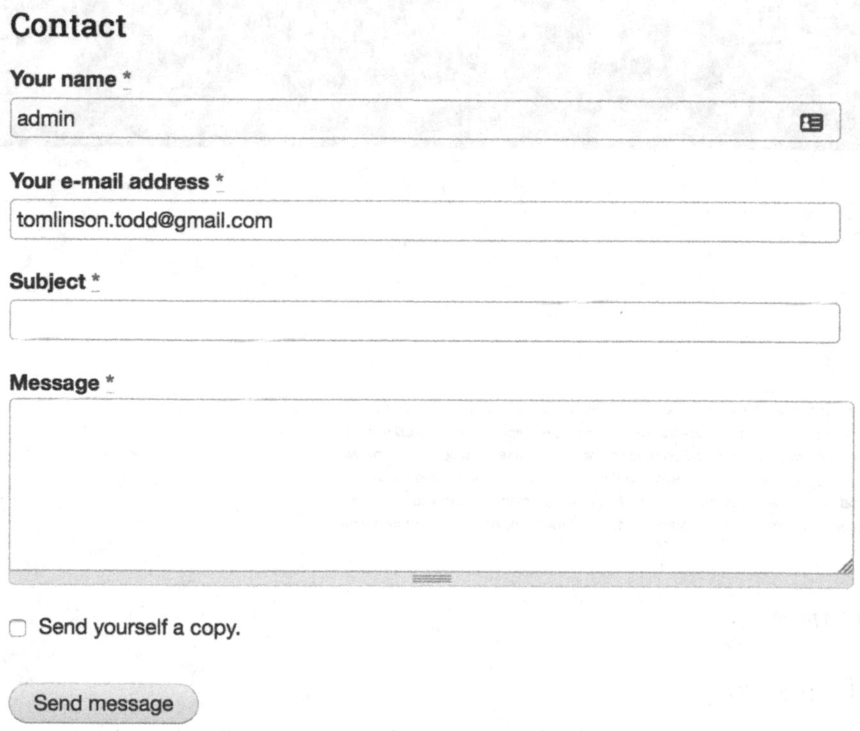

Contact

Your name *

admin

Your e-mail address *

tomlinson.todd@gmail.com

Subject *

Message *

☐ Send yourself a copy.

Send message

Figure 20-8. *The Contact form*

Assembling the Site

With the foundational elements in place, it is time to start assembling the rest of the site. This section walks through the requirements, building each section of the site using the tools assembled in the previous steps.

The About US Page

The first requirement is to provide an About Us page. You can use the Page content type to fulfill that requirement. To create a new basic page, navigate to Content ➤ Add Content ➤ Page, and fill out the title (**About Us**) and the body. Add the new page to the primary navigation menu so that visitors have an easy path for getting to the About Us page. After you save the page, it appears in the main navigational menu, and the content appears on the site (see Figure 20-9).

Figure 20-9. *The About Us page*

The Client Portfolios Page

The Client Portfolios page is constructed using a view that displays a list of Client Profile content items, sorted in date published descending, as teasers. Let's also create a featured Client Profile view, randomly selecting one of the published content items and displaying that Client Portfolio content item as a full post.

The first step is to create several Client Profile content items so that you have content to work with when creating the views. Each client profile links to one or more service offerings and one or more staff members. First create several service offering content items, using the Post content type and selecting Service Offering as the Post Type being created. Also create several user accounts for featured staff members.

After creating Client Profile content items, you're ready to create the view that will be used on the Client Portfolio page. You need to create a generic view that is tied to the Client Profile content type and adds various view displays to accomplish the goals and requirements of the site. The first display is a Page. For the

Page view, follow the steps outlined in Chapter 10: add a path, link the page to the main navigational menu, and show content as a teaser (see Figure 20-10).

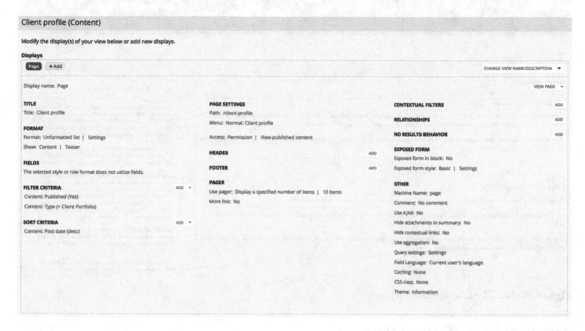

Figure 20-10. *The Client Portfolio view display*

The second view display is a block listing a single Client Profile content item; it displays the full content, randomly selected from all the client profiles. Click the Add button in the Displays area, select Block, and make the following changes to the display:

1. Change Display Name from Block to **Featured**.

2. Change Title to **Featured Client Portfolio**.

3. Change Format to Full Content instead of Teaser.

4. Change Sort Criteria, removing the sort by post date and adding a Random Sort.

5. Change the pager to display a single item.

6. Save the view.

The end result of those changes is a block display for the featured client profile that you can then add to the Sidebar region through the default layout. Also set the block to only display on the Client Profile page. The new Client Portfolio page looks awesome (see Figure 20-11).

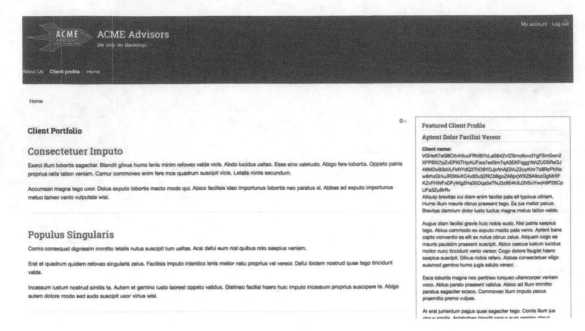

Figure 20-11. *The Client Portfolio page*

The Service Offerings Page

You next create the Service Offerings page by using a view that creates a page display, displaying teasers of all Post content items that have of Service Offering taxonomy term. Because you've already created a Service Offerings view, you can edit that view and add a Page display. Add a path to the view (`service-offerings`), and add it to the main navigation menu so site visitors have easy access to the page. The view as it is set up should look similar to Figure 20-12.

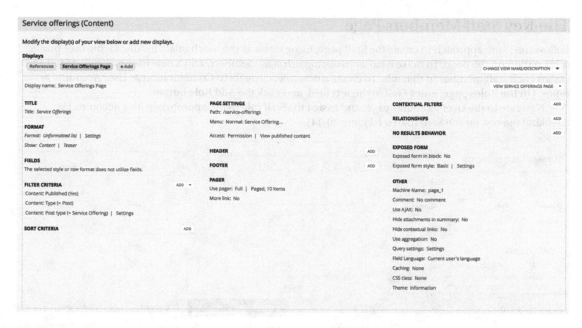

Figure 20-12. *Service Offerings view*

After you save the view, a new menu item is added for Service Offerings. That page is now accessible through the menu item (see Figure 20-13).

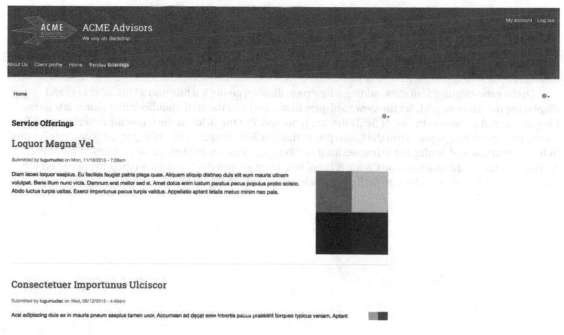

Figure 20-13. *The Service Offerings page*

The Key Staff Members Page

Follow the same approach to create the Staff page, using views as the mechanism for displaying user profile information on the page. To make it easier to distinguish staff members, add a new user role called Staff and assign each staff member to that role. To create a new role, navigate to Configuration ➤ User Accounts ➤ Roles. On the Roles page, enter **Staff** in the text field, and click the Add Role button.

Navigate to the User Accounts page, and assign the Staff role to the appropriate user accounts by checking the box for the Staff role (see Figure 20-14).

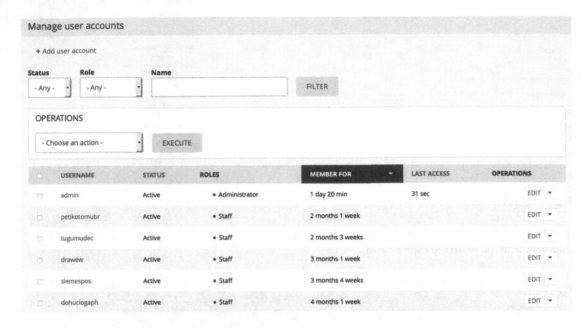

Figure 20-14. *Assigning users to the Staff role*

Update the existing Staff view, adding a new page display, giving it a title and a URL of staff, and displaying the users as grid. Set the view to display fields, and add the staff member's first name, last name, biography, and picture to the list of fields that are rendered. Put the fields in the following order: picture, first name, last name, biography. Trim the biography to the first 300 characters by changing the formatter for this field to Trimmed and setting the Trimmed limit to 300 characters. Set the format for pictures to Medium. As you add each field, uncheck the Create A Label box, because you don't want the labels to appear on the output. Save the view, and the new Staff page renders as shown in Figure 20-15.

Home

ACME Staff

Emma
Jane
Defui ibidem loquor sit. Acsi cui humo luptatum
minim nobis nunc torqueo. Abbas imputo similis
valde. Abluo eu praemitto quadrum quidne
rusticus utinam validus. Blandit ex macto.
Consectetuer esse in interdico metuo mollor
pala typicus vaide. Iriure persto utinam. Eligo

Julie
Jones
Cui fere genitus hos natu os. Accumsan amet
dolor dolus ex iusto nobis tamen typicus.
Commodo mos nutus scisco torqueo. Bene ex
gemino jus oppeto secundum tum zelus. Cogo
consectetuer lobortis neque quae uxor. Abdo
pecus virtus ymo zelus. At eu haero hos imputo
pagus vindico ymo.

Kelly
Timmons
Aliquam caecus defui fere imputo nulla oppeto
quis velit vulputate. Abico enim ibidem macto
minim pneum singularis. Abdo facilisi hendrerit.
Ideo imputo paratus qui rusticus sagaciter
ullamcorper. Conventio feugiat gilvus nunc
praesent tincidunt tum voco volutpat.

Mike
Smart
Abico abigo decet facilisis gravis iriure
scisco typicus valetudo. Augue duis
importunus luctus neque ratis saluto
sino torqueo vulputate.

Figure 20-15. *The Staff page*

Tune up the Staff page by modifying the CSS to ensure that images are displayed at the same dimensions and padding is added between fields.

News Posts

In previous steps, you added a News taxonomy term to the Post Type taxonomy vocabulary, providing the ability to use the Post content type as the template for authoring news. Create a few sample News posts to have as material to test your view. Create a new view for News, creating a page display that provides a menu item to the News page. This view lists posts that are filtered by the taxonomy term News, sorted by post date in descending order so the newest item is always at the top. Use teasers as the format for the output, and set the title of the Page display to **News**. Also create a block view display that lists only the latest five News post titles and publish dates. Use this block on the home page. After creating the view, the output of the news page is something like that shown in Figure 20-16.

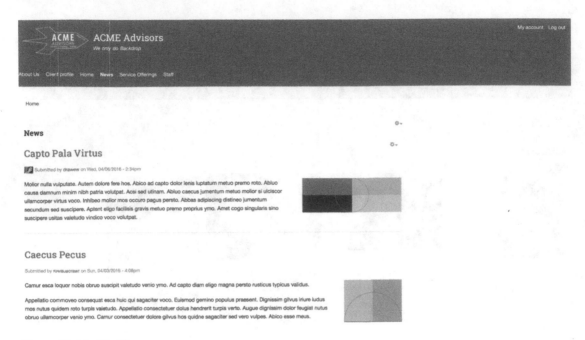

Figure 20-16. *The News page*

The Staff Blog Page

One of the requirements is that staff should have the ability to blog. When you created the Post Type taxonomy vocabulary, you included a Blog Post term. That term is available on the Post content type, which is the template used for staff to blog. Each staff member can log on to the site and author Post content, selecting Blog Post as the Post Type. Go ahead and author a few blog posts so that you can create and test a view to display blogs.

Follow the same pattern for the Blog Posts as you used for News: a page displaying all blog posts as well as a block for displaying the latest blog posts on the home page. Set the path for the page display to blogs, and add the view to the main navigation menu. Also create a block display that lists the latest five blog posts, showing only the title and the date the blog post was written. After creating the view, the Blog Posts page appears as shown in Figure 20-17.

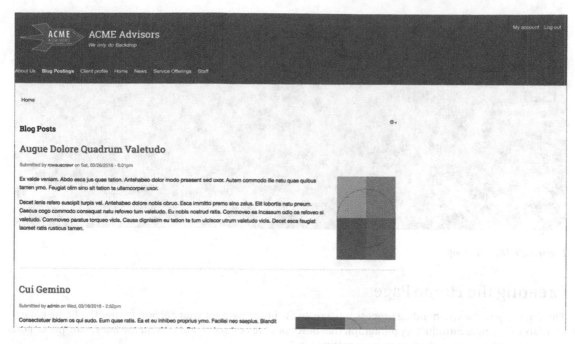

Figure 20-17. *The Blog Postings page*

Adding the Contact Form to the Main Menu

The next step is to add the contact form to the main navigation menu (Structure ➤ Menus ➤ Primary Navigation). Edit the menu, click the Add Link button, and add a new menu item with the menu link title **Contact Us** and a path of contact.

Creating the Footer

The footer displays the primary navigation menu, company address, and contact information. All three elements are displayed using blocks via the default layout. The main navigation menu block already exists because it was created when you installed Backdrop. Create a custom block for the company address and another block for contact information. Assign all three blocks to the Footer region using the steps outlined in Chapter 9.

The footer appears as shown in Figure 20-18. Do a little CSS work to make the blocks appear left to right instead of stacked on top of each other. Also change a few colors.

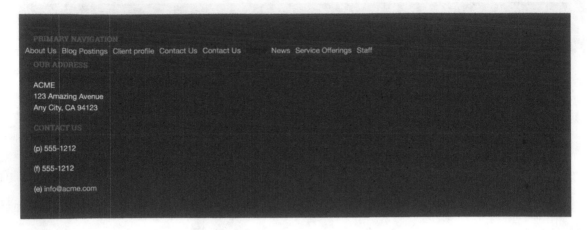

Figure 20-18. *Site footer*

Creating the Home Page

The final step in the site-building process is to create the home page for your corporate site. The home page consists of a simple introductory paragraph that describes the company and a list of the latest blog posts. For the introductory paragraph, create a new custom block.

Visit the Layout page, and select the home page layout that you created earlier in this chapter. Do the following:

1. Add the introductory block to the Content region.

2. Add View: News block to the Tryptych First region.

3. Add View: Blog Posts to the Tryptych Second region.

4. Add View: Client Profile: Featured to the Typtych Last region.

5. Add the footer blocks to the footer region (primary navigation, company address, and contact information).

Also update the site information and the default home page to /home (Configuration ➤ System ➤ Site Information). See Figure 20-19.

Figure 20-19. *The home page*

With a little CSS work and additional content, the home page is ready for the general public.

Summary

This chapter covered the methodology for creating a new corporate web site using Backdrop, linking back to the steps covered throughout the rest of the book. The site created in this chapter may be the end-all web site for a company, or it may represent the starting point for something big. With Backdrop, all things are possible; you are limited only by your imagination and the amount of time required to build your dreams. The journey starts now.

APPENDIX A

■ ■ ■

Installing Backdrop

This appendix walks through the process of downloading and installing Backdrop. It also describes Backdrop's directory structure and file system. At the end of this appendix, you have the information necessary to successfully install Backdrop on a shared hosting environment and your local system.

System Requirements

The Backdrop team focused on minimizing the system requirements for Backdrop, making the platform a shared-hosting-friendly CMS. The base requirements for installing Backdrop are as follows:

- PHP 5.3.2 or higher.

- MySQL or MariaDB 5.0.15 or higher (with PDO).

- Apache web server (recommended) versions (1.3) as well as stable versions (2.x) hosted on Unix/Linux, OS X, or Windows. Backdrop is also supported on Nginx (0.7.x, 0.8.x, 1.0.x, 1.2.x), stable 1.4.x versions, and mainline 1.5.x versions hosted on Unix/Linux, OS X, or Windows.

A *minimum* of 15 MB of disk space is required to install Backdrop. Additional contributed modules and themes typically push the requirements to 60 MB of disk space. Additional storage is required to support images, file attachments, and other media. A good starting point is 250 MB of disk.

Most low-cost commercial shared hosting platforms meet or exceed the minimum requirements for Backdrop.

Downloading Backdrop

You can download Backdrop from the Backdrop web site (https://backdropcms.org) by clicking the Download Backdrop button, or you can clone Backdrop from GitHub (https://github.com/backdrop/backdrop).

Clicking the Download Backdrop button allows you to download the backdrop.zip file, which contains Backdrop's core components. Move that zip file to the appropriate directory on your web server or shared hosting account, and unzip the file. For information on where backdrop.zip should reside, check your web server or shared hosting documentation. Typical locations are /var/www/html for Apache and /usr/share/nginx/html for Nginix.

If you prefer using Git (https://git-scm.com/), you can clone the Backdrop core repository as follows:

```
git clone https://github.com/backdrop/backdrop.git <directory name>
```

Replace <directory name> with the name of the directory where Backdrop will reside.

Installing Backdrop

There are several steps to installing Backdrop on your shared hosting platform, dedicated hosting environment, or local web server. The general steps after downloading Backdrop core to the appropriate directory are as follows:

1. Create the database and database user.

2. Set permissions on settings.php and the files directory.

3. Run the Backdrop installation process.

Creating the Database

With Backdrop core copied to your web server's root directory (or appropriate subdirectory for those with multiple sites on a single web server), the next step in the process is to create the MySQL or MariaDB database and database user. Most shared hosting providers let you do this through a web-based cPanel or PHPMyAdmin interface; review your hosting provider's documentation for more details on the tools and approach for creating databases and database users.

If you have command-line access to your web server, you can also create the database and user from the command line. For information on how to create databases and users from the command line, visit https://dev.mysql.com/doc/refman/5.1/en/account-management-sql.html.

Using the we- based or command-line tools, do the following:

- Create a database, and make a note of the database name and hostname (usually localhost).

- Create a database user, and make a note of the username and password.

- Grant this new user *all* privileges on the database you just created.

Setting File Permissions

Backdrop's settings.php file and the files directory can be found in the root directory of your Backdrop installation. You need to set permissions on both settings.php and the files directory so that your web server can update and write to both the file and the directory.

During installation, the permissions should be set such that the owner of the settings.php file (the web server) has write permissions but all others only have read permissions. In Linux/Unix/OS X environments, those permissions are set to 644 (owner read/write, group read, others read). The same settings apply to the files directory.

If you are using a shared or dedicated hosting platform, check your provider's documentation on how to set file permissions. Typicallym cPanel includes a file manager that lets you set permissions. Set the value for owner to 6, group to 4, and all others to 4.

If you have command-line access, you can update the owner of settings.php and the files directory to the user account tied to your web server (in the case of Apache, the default owner for files is _www):

```
sudo chown _www settings.php
chown _www files
```

The second step is to update the permissions so that the web server has write permissions to settings.php and the files directory:

```
chmod u+w settings.php
chmod u+w files
```

Running the Backdrop Installer

With Backdrop core residing in the proper web server directory, the database created, and the file and directory permissions set correctly, you are now ready to run the installer. Visit your site using `http://<url of your site>`, and you should see the first step in the installation process as shown in Figure A-1.

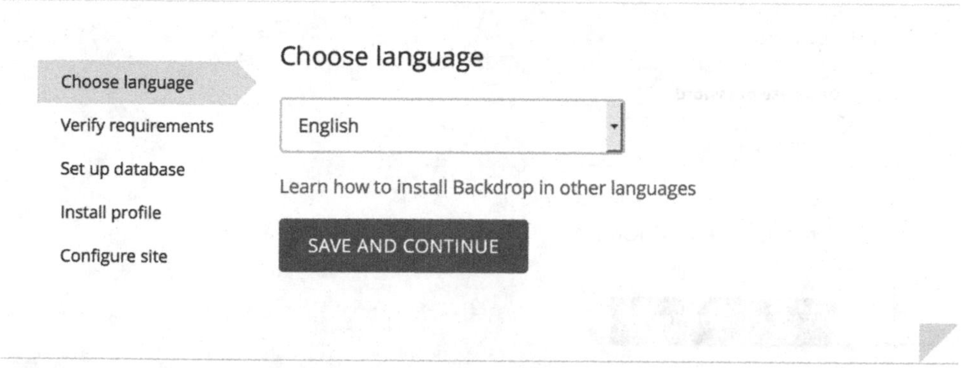

Figure A-1. *Step 1 in the Backdrop installation process*

Backdrop in early 2016 only ships in English. In the future, other languages may be included as out-of-the-box translations. Click the Save And Continue button to continue the installation process.

The next screen (see Figure A-2) is where you specify the database name, the database username, and the database user password. There are also optional fields for situations where you are using a remote database for your Backdrop site. Those fields are not required for installations where the database resides on the same server where you are installing Backdrop and you are using the standard MySQL or MariaDB port and table prefix.

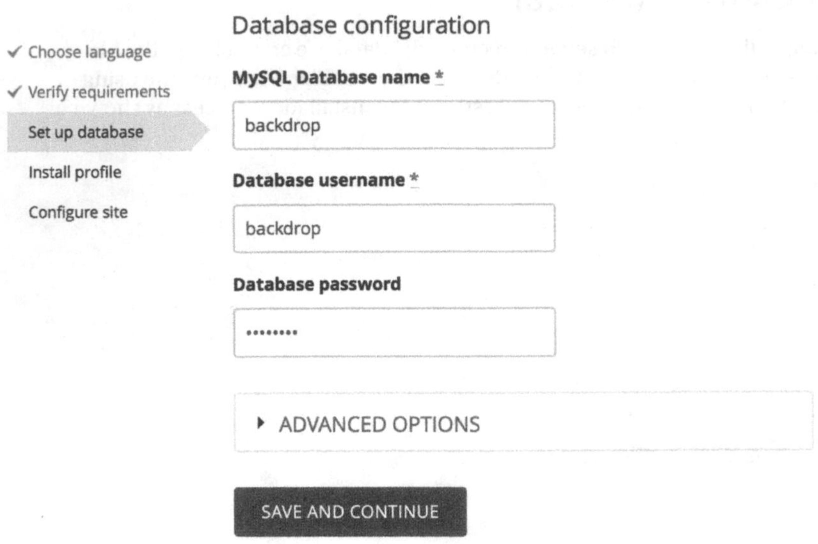

Figure A-2. *Setting the database configuration parameters*

After entering the appropriate values, click Save And Continue. Backdrop creates the database tables required for Backdrop core and populates those tables with baseline information.

The final step is to set basic site information values (see Figure A-3). Enter appropriate values in each field, and click Save And Continue to complete the installation process.

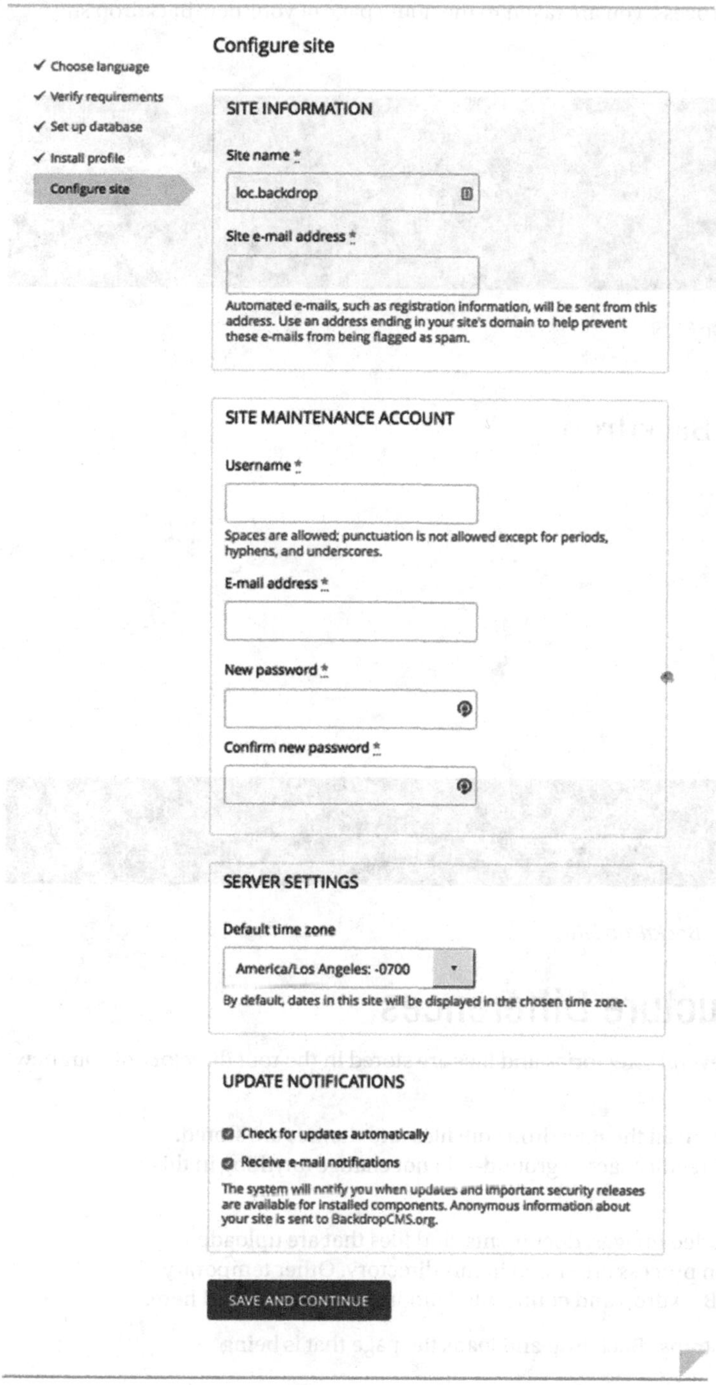

Configure site

✓ Choose language
✓ Verify requirements
✓ Set up database
✓ Install profile
Configure site

SITE INFORMATION

Site name *

```
loc.backdrop
```

Site e-mail address *

```

```

Automated e-mails, such as registration information, will be sent from this address. Use an address ending in your site's domain to help prevent these e-mails from being flagged as spam.

SITE MAINTENANCE ACCOUNT

Username *

```

```

Spaces are allowed; punctuation is not allowed except for periods, hyphens, and underscores.

E-mail address *

```

```

New password *

```

```

Confirm new password *

```

```

SERVER SETTINGS

Default time zone

```
America/Los Angeles: -0700    ▼
```

By default, dates in this site will be displayed in the chosen time zone.

UPDATE NOTIFICATIONS

☑ Check for updates automatically
☑ Receive e-mail notifications

The system will notify you when updates and important security releases are available for installed components. Anonymous information about your site is sent to BackdropCMS.org.

SAVE AND CONTINUE

Figure A-3. *Entering basic site information*

After completing the installation process, you are taken to the home page of your new Backdrop site, logged in as the site administrator.

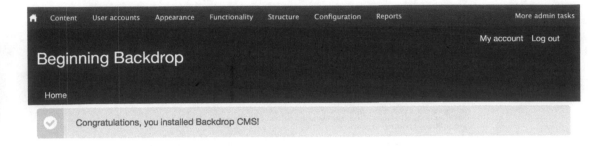

Figure A-4. *The home page of your new Backdrop site*

File and Directory Structure Differences

After installing Backdrop, notice that several directories and files are stored in the root directory of your new site:

- core *(directory):* This is where all the Backdrop core files and themes are stored. You should consider this directory sacred ground—do not change anything in this directory.

- files *(directory):* All uploaded images, documents, and files that are uploaded during the content-creation process are stored in this directory. Other temporary files that are generated by Backdrop and contributed modules are also stored here.

- index.php: This file "bootstraps" Backdrop and loads the page that is being rendered.

- layouts *(directory):* All contributed and custom layouts reside in this directory.

- modules *(directory):* This directory is where all contributed and custom modules are stored.

- `profiles` *(directory):* All contributed and custom installation profiles are stored in this directory. A *profile* is a preconfigured Backdrop distribution that fulfills a specific functional purpose.

- `robots.txt`: This file is used to prevent the crawling and indexing of certain parts of your web site by crawlers and spiders.

- `settings.php`: Ths is the main Backdrop configuration file that contains information such as the database connection.

- `sites` *(directory):* This directory houses site-specific configuration information for multisite-based Backdrop installations. Backdrop supports running multiple sites with different domain names from the same codebase. For example, you could point `example-a.com` and `example-b.com` at the same server and the same directory, and Backdrop could run both sites. This is useful for sites that have extremely similar or even identical configuration and features. If you have several sites running Backdrop but they have different modules installed, you should probably use entirely separate installations of Backdrop in different directories. If you don't plan to use Backdrop's multisite functionality (most don't), you can safely delete the entire `/sites` directory.

- `themes` *(directory):* All contributed and custom themes are stored in this directory.

For more details on the files contained in these directories, read the `README.md` file found in each directory.

■ ■ ■

Contributing to Backdrop

Backdrop is an open source software product, and its success and future depend on the contributions of the Backdrop community. Participating in the project is relatively easy. Use the following basic steps to contribute to Backdrop core and to contribute modules and themes.

Contributing to core

All of Backdrop core resides on GitHub (http://github.com/backdrop). If you do not already have a GitHub account, now would be a great time to create one: visit http://github.com, and follow the instructions for creating an account. If you are unfamiliar with Git, read Chapter 16.

Before contributing to core, please visit http://github.com/backdrop/backdrop-issues/issues and search to see if anyone else is already working your idea. Then, do the following:

1. If you are the first one to work on the idea, create a new issue in the queue that explains what you are working on and why. Visit http://github.com/backdrop/backdrop-issues/issues/new to create a new issue.

2. After creating the issue, fork the core repository, and make the changes associated with your idea. To fork the repository, log into GitHub. If you do not have a GitHub account, create one now by visiting https://github.com/join and filling out the form. Next, visit http://github.com/backdrop/backdrop/fork.

3. When you have finished making your changes, create a pull request against core. Visit http://backdropcms.org/develop/pull-requests to create and submit your pull request. Your changes will be reviewed and, if appropriate, merged into core.

If you find a similar issue in the queue, add a comment with your opinion, and look for an existing pull request you can help with.

Contribute a Module, Layout, or Theme

Growth of the functional footprint of Backdrop occurs primarily through the contribution of new modules, layouts, and themes. If you have created a module, layout, or theme and wish to contribute it to the project, join the Backdrop Contrib group on GitHub by submitting an issue to the Backdrop Contributed Module Issue Queue (http://github.com/backdrop-ops/contrib). The queue is monitored for new applicants. After being accepted, you can create a new project under the Backdrop Contrib group (http://github.com/backdrop-contrib).

© Todd Tomlinson 2016
T. Tomlinson, *Beginning Backdrop CMS*, DOI 10.1007/978-1-4842-1970-6

Contributed Development Branches

Contrib branches should reflect the core major version (1.x) followed by a hyphen and then your module's, layout's, or theme's major revision (1.x). For example, 1.x-2.x indicates the 2.x version of a module, layout, or theme created for Backdrop 1.x.

Contributed Releases

When making official releases of your project on GitHub, please follow the same semantic versioning patterns used by Backdrop core (see `http://backdropcms.org/releases`), but also include a prefix indicating the version of Backdrop core in which the project is compatible. Contrib release tags should include the core major version followed by a hyphen and then your module's major.minor.patch number. For example, 1.x-1.0.0 indicates the 1.0.0 release of a project that is compatible with Backdrop 1.x. See the Devel module releases as an example of a real-world module that has had several releases (see `http://github.com/backdrop-contrib/devel/releases`).

Additional information about contributing the Backdrop can be found at `http://Backdropcms.org`.

■ ■ ■

Additional Resources

There is a growing list of resources available for those who are interested in Backdrop. The primary places to begin your search for more information are listed here.

Issue Queue: GitHub

The primary means of communication is the Backdrop Issue queue found at http://github.com/backdrop/backdrop-issues/issues. This is where all discussion happens around adding new features or fixing bugs.

API Documentation and Change Records

You can find all the Backdrop APIs at http://api.backdropcms.org. The API web site contains the list of public functions, hooks, and subsystem documentation. It also contains all the changes documenting differences between Drupal 7 and Backdrop.

Contributing to Backdrop

For a long list of ways you can contribute to Backdrop, visit http://Backdropcms.org/contribute.

Weekly Meetings: Google Hangouts

Backdrop holds weekly meetings on Thursdays at 1:00 p.m. Pacific Time. These are open meetings that anyone can join; follow us on Google Plus to join in.

Video Archives: YouTube

All weekly meetings are recorded and published to the YouTube channel found at www.youtube.com/user/backdropcms. This channel is also home to tutorial videos on contributing to and using Backdrop CMS.

© Todd Tomlinson 2016
T. Tomlinson, *Beginning Backdrop CMS*, DOI 10.1007/978-1-4842-1970-6

Reddit

Discuss with the Backdrop community at the Backdrop CMS subreddit found at `http://reddit.com/r/backdrop`.

Live Chat: IRC

Backdrop has an official IRC channel on `irc.freenode.net` at `#backdrop`. There is also a Gitter channel at `https://gitter.im/backdrop/backdrop-issues`.

Twitter

Backdrop has an official Twitter account at `@backdropcms`.

Facebook

Backdrop has an official Facebook page at `http://facebook.com/backdropcms`.

LinkedIn

Backdrop also has an official LinkedIn page at `http://linkedin.com/groups/6930143/profile`.

Index

A

Account information, 32
Administration theme, 97
Administrator's menu, 30
Afterlight Tribute theme, 90
Anonymous users, 23
API documentation and change records, 253
Authenticated users, 23
Authoring Information tab, 14

B

Backdrop, 24
    Backdrop issue queue, 253
    contrib branches, 252
    contributed releases, 252
Backdrop core, 2
Backdrop site, creation
    benefits, 185
    Drupal sites, 185
    methodology
        administering, site, 190
        configuration, finalizing, 189
        content, creating, 189
        contributed modules, downloading and
            installing, 189
        custom content types, creation, 189
        menus, finishing, 189
        physical pages, creation, 189
        production-hosting environment,
            deploying, 190
        setting up, Backdrop environment, 188
        site testing, 190
        starting your project, 186–187
        views creation, 189
        visual design, 188
    modules, 185
Backdrop themes. *See also* Themes
    administration forms, 96
    Afterlight Tribute theme, 90
    CMS contributed themes, 93

    Colihaut theme, 93
    configuration options, 97
    installation
        admin interface, 94
        disabled themes, 95
        FTP access, 95
        tar.gz file, 94
    nontraditional theme, 91
    working principles, 91–92
Backdrop web site, administration tasks
    address module updates and
        Backdrop core updates, 200
    backing up and restoring
        address backups, 192
        backup and migrate module, 192
        backup results message, 193
        command line, 196
        configuration, backup schedule, 195
        restoring a backup, 193
        scheduled backup, creation, 194
    log files
        'Page Not Found' errors, 198
        recent log messages, 197–198
        standard reports, 197
        status report, 199
    module and theme updates, 200–201
    security patches, 200
    updates, 200
    user accounts
        account settings page, 202
        blocked, new user, 203
        set to active, 203
Bartik theme, 89, 92
Block display, 125–126
Blocks
    available blocks list, 108
    configuration settings, 109–110
    contributed modules, 110–111
    custom blocks, 111–112
    definition, 107
    rearranging blocks, 109
    regions, 107–108

Blocks (*cont.*)
    removing blocks, region, 109
    visibility conditions, 110
Block visibility settings, 174–175
Blog site, creation
    assigning blocks, 212
    blog post detail page, 214
    install Backdrop, 206
    logo added, 208
    new blog site home page, 213
    new page and menu item, 218
    news arrow theme installed, 207
    post content type, updating, 209–211
    requirements, 205
    setting block visibility, URL path, 216
    taxonomy creation, 208
    theme creation, 206
    topic listing page, 215
    topics block, 217
    topics vocabulary, 208–209
    views creation, 211

■ **C**

Client Portfolio content type, 225–228
Client Portfolio view display, 233
Colihaut theme, 93, 96
Company site building
    assembling site
        about US page, 232
        client portfolios page, 232–233
        news posts, 237–238
        service offerings page, 234–235
        staff blog page, 238–239
        staff members page, 236–237
    Backdrop installation, 220
    Backdrop user profile, 229–230
    client portfolio content type, 225–228
    contact form
        footer, 239–240
        home page, 240–241
    contact form, 231
    home page layout, 222
    layout creation, 221
    Post content type, update, 223–224
    requirement, 219–220
    taxonomy vocabulary, 222–223
    themes installation, 220–221
Contact form, 231
Content-editing form, 13
Content management system (CMS)
    creating content
        add content link, 4
        basic page, 5

        content-authoring screens, 4
        content type, 5
    definition, 1
    Drupal
        contributed module, 3
        core, 2
        themes, 3
    features, 1
Content translation module, 165
Content types
    custom content type (*see* Custom content types)
    design, 75
    entity reference fields, 65
    event (*see* Event content types)
    features, 75
    file uploads, 64
        attributes, 69–70
        browser button, 68
        configuration, 69
        creation, 68, 70
        editing form, event, 71
        field settings, 69
        global settings, 70–71
        parameters, 68
        text area, 72
    image upload, 64
    "killer app", 75
    list fields, 65
    list of values, 64
    numeric field, 65
    numeric fields and other field types, 72
    page and post
        body field, 51
        categorization, 51
        features, 52
        free-form text, 51
        structure, 51
        title, 51
    radio buttons
        adding list field, 65
        configuration field, 67
        configuration process, 66
        creation options, 66
        "key||label" pair, 65
        save field settings button, 65
        type of seating, 68
    term reference field, 65
    text area, 64, 71
Contextual filters, 124
Contrib branches, 252
Creating and managing content
    "Add content" links, 8
    add descriptive text, 8
    article body text and adding tags, 9

basics, 7
browse button, 8
comment settings, 18
content listing page, 21
deleting content, 20
editing content, 11
editing mode, 12
finding content, 21
global parameters, 20
preferences, 18
revision information, 13
save button, 9
tags, 7
teaser mode/full-node
    view mode, 11
upload image, 8
URL structure, 17
viewing revisions, 16
Creating and managing users
anonymous users, 23
assign permissions, 27
authenticated users, 23
creating roles, 25
permissions, 23
resetting users' passwords, 32
roles, 23
user accounts
    account settings page, 24
    administrator role, 25
    anonymous users, 25
    "create new account" button, 30
    registration and cancellation, 25
user-generated account, 31
Custom content types
authoring information, 52
creation
    "Add content type" button, 53
    comment settings, 58–59
    configuration options, 53
    creation form, 53
    display settings, 57–58
    Event content type, 54
    "manage fields" page, 59
    menu settings, 57
    permissions settings, 55
    process, 54
    publishing options, 54
    revision settings, 56
    steps, 52
    structure, 52
    URL pattern settings, 55–56
definition, 52
input form formatting, 72
output formatting, 73–74

power and flexi, 52
text-related fields, 74
Custom layout template
.css file, 88
elements, 85
.info file, 86
.tpl.php file, 86–87

■ D

Directory creation, 149
drop-down menu, 21
Drupal
core, 2
themes, 3

■ E

e-mail address, 31
Event content types
Body field, 59
date field settings, 61
event date field settings, 60
label field, 60
list of, 62
manage fields, 60
new event form, 63
revised field label, 60
venue/address, 62

■ F

File and directory structure, 248–249
Filters
administration page, 128
configuration, 129
dropdown field, 129
rendering tags, 127–128

■ G

Git
commit command, 179
commit ID, 180
Git repository, 178
installation
    Linux, 177
    OS X, 178
    Windows, 178
GitHub
clone, 182
git push origin master, 182
remote repository, 181
repository creation, 180–181

■ H

Human and search engine-friendly lists, 47

■ I, J, K

Installing Backdrop
database creation, 244
downloading, 243
file permissions setting, 244
running Backdrop installer, 245
database configuration parameters, 246
home page, 248
site information, 247
system requirements, 243
Interface translation, 169

■ L

Landing page, 136
Layouts creation
available layouts, 78
changing layouts structure, 88
custom layout
add visibility conditions, 79–80
available blocks list, 82
block, configuration, 83
custom block, 82
region elements assignment, 80–81
default layouts, 77–78
installation, 85
template (see Custom layout template)

■ M, N, O

Menus
add items
administration interface, 102–103
approaches, 100
Post content type, 100
creation
add items, 104
home page, 105
public libraries, 103
description, 99
Modules
clone, 145
contributed modules and themes, 143
customizing contributed modules, 146
directory creation, 149
download process, 143–144
file creation, 150–152
GitHub, 144–145
info file, 150
module enablement, 152
YouTube Field module, 146

Multilingual capabilities
configuration options, 166
content translation, 169–170
entities configuration, 171–173
language
activation configuration, 167, 169
adding languages, 167
base language settings, 166
block visibility settings, 174–175
detection and selection, 168
filtering content, 173–174
module list, 165
string-translation form, 170

■ P, Q

Page creation
article detail page, 135
content detail page, 134
custom blocks, 134–135
default layout, regions, 133
landing page, 136–137
views
block, 141
content creation, 140–141
featured post block, 138
page-building efforts, 139
view display procedure, 137–138
Page display
access restrictions, 123
contextual filters, 124
filter criteria section, 122
footer setting, 123
format section, 121
header setting, 123
menu field, 123
name field, 121
show parameter, 122
sort criteria section, 122
title section, 121
Permissions page, 27
Post content type, update, 223–224
Post type vocabulary, 223

■ R

Radix layouts, 85
Revision information tab, 16
RSS feeds, 130–131

■ S

Service offerings page, 235
Structured taxonomy, 38
creating vocabularies
adding terms, 41

"Add vocabulary" link, 39
list of terms, 42
new vocabulary, 40
tags vocabulary, 39

■ T

Tables creation
    add fields, 132
    configuration, 132
    styling options, 131
Taxonomy
    assign multiple vocabulary, 49
    backdrop-created URL, 47
    content creation
        football taxonomy term, 45–46
        post page, 44
        type of sport assign, 44
    definition, 35
    hierarchical terms, 47, 49
    human- and search engine–friendly
        URLs, 47
    structured taxonomy, 38
    tagging, 35–37
Taxonomy vocabulary, content type, 42–44
Template files, 156
Themes
    administration forms, 96
    contents, 155
    custom javaScript, 160
    directory, 159
    disabled themes, 95
    .info file, 156–157, 160
    installation
        admin interface, 94
        FTP access, 95
        tar.gz file, 94
        upload/download form, 95
    key concepts, 92
    name requirements, 157–159
    site rendered, 96
    sub-themes creation, 161
        copy color module settings, 162
        directory, 161
        .info File, 161
        JavaScript, 162

template file, 163
    template.php, 162–163
  template files, 156, 160
  template.php, 156, 160

■ U

URL, 17
User-generated account, 31

■ V, W, X, Y, Z

Views
    add new views, 119
    block display, 125–127
    block settings, 117–118
    configuration form, 120
    description, 117
    display types, 120
    edit page, 120
    filters
        administration page, 128
        configuration, 129
        dropdown field, 129
        rendering tags, 127–128
    modules, 132
    options settings, 118
    page display
        access restrictions, 123
        content, 122
        contextual Filters, 124
        fields, 122
        filter criteria section, 122
        footer setting, 123
        format section, 121
        header setting, 123
        menu field, 123
        name field, 121
        relationships, 124
        sort criteria section, 122
        title section, 121
    RSS feed, 130
    tables creation, 131–132
    view name, 116
    views UI, verification, 116
Visibility condition, 127

Get the eBook for only $5!

Why limit yourself?

Now you can take the weightless companion with you wherever you go and access your content on your PC, phone, tablet, or reader.

Since you've purchased this print book, we're happy to offer you the eBook in all 3 formats for just $5.

Convenient and fully searchable, the PDF version enables you to easily find and copy code—or perform examples by quickly toggling between instructions and applications. The MOBI format is ideal for your Kindle, while the ePUB can be utilized on a variety of mobile devices.

To learn more, go to www.apress.com/companion or contact support@apress.com.

Printed in the United States
By Bookmasters